The
BLARNEY
STONE

The
BLARNEY
STONE

BY

John Hewlett

AVENEL BOOKS
New York

This 1983 edition is published by Avenel Books,
distributed by Crown Publishers, Inc. by arrangement with
Hawthorne Books/E.P. Dutton, Inc.

Manufactured in the United States of America

Library of Congress Cataloging in Publication Data

Hewlett, John.
   The Blarney Stone.

   Originally published: New York : Appleton-Century-
Crofts, c1951.
   1. Blarney Castle (Blarney, Cork)—Blarney Stone.
2. Blarney (Cork)—Castles.   I. Title.
DA995.B58H48   1983   9419'56   83-15819
ISBN 0-517-425823

   h g f e d c b a

Dedicated to

LORRAINE MOORE

Contents

CONTENTS

Foreword

During this year or any year of our Lord reasonably free of world wars, plagues, pestilences and depressions, scores of thousands of persons will labor up the tortuous heights of a 180-foot ruin of an old castle in Ireland. Once on the battlement of a crumbling turret commanding a fine view of emerald valleys and the lofty chain of the Boggeragh Mountains, these pilgrims to the "Mouldering Hall of Kings" will carefully empty their pockets of change, place their valuables in a safe spot to prevent them from cascading downward into the branches of the elms, lie flat upon their backs, grasp two rusty upright iron bars, have their ankles held by two strong men, and inch their torsos backbreakingly through an opening above a sheer drop of nearly two hundred feet. Now they can stare fearfully into the purple fog of Irish skies above, or toward the death that threatens in dangerous greenery below. But these views, as excellent as they are, are not the object of their remarkable acrobatics. Twisting bone and sinew in the hazardous process, these visitors who pay about 14½ cents for the privilege (the shilling being worth what it is at the current exchange) by main force of strength will raise their shoulders and heads about two feet up and bestow with their lips a kiss upon a block of limestone, measuring approximately 4 feet in length by 1 foot 1 inch in width and 9 inches in depth, embedded in the wall.

This piece of rock is variously stated to be the original Jacob's Pillow, a part of the Stone of Scone, the Coronation Stone of England which was so sensationally taken from Westminster Abbey on Christmas Day, 1950. This rock is reputedly a

fragment of that prized seat on which 27 English monarchs have
been anointed and crowned since Edward I stole it from the
Scots at Dunstaffnage Royal Castle in his spoilations of their
country, and set it up in Westminster in the year 1296.

The Coronation Stone enjoyed many marvelous wanderings
after it served as Jacob's Pillow, during his vision of angels
descending and ascending from heaven at Beth-el.

*And Jacob went out from Beer-sheba, and went toward
Haran.*

*And he lighted upon a certain place and tarried there all night,
because the sun was set; and he took of the stones of that place,
and put them for his pillows, and lay down in that place to sleep.*

*And he dreamed, and behold a ladder set up on the earth, and
the top of it reached to heaven: and behold the angels of God
ascending and descending on it.*

When Jacob awoke he said, *Surely the Lord is in this place;
and I knew it not.*

Then the Patriarch *rose up early in the morning, and took the
stone that he had put for his pillows, and set it up for a pillar,
and poured oil upon the top of it.*

In the custody of the prophet Jeremiah it toured Egypt, then
we find it roving in Spain, Sicily, Greece, and finally in Ireland,
at Tara, now the *Lia Fail,* or "Fatal Stone," used as an oracular
throne of Irish kings. It was also said to be the deathbed pillow
of the Irish St. Columba on the Island of Iona.

Following St. Columba's passing, legend says the Coronation
Stone was removed to Argyl in Scotland, where it was venerated
as the prophetical power of royal succession.

Years later, when Cormac McCarty, builder of Blarney Castle
and a great and puissant Irish king, provided Robert Bruce with
5,000 kerns to fight Edward II in Scotland at the Battle of
Bannockburn, the great liberator of the Scots gratefully rewarded

the Irishman with a piece of the "Fatal Stone" that the jealous and rightful owners had surreptitiously broken from the original when the hosts of Edward I threatened the sacred relic.

McCarty placed this monument of faith atop his strongest of twenty-six Irish castles, Blarney, where it remains to this day. There it has been imparting "sweet, eloquent persuasiveness" ever since to all of those who brave the back-breaking ordeal of kissing it.

The British hullabaloo over the Christmas removal of the Coronation Stone from Westminster, and their expenditure of $5,000 an hour in a frantic search by Scotland Yard and thousands of police, the army, navy, the air force, "private eyes" and country constables, in a national hue and cry of ludicrous proportions which extended to blockading the Scottish border, searching Scottish trains, busses and motor cars, may be traced to the Latin prophecy once engraved upon a brass plate on its surface. This couplet was translated by Sir Walter Scott as follows:

> Unless the fates be faithless grown
> And prophets' voice be vain,
> Where'er is found this sacred stone,
> The Scottish race shall reign.

The current push for freedom by the clamoring Scottish Nationalists is of deep concern to the British. In the hands of the Scots, their Coronation Stone could spell the doom of Empire.

The Scottish question is becoming an exasperating problem. Many of the 2,000,000 citizens want semi-independence at least, home rule, commonwealth status. The demand has become so boisterous that it is more than merely irksome to English ears. It has given the English a splitting headache. They are mazed as the Scots fight their plight under the present state of their "freedom's" tenures in a manner suggesting violence.

England has made a cricket ball of Scotland's economy. During the depression of 1930, 1,500,000 Scots were thrown to the dole in the interest of England's selfish purposes. The British closed their Scottish shipbuilding yards and other industries on the Clyde, and kept their own humming.

Ninety-four per cent of Scotland's soil is barren. English landlords refuse to permit the Scots to turn 3,000,000 acres of land, set off for the owners' sport of stalking deer, to productive sheep and cattle raising for meat and wool to help the Scots improve their national well-being. The Scots want their deplorable transportation systems bettered. They want to boss their own affairs, tax themselves, control their own industries, listen to their own uncensored radio broadcasts. They are "up to here" in the programs of the British Broadcasting Corporation. The Scots want freedom. They ask for the most unreasonable of concessions. Lesser rumblings have led to revolutions.

Already bereft of many of their dominions in the march of autonomy so that the sun does set on soil no longer liege, the Crown worriedly remembered another translation of the Coronation Stone's foretokening text:

> If fates go right, where'er this stone is found,
> The Scots shall monarchs of that realm
> Be crowned.

The jubilant Scots from Glasgow to Scone quoted still another version as they anticipated final liberation from the British through the fulfillment of the stone's prediction:

> Except old saws do fail,
> And wizard's wits be blind,
> The Scots in peace must reign
> Where they this stone shall find.

The stone's disappearance from Westminster created an understandable crisis that soon became a veritable panic as the tradition-bound English government weighed its enormity in

stunned horror. It was a calamity and a threat to the royal line
so dire as to make the foundations of its posterity tremble. The
Coronation Stone is a symbol to England of its perpetuity and
solidity, an investiture of the very authority to which it owes its
existence. The fact that it was stolen from the Scots makes no
difference. By dint of asseveration and ebullition of scorn, the
English have persuaded themselves of rightful ownership, flaunt-
ing the curse of Moses: *Cursed be he that removeth his neighbor's landmark.*

The terror that the straying of a pebble worth a Yankee dime
struck to the heart's core of the nation was unprecedented; even
the threat of Napoleon and the Asiatic hordes of Genghis Khan
reaching toward the gates of Vienna being so much fish and
chips in comparison. The bombings by Hitler, the crisis of
Dunkerque, were all the same. The end of the world as the
English knew it was at hand as a prophecy of doom hung over it:

> The Scottis sall brwke that realm as native ground,
> Geif weirdis faill nocht quhairever this chair is found.

Across the Channel the Irish found an inspiration for gay and
rollicking fun over the possibility of a riotous spectacle: For a
while, in those terrible days of disaster, it appeared likely that
all future English kings, if any, would of necessity have to be
inaugurated in Ireland while sitting on the Blarney Stone, the
only other piece of the Coronation Stone available, their royal
dignity teetering in more ways than one over the alarming heights
of McCarty's castle!

And would that have been a great day for the Irish!

> If fates goe right, where'er 'tis pight
> The Scot shall find, and there his Raigne assign'd.

The Irish and the Scots are of the same race, anyway. Is it
possible that England, because of their fortuitous possession of a
magical slab, may some day have an Irish king?

That would be one way, at least, to recover Ulster.

When the Blarney Stone was part of the Coronation Stone on the hill of Tara, the celestial object that had been rescued from the bottom of the sea where storm-tossed mariners had cast it on a voyage from Egypt, it proved an uncomfortable seat for spurious claimants to the thrones of Ireland, separating the wheat from the chaff in a manner all its own. When a pretender sat upon it, the *Lia Fail* roared out a protest that made the occupant jump right back into the ranks of the commoner. When a legitimate heir took his place, it remained silent and a new worthy king was hailed.

Some say the Blarney Stone was that which gushed forth water in the wilderness when struck by Moses. Others that it was the cornerstone of Solomon's Temple, and was brought to Ireland after Titus destroyed Jerusalem.

Still another legend asserts the Blarney Stone is a part of the original "great Stone of Abel" whereon the Philistines set down the sacred ark of the Lord in the field of Joshua, the Bethshemite, before the plague-stricken thieves returned it to the Israelites.

It may be a stone brought to Ireland from the environs of Bethlehem during the Crusades. The holy warriors claimed that it was a fragment of the "Stone of Ezel," behind which David hid on Jonathan's advice when he fled from his Biblical enemy, Saul.

Whatever may be the origin of this remnant of Ireland's ancient glory, her "precious Phoenician inheritance," it possesses always the remarkable power which "can communicate to the tongue that suavity of speech, and that splendid effrontery so necessary to get through life."

Queueing up in daily thousands before the turnstile are every manner of men—men in the kilts of Ireland and Scotland, the turbans of India, the military uniforms of a score of nations, the suits of Bond Street and Broadway. And sandaled women of the Orient, ladies of the peerage, schoolteachers from Kansas, ste-

nographers from Brooklyn—all of these, the plain housemaid
and her grand bejeweled mistress, who have measled the block
with enough rouge to paint a mountain; for women, too, have
use for the gift of the Blarney Stone, which arms them with their
second most potent weapon in the eternal war of the sexes. The
oil baron and the cattle rancher, the butcher, the baker, the
candlestick maker—and nuclear scientist—have been drawn by
an irresistible magnet which holds them in common thrall. But
when boy meets girl and both kiss the Blarney Stone, irresistible
object meets immovable force.

Some of the visitors will have invested in the fey osculation of
a rock sums amounting to thousands of dollars, because annually hundreds of travelers from all parts of the earth come at
great expense by air and sea to this enchanted fairy ground of
Ireland solely for the purpose of wooing the mysterious gifts
which the oblong slab to which they now pay homage reputedly
bestows.

Down through the centuries this highly endowed part of the
ancient castle has been a mecca for men and women who have
besought the powers of its mystery at the risk of their lives. And,
indeed, the old talisman has claimed the broken bodies of many
worshipers, where all perforce have worshiped not upon their
knees but flat upon their backs in one of the strangest rituals in
the world.

Once upon a time, before the construction of the iron bars,
visitors who came to kiss the responsive stone were necessarily
held by their ankles and lowered head first over a terrifying wall.

The promised reward for this journey to the famous site and
the planting of respectful lips upon the stone is the imparting
of a charming ingredient to the conduct of mankind which is an
eternal essential of all human behavior and relations. It has become known as "blarney."

It is the fateful piece of limestone itself that epitomizes the

difference in the temperament and spirit of the Irish from all
other people's. The Blarney Stone therefore is not a rock at all
but is actually the mysterious heart of Ireland that beats and
flows its magic blood through the veins of all of her sons and
daughters wherever they may be and under whatever flags they
may fight and die, and whether or not it is mixed with that of
other races; the Blarney Stone is the "mother heart" of them
all. The "blood" of the Blarney Stone, whether one drop or
gallons, makes every Irishman an Irishman. It is veritably a
symbolical keystone of their nation and the link which ties them
more than any other single thing to the Ould Sod. It is truly
their fateful shrine and the fountain of their wit and humor,
their ready tongue and the eternal gift of gab for which they are
famed. It is a treasure beyond compare, a treasure of soft voice.

Insensitive enemies of blarney have called it by many names
that have served in some quarters to profane it. Queen Elizabeth
dubbed a blarneyer "a jugglyng traytor." This was the most
ungracious utterance to which her majesty ever gave voice. It
may be said, however, that she was highly disgruntled at the
time over the behavior of an Irishman. This strangely choleric
queen should not have been surprised at the Irish for anything
they did, since she herself was half Irish on the side of her
mother, Anne Boleyn.

Lowell, in his *Fable for Critics,* was one of a woefully mis-
informed number who subscribed to an unfortunate definition,
as follows:

> The cast clothes of Europe,
> Your statesmanship tries,
> And mumbles again the old *blarneys* and *lies.*

In another offensive libel there came from the pen of the
historian Windele, more than a century ago, the following lines:

> In unvarnished prose, the touch of the Blarney makes
> a liar of the first magnitude; but a smooth and graceful

liar; its eminent perfection is a sweet and persuasive tongue, in whispering the softest words into the ears of women—full of guile and blandishment and potential flattery, and uncontrollable in its sway over the credulity. Miss Plumtre translates Blarney into the single word "Rodomontade," a faculty of speech remarkably perceptible in the vicinage around, whose inhabitants, it is said, have been mistaken by Boullaye le Gouzand Latocnaye for a colony from Gascony. They are of a truth a swaggering, vainglorious, wheedling population.

Horrors!

The Blarney Stone's only rival, did it exist today, might be the tablets of the Ten Commandments, but the Blarney Stone carries no injunctions which would burden the easy mind or tongue; lies and blarney themselves are miles apart. "Thou shalt not lie" has no place in the spirit of the Blarney Stone, that imposes no weight on the conscience, for a blarneyer does not lie. Neither is blarney boloney. About this fine shading of difference, Monsignor Fulton Sheen, of New York, has written a profound opinion.

> There is a world of difference between "Blarney" and "boloney." "Blarney" is the varnished truth. "Boloney" is the unvarnished lie. "Blarney" is flattery laid on just thin enough to like it. "Boloney" is flattery laid on so thick we hate it.
>
> I firmly believe that if the world had a little more "Blarney" and a little less "boloney" it would not be in the mess it is today.
>
> During the World War there was a policeman stationed at New York's 42nd Street and Broadway; I believe he was Matt McGrath, the weight-thrower. He used to address every private who passed him by as "Captain." He explained: "It made them feel good." That was "Blarney." It is worth noting that that cop never called any one of the privates "General"; that would have been "boloney."

"Boloney," then, is flattery laid on with a trowel; "Blarney" is flattery laid on with the lips; that is why you have to kiss a stone to get it.

Other authorities are quoted to give the lie to those who give it to blarney.

Webster . . . . To flatter or cajole with complimentary talk; coax or wheedle with praise or compliments; blarneyer, "so he blarneyed the landlord."

Funk and Wagnalls . . . . . Wheedling flattery, smooth and ready talk, in allusion to the Blarney Stone in Blarney Castle, Ireland, said to give those who kiss it a cajoling tongue.

Richard Caulfield . . . . On the word Blarney, urn of flowers is said to be its derivation.

Oxford Dictionary . . . . . . Blarney. . . . To flatter or Beguile.

John T. Collins . . . . "Blarney" does not mean soft, (Of the Cork Historical golden, or smooth talk. It is derived and Archaeological from the Irish words meaning a Society) field, or the little field. It takes the article *the* before the name. Letters which passed between the owners and the Queen's Court during the time of Elizabeth were always sent from "the Blarney" and in all documentary evidences "the Blarney" is used.

Chamber's Dictionary . . . . Blarney—cajoling talk. The gift of *Blarney* is conferred on those who kiss the Blarney Stone.

J. S. Coyne . . . . A popular tradition attributes to
(From *Cork Historical* the Blarney Stone the power of en-
and Archaeological dowing whoever kisses it with the
Journal, 1912, Vol. sweet, persuasive, wheedling elo-
18, p. 104) quence so perceptible in the language of the Cork people, and
which is generally termed *Blarney*.
This is the true meaning of the
word, and not as some writers have
supposed, a faculty of deviating
from veracity * with an unblush-
ing countenance whenever it may
be convenient.

Irish Tourist . . . . The famous Blarney Castle and the
Association magic Blarney Stone with its tradi-
Handbook tional power of conferring eloquence on all those who kiss it are
known to the world. Its meaning
has become established to be "fair
words and soft speech." Or pleasant talk intended to deceive without offending.

The satirical *Survey of Ireland,* written by the 15th century
author, Aenghus na N-Aor, or just plain Angus O'Daly, tells us
intimately how the owners of the Blarney Stone themselves
practiced the gift of blarney. On a visit to McDermod McCarty
at Blarney Castle in the 1600's, he says, "Flattery I got for food
in great Musgraidhe of MacDiarmoda."

The Rev. C. B. Gibson gives us this "versified paraphrase of
the Irish" by the poet Mangan:

MacDermod of Muskerry, you have a way,
Which at least I must term odd, you gave me, MacDermod,
With a great deal of blarney, a wine-glass of whey.

* Mr. Coyne, we think, is being a little harsh.

Before I could reach Ballincollick,
I thought I'd have died with your frolic.

Another translation from the Gaelic is:

Flattery I got for food
In great Muskerry of MacDiarmada
So that my chest dried up from thirst
Until I reached Baile-an-cholaig.

Withholding food from a guest while entertaining him with blarney, certainly does not make a liar of a host. If O'Daly had eaten too much, he might have suffered from colic anyway. Furthermore, there is no historical evidence that O'Daly had been invited to Blarney Castle, or was even expected!

If McCarty had known he was coming. . .

When a guest just pops in, a certain amount of blarney is always required to distract his mind from an empty board. It is certainly a better and more polite method than bawling him out for coming at all.

Acknowledgments

This is to advertise with gratitude the labors of so many *fey, shee*-bound mortals who gave to this book the best in their enchanted powers. To those who sifted the dust and bones of donjon, tunnel and raft in search for new clues to the tantalizing secret of the Blarney Stone; who braved the bats of ancient subterranean galleries, and worked over the sneezy must of medieval lore; who, when the moon shone blood-red in eclipse on a wild night that idiots loved and drove Irish dogs wild, grubbed in the decaying vaults and tombs of Iniscarra, scraping lichen from some moldering epitaph, clutching "sticks" that halfway through they found were human ribs. *Inne thys burying ground lyeth the bodye.* You know "he walks," whoever he is. A jolly place to research while resentful whooshing owls whirred the fungi with their wings from the crumbling ivied walls.

And through the great old castle itself, "the Mouldering Hall of Kings," they raked the floors and read the walls of keep and dungeon and oubliette for the mark of the shamrock and Latin keys to the mystery of the most famous rock in the world, scuffed their shins and risked impalement on the stalagmites sprouting in long-closed caves, and braved the gloomy "murdering hole." Their enchanted hands and minds never tired, and without their discoveries this, the first and only book ever written on the Blarney Stone, would have failed of its purpose.

Especially to Jeanne Perkins Smith of New York, for years of research and editing, and to her always sure and bewitching hand that finally touched more than 3,000 pages of notes resulting from the combined labors of all who followed with ingenuous

faith the marvelous peregrinations of the "palladium of Ireland."
Artlessly they choose to believe in the power and the magic
which have enabled the beguiling font of eloquence to endure
for so many centuries in the affections of all peoples and even
unto this day as it continues to bestow its generous benison
upon the tongues of the world.

And to all of these for their help and encouragement, as the
Irish say, *God bless!* Martha Foley, America's famous lady of
letters, and herself a descendant of McCarty kings and queens;
W. O. Sorensen, a beloved and philosophical chauffeur of Cork
City, with a predisposition for graveyards, and Norman skulls
and bones; Tim O'Dwyer, a reaper of Blarney Village; Thomas,
a butler of the New Castle; the late lamented dear old Puff, the
royal Pekingese who in his own dog's way kissed the Blarney
Stone himself; Katy Ford, the gatekeeper of the Old Castle;
Mary Ellen Hyan, of Inagh, in County Clare; Marguerite Alice
O'Hara, a Pennsylvania colleen, and communicant of the Alle-
ghany leprechauns, who gave these lines her lore. (It has been
seldom and long ago that man has shared such magic.) Jim
Bishop, the ould colleague; Rex Smith, of American Overseas
Airlines; George H. Lyon, James and Helen Thurber, Dr. Franz
Horch, Archie Ogden, this author's editor; Houghton Furlong
and Coburn Gilman, Dawn Powell, Dorothy Kiley, Agnes
Keeley, Maggi McNellis, Lisa and Gorham Munson, Clip Bou-
telle, Red Neubert, of R. H. Macy & Co., of New York; General
Clark Howell, publisher, *The Atlanta Constitution;* Dr. O'Hig-
gins, Minister for Defence, Republic of Ireland, and James
Douglas Caldwell, Nunnally and McCrea Co., of Dixieland.

And to all of the woodsmen and the foresters and the dairy-
men of the great Blarney demesne, who added to the lore of
this volume and gave the best they could remember and then
remembered more. And the old folk of the village, custodians
of rare oral literature of ancient Blarney's past, who hour after
hour sat patiently over stout or tea in their thatched cottages or

in the pub of Muskerry Arms or within the beneficent rays of the sentinel looming over their lives and, giving charming voice, recited elvan lore and ancient glories. Of love, wars, the supernatural, their Gaelic tongues as sweet as cream with rhythm, in magic telling of nature. No Druid *fili* on his *cromlech* in Blarney's ferny Rock Close could compare.

And to Adrian Hamilton, the "Crown Princess" of Blarney Castle, a modern Alice in Wonderland, the loveliest young sprite who ever took disguise in mortal form.

And to the shades of Spenser, Pope Adrian IV, St. Patrick, Sir John Suckling, John Salisbury, J. Windele, John Hogan, Father Peter Lombard, Dean Swift, Father Francis Sylvester Mahony, Daniel O'Connell, O'Sullivan the Red, Francis Tucky, Lord Roger Orrery, Thomas Crofton Croker, Sir Walter Scott, Queen Elizabeth, Father Edmund Hogan, John Hogan, Father C. B. Gibson, Father Matthew Horgan, Cormac McCarty, Richard Milliken, William Maginn, Sir George Carew, Henry VIII, the Monks of Lismore, Rudyard Kipling, Pliny the Elder, and countless others, forgiveness for their omission to be sought by the author in heaven.

Also sincere appreciation is extended to the following: Joseph Reilly, editor of the *Blarney Annual of Fact and Fancy,* County Cork; the librarians of the New York Public Library; the Congressional Library, of Washington, D. C.; the British Museum, of London; the Cork Public Library and the Cork Historical and Archaeological Society, of Cork City; and last, for emphasis alone, to all of those droll and inspirational *O'Boys* of old Blarney Village, O'D., O'K., O'S., O'L., O'T., O'M., O'H., O'F., O'R., O'B., O'C., O'N., O.G., O'W., O'U., and O'O., who freely, even as Queen Mab delivers men of their dreams, delivered themselves for this volume of unrestrained torrents of that ingredient that has made their home town famous everywhere.

Some of the stories they have told so disportingly on themselves were wracked from the memories of lifetimes in Blarney.

Some of the clashes in O'K.'s Snug Pub are compounded of episodes involving the British, American tourists and other visitors over various periods of their histories. These often amusing and, in some instances, almost tragic happenings are grouped in the interest of cohesion and continuity.

A few names have been changed, such as that of lovely Maggy, whose "wrong bottom" was spanked by the midwife; and some other characters, now and then, have been disguised, as promised, to save reputation and prevent almost certain social reprisals. Certainly these are gentle and considerate liberties to take with the story of the Blarney Stone, but ones that have not been permitted in any way to allow of distortion or to impair the blarneyed truth.

But most of all to you, for giving these blind words the sight to see your face.

John Hewlett

The
BLARNEY
STONE

Chapter One

The Season of the Pooka

Here, on the top, exists the wondrous stone,
Which to the tongue imparts that soft'ning tone;
Its high pretentions are acknowledged wide,
And with the nation 'tis identified:
Nor can its long-established fame subside
Throughout the world, till tongues themselves have died;
But this strange feature multitudes have got
Who know no other of the charming spot.

—*Hogan,* 1842

Now will I dip my pen in a thundercloud, for 'tis a strange and stormy fluid this script will need, and the gossamer dew of faeries' wells. Uncommon hues they are, indeed, but as kindred to this story as is blood to Ireland's wounds, and the ghosts of the *shee* to its primeval yews, and the echoes of the cobbling leprechaun in the old groves of Blarney, where a lucky one to this day may even milk an enchanted cow.

It is to search the pages of a history sometimes written with fog, rather than with ink, scribbled with the point of a pike and not the quill, a record brushed upon the parchment of the ages by the wings of sprites dripping with the disappearing mist of Ireland's changing skies.

Deep must it dig into the ould sod soaked with the blood of saints and martyrs, and spade and dip for McCarty gold, for "this is fairy gold, boy, and 'twill prove so." And "bell, book and

1

candle shall not drive me back when gold and silver becks me to come on."

These will be the sentiments of this pen as they were in *Winter's Tale* and in *King John,* and more, for the lure of a treasure greater than Shakespeare ever dreamed drives it deep for buried maps splashed in brave and careless gore, and becks us to come on. It has been called a hopeless task but in the Pope's Green Island we will search away in the solitudes where the feathered ring ouzel pipes a keening ullagone and the field-fare laughs at us while on the wing. But the last laugh yet will be our own, and the reward is great, for "by oak, ash and thorn!" we would find the lost secret of the Blarney Stone—that "pebble of destiny," imparting merely for the fee of a single kiss a golden reward of golden talk, sweet persuasiveness, fair words, soft speech and, say some, the greatest of capacities for the varnished truth. The start must be made almost at the beginning of Creation itself.

Now, when the three-storied Ark of gopher wood finally settled to rest upon the Mountain of Ararat, its eight human voyagers hailed the promising bow that the Lord set in the cloud. The covenant they saw in the sky was the first rainbow in the world, the father of all rainbows to follow, and since there is no Biblical word to the contrary, most likely a perfectly normal rainbow in every respect. That is to say, its bands diffused seven shades of violet, red, indigo, blue, green, orange and yellow. But it might well have been entirely green.

For aboard Noah's ark that day were the seed of an especially proud and mighty race of men with whom that verdant tint has been immemorially synonymous. All of Noah's passengers gazed in wonder at the dazzling spates of colors in the heavens and saw the glowing roads that their sons after them would surely follow.

There were seven roads in this first rainbow of the Lord, and their descendants would pursue them all to many lands, to many beginnings and many endings, and some of them would find their pots of gold. But the pilgrims who took the green road in the arc found that the end of the rainbow was an emerald.

Shem, Ham, and Japeth, sons of the great Biblical mariner, rubbed their eyes at the glorious pattern and then dutifully went ashore to become *fruitful and multiply and bring forth abundantly in the earth and multiply therein, and to overspread the whole earth* as the Lord desired; and the Lord made nations of their lines and out of them came kings.

And some of these kings who came after them followed the yellow road of the rainbow to the lands of gold, and other monarchs who went down the thoroughfares of violet, blue, indigo and red found rich jeweled sovereignties of diamonds, rubies and sapphires. Untold numbers of them through the succeeding generations traversed all of these glittering and tempting highways, indiscriminately straying afield from one to another, tarrying by the wayside on one precious road, abiding for a spell here and lingering there for a little season, acquiring new and alien baubles as they went errantly on their ways. They became a multitude of races and scattered themselves over the face of the earth and acquired motley characteristics as their complexions and their strains mixed with all of the pigments of the spectrum, soon having no place that now they could truly call their home. They were neither of the kingdoms of the diamond nor of the gold, nor the ruby nor the sapphire, and but for a single race alone, all men were as mongrels upon the known continents of the earth.

For there was one and only one line of those kings who descended from the sons of Noah that deviated not.

Tenacious of their objective, erring neither to the right nor to the left, tempted by no other hue, save one, these staunch rulers held to their course on the green road which led through Phoenicia and Spain, achieving glorious exploits along every mile until they came finally to the end of the rainbow's trail and found that it was Ireland. Now in this land began the reign of kings more numerous than that of any other in the world. And they ruled in an unbroken line for more than 2,500 years over a people whose blood in its descent had been kept as pure and undefiled as was the world itself when God washed out all of its wickedness with the flood.

This pilgrimage that started down the 16,000-foot slope of the highest peak in the land that is now called Turkey required many centuries. It ended on the emerald isle during the reign of Belshazzar, the last king of Babylon, in the times of the miracles of Daniel and the appearance on the wall of handwriting unknown to any magician in the valley of the Euphrates.

While the world was still young, Delus and his five sons divided Ireland into five provinces, Connacht, Ulster, Meath, Leinster and Munster. There was no interference from any unfriendly man. The Milesians had rid the land of all of the Tuatha Dé Danann, who came before them to conquer the Firbolgs, a dark, dwarfish people who arrived in the Stone Age out of somewhere in canoes and were the pygmies who later inspired Dean Swift to write *Gulliver's Travels to Lilliput,* because of their fabled visit to the court of Fergus MacLeite, King of Ulster, in the second century B.C. Even though they were gods, the Tuatha Dé Danann could not prevail against the destiny of the invaders from Mt. Ararat via Phoenicia and Spain. They retired into their faery mounds, and now the Irish had none left to fight except themselves.

Now we have in Ireland Kings Heber and Heremon, two of the sons of Milesius, King of Spain. It was through their seed that was born Eogan More, son of Alioll Ollum, King of Munster, and today, say the most careful historians of Europe to this effect, "there exists no Irishman of the race nor one who ever lived who was not descended from one of the three sons of Eogan More."

But only one family even among the Irish, and of no other race in the world today, can produce an accurate tree ascending to the survivors of the flood, a posterity without compare in the records of mankind's antecedents, a genealogy of stock so vaulted that all others of different names are as newcomers to the society of Europe: this is the celebrated royal Hibernian house of McCarty, Clancarty, Barons of Blarney, Kings of Cork, Earls of Glencare, Viscounts of Valencia, Knights of Muskerry, descendants of Heber the Fair, son of Milesius, the Spanish hero and father of the Hibernian race—and Noah, grandson of Methuselah, and second father of the world. Their very name itself is derived from Cartheigh, meaning inhabitant of the rock.

The great variety of spellings found in the old records of Clancarty for both family and surnames, the latter not being in use in Ireland until 1702, when Edward VII sought to end the confusion of identities by forcing the Irish to adopt them, leads to a fascinating bewilderment. The result in the case of Clancarty defeated the very purpose of the statute, making a mockery of it and presenting a superabundance of nomenclature seldom encountered anywhere in history except among the Indian Raj.

McCarty is found spelled MacCartee, MacCartie, MacCarthy, plain Carty, and so on and on; and all of these are one and the same. Their given names and titles are myriad and even more perplexing. Dermod is also Dermoty; Cormac is Cormoc, Cormack and McCormock. There are Tiege, McTieg, Og and Oge. Muskerry is also Muskerrie, Muskery, Mouskerry, Muscrey and Mouthcerry, which must be lisped as Castillian Spanish.

The most illustrious member of this ancient line was Cormac Dermod Carty, famed in Europe as the builder of Blarney Castle in County Cork, and world-renowned for his long and intimate possession of a remarkable stone atop its battlements.

Every scrap of this famous man's history is reverently preserved in Erin. It is not the habit of the Irish people to forget anything, whether important or unimportant, especially in

matters pertaining to their bard-singing past. A dogged memory
is one of the notable characteristics of the Hibernian, and ample
proof of this heritage is not lacking anywhere in the accurate
records of centuries. But since they were unable to read or write,
there was required for this purpose an almost endless oral literature to keep alive their facts in the national memory.

When St. Patrick arrived in 394 A.D. he found a people whose
only writing was accomplished with the ogam, hieroglyphic-
looking carving based on a conception of the Latin alphabet
and apparently used exclusively for inscribing tombstones and
making mysterious and frequently undecipherable characters on
the boulders of the field, which some later and more literate but
indifferent Irish peasants used to build barns.

Yet it is unlikely that there was a single Celtic aborigine but
knew of his proud Phoenician origin, of the valorous deeds of
the Milesians in Spain, who could not recite the proof of his
relationship to the builder of the Ark and declaim with heroic
exaggerations the exciting lore his forebears heard from the lips
of the *filid,* Ireland's professional historians, the most learned of
whom knew as many as 350 stories of battles, hostings, naviga-
tions and immigrations, love and catastrophes. And more they
heard from the darlings of their folklore, the bards, who with
elvan singing of the glories of Ireland made real and brought
back again the lost worlds of enchantment.

The oral preservation of Ireland's voluble history, therefore,
required a retentive memory and a lot of talking over a period
that must be calculated in dozens of centuries if we base the
beginning on the Biblical calendar once decreed by the English
Parliament, which made it legal and official that the world was
created on October 23, 4004 B.C.

The first was easy. Memory, the Irish came by naturally. The
second was simpler still, for some of Ireland's foremost writers
themselves declare that her settlers brought with them from

Tyre and Sidon the very font of eloquence itself. That was the Blarney Stone.

To the pages of Blarney's history now must be added a new story, that of the quaint and curious Season of the Pooka. That is now indelibly a part of the district's past, and for ages to come the people of Blarney Village will talk about it and keep it alive until such time as the historians of Dublin and Cork get around to setting it down officially. "Season of the Pooka" is the name by which posterity will refer to those exasperating weeks during the Holy Year of 1950 when visitations of annoyances and vexations, trials and tribulations, left scarcely a cottage untouched.

Now the pooka of Ireland is not to be confused with the gentle homebody faery of Shakespeare who served King Oberon. The Irish puck or pooka is a malignant sprite bent on no conceivable good. A pooka is a devil of a puck, a mischief-making sprite. A pooka can do to man whatever he takes a notion to do.

At his hellish worst he can be especially tricksy with the tempers and dispositions, just as he was all summer long in that unlamented season of his emergence from the bog that he usually haunts in the form of a horse.

Those good people of Blarney who take no stock in pookas, and there are many of them too, believe the long drought and the unprecedented heat wave caused tempers to snap and bad manners to prevail, for Ireland was sorely punished that summer by an unrelenting sun. To this unorthodox group, the Season of the Pooka is put down as a lot of superstitious and nonsensical rot.

Even so, the tormenting dry spell itself is said by the less skeptical to be of pooka origin.

Whatever the reason, the Season of the Pooka was and will remain remarkable for all time to come if for no other reason than the role played in it by the world-famous Blarney Stone.

Furthermore, the ghosts and faeries of Irish folklore have taken a definite and serious place in scholarly Irish history, and will never be dislodged.

Ireland itself is a land of ghosts and faeries. But as to Blarney, they have taken it over as their own private preserve. There are probably more authentic sprites in Blarney than any other district in the world. It is their stamping ground, their happy hunting ground, their clanking ground. It is probably the place where all ghosts wind up, anyway, no matter where they were born. Every house and chimney and attic in Blarney has its own private spirits. They create a most desperate housing problem. They are thruppence a horde and some are actually kept as pets. But somehow there is always room for more.

They have the run of the land and none in any other district have as many privileges or command more respect.

There are elves galore and spellbound cows, chickens and geese, and ghosts of every "crayture," hairy, feathered and finny. There are ghosts of salmon in the Martin River of Blarney Castle that leap in the most peculiar ways for the ghosts of flies. Too many sober fishermen have seen their enchanted acrobatics for any doubt whatever to exist in a reasonable mind. All Ireland *is* reasonable in evaluating such matters.

The faeries, as one will learn in Ireland, are the souls of the dead who passed on without the benefit of extreme unction by a priest.

The Irish know that faery circles where the sprites have danced the night before can be found even by the near-sighted any morning in the fields of Blarney. They shine brighter than any others in all of Ireland.

Not even rich millionaire Americans who buy up old houses, get rid of the drafts and the rats, and bathroom them up like New York, are freed of them. The "little people," never before accustomed to a drip of hot water or anything better than a medieval sitting tub, now thoroughly spoiled, stay on to enjoy the modern conveniences, more attached than ever to the premises, and so clean that they are shortly visible even in the broad open daylight.

Hard by Blarney Castle, camouflaged by a bower of vines and guarded by yew trees and ilexes 3,000 years old, is the celebrated Rock Close, one of the surpassing natural beauty shelters of Europe. There, where the Druids made human sacrifices on their *cromlech,* which still remains intact, and trained snakes to make golden eggs with the saliva of their mouths (for which we have no lesser authority than Pliny himself, who claimed that he personally had seen one!), lives a witch. She is the custodian of the celebrated witch's cave. A fearsome creature she is too, and a sinful wastrel of firewood. The local people avoid the Rock Close at night, and even the avenue that runs by it, for fear of meeting her.

Now here is a witch that no mortal has *ever* seen, not that anyone in Blarney would wish to, but the evidence of her existence is proved every day of the year and there is not a child who cannot describe her appearance in detail.

In the daylight she lives in a grotesquely shaped stone about five feet high. Her body is hidden inside but her face leers horribly frozen from the top of the slab and tens of thousands of tourists have seen her features there. She is safe in that form, but when the sun goes down, the stone trembles like grandmother's jelly on a cold, frosty morning and the witch comes to life. She immediately proceeds to a prehistoric cave near the Druid's sacrificial altar and loses no time in building a roaring fire. The cave was constructed centuries ago by the early dwellers of Ireland and equipped with a fireplace to cook the extinct pre-Ice-Age bear, the mammoth, and the giant Irish deer that roamed the acres of Blarney and grazed on shamrocks that probably grew as high as privet hedges. The chefs who roasted them left their kitchen middens by the hearth.

The old witch, who succeeded the cave dwellers as an occupant, hustles about and mixes the ingredients of her brew to heat in the cauldron. The fire is roaring by this time, but she piles on more and more fuel, for there is always plenty of wood on hand. It is left there every day by neighboring peasants to keep the witch so busy at night with her fire that she will not think to go abroad and terrify the countryside looking for a warm Irish hearth.

The average Blarnearian is confident that she is the only Ice Age witch in existence today and that once she cooked for the cave dwellers. She still shivers, they say, from the great cold she suffered when Ireland was caught in the freeze of the world. That explains why she uses so much wood, considering the precious little it takes to make a pot boil.

Every morning the fireplace is filled with ashes and no matter how many times it is cleaned out, the ashes are there again.

Also in the Rock Close nearby, there is an archway of limestone rocks, water-worn into fantastic shapes. Beneath it a rough stone stairway leads down to a thicket of bamboos, growing in a swamp. These steps are known as "The Wishing Steps," and legend says that if anyone walks down these, turns round three times at the bottom, and climbs up again, without opening his eyes or ceasing for one moment to think of his wish, that this will be fulfilled within the year. As the steps are slippery, and uneven, and the feat of turning around three times in a swamp with eyes shut not only destroys all sense of direction, but entangles the wisher in bamboo and trips him with briars, it is readily understood why so very few people make the attempt at all. But some do, in all seriousness, and indeed often return, suitably clad and shod, to make a second attempt, after the fulfillment of some previous wish.

It is told that the granting of wishes is the shivering witch's way of paying for her firewood.

All of these sprites are a part of the national scene and character, the population of a "Secret Commonwealth," of which the pooka of Blarney is a definite, if also a disreputable, citizen.

His manifestations left many scars, and none that the eye could see, because none of the scars were physical; all of them were psychological, but no less damaging or annoying for all that. The pooka shortened the patience of old friends, lured strange visitors to the village, increased man's thirst for drink, encouraged his high jinks in the pubs, gave him a foolish and unrestrained tongue, provoked a sense of uneasiness and created tension and suspicion. The Blarnearians were in the most disturbed and restless of moods just when the greatest influx of tourists and pilgrims to the Blarney Stone overran their countryside, and when they certainly should have been on their best behavior.

Americans, particularly, came in such numbers as were never counted before, and their strange habits which had formerly been regarded with euphemism, to say the least as charitably as possible, especially since they brought prosperity wherever they went, now only grated on the nerves of their traditionally genial hosts.

To this mecca, one of the most visited places in Europe, they had come demanding ice and Camels and Chesterfields and prompt telephone service and rooms with baths, both tub and shower. They had come in every manner of conveyance—they came on bicycles, motorcycles, in $16,000 Bentleys, taxicabs, busses, smart gigs, Model T's, on saddle mares, stallions and geldings, in shandrydans, new Packards, Lincolns and Cadillacs fresh off the steamer at Cobh—and the assembly lines of Detroit —in jaunting cars, one-horse, calash-topped chaises, donkey barrel carts. And afoot, like sunburned English summer hikers, in short pongee pants and brown cotton sweat neckerchiefs. The clutter of divers vehicles filled the square, and daily long lines of pilgrims queued up at the shilling turnstile leading to the old castle and the Blarney Stone.

So have men for centuries come in numbers to woo the Blarney Stone and pay it slavish homage.

Sir Walter Scott, lame from youth, in 1825 limped painfully up Blarney Castle's spiral newel stairs, negotiating the 118 sloping steps to the summit with a grimace on every landing, and faithfully flattened himself upon his back and planted his lips upon the mystic Stone, although the effort cost him the greatest discomfort.

Winston Churchill, when he was the First Lord of the Admiralty, journeyed to Blarney and squeezed himself up the venerable keep's narrow staircases that were made by builders who had not envisioned the possibility of any warrior's plumpness.

All of the historical area was of especial interest to the great English declaimer, for it was his illustrious ancestor the Duke of Marlborough, who besieged the walls of Cork in the same bloody undertaking in which the defenders slew the Duke of Grafton, bastard son of Charles the Second.

By a coincidence, even the Admiralty yacht which brought Churchill to Cobh, was named *Enchantress,* but now the celebrated visitor was prepared to pay court to the greatest enchanter of all.

Dutifully, that burgeoning master of eloquence and rhetoric placed his cigar on a merlon of the battlement from whence once upon a time the Clancarties had poured scalding oil upon many of his besieging countrymen, and obediently adjusted his mass in the traditional position. 'Tis said that from the very moment he implanted his buss upon the limestone, the fluency of his utterances was never so manifest. Now 'twas acclaimed far and wide that Churchill with new powers could charm even the timid meadow pipit to his finger from the furze. Only the most dissentious of men, recklessly contemptuous of history, would dare challenge this specific proof of the Blarney Stone's magic. In its most benevolent mood that day the palladium of

Ireland let bygones be bygones and generously bestowed the gift
of adroitness upon a hated British tongue. Some of the following doggerel is singularly apropos:

> There is a stone that whoever kisses,
>   O, he never misses to grow eloquent.
> 'Tis he may clamber to a lady's chamber,
>   Or become a member of Parliament.
>
> A clever spouter he'll sure turn out, or
>   An out-an-outer to be let alone!
> Don't hope to hinder him, or to bewilder him,
>   Sure, he's a pilgrim from the Blarney Stone.
>   —*"Father Prout"*

There are to be found among the Irish, however—a people
who, it may be said, are not entirely without prejudice in matters where English statesmen are involved—some who have
labeled Churchill's oratory a type replete with "circumflexion,
circumbendibus, circumambience, circumvention and circum-
volution, all circumvolving circuitousness and circumfusion."

Nevertheless, the Blarney Stone made of Churchill the greatest
diplomat of his generation.

Few are those who have spurned an opportunity to kiss the
great palladium, and strangely, or shockingly, the only ones
vigorous research has brought to light have themselves been
Irishmen! One was Kevin Collins, the Dublin journalist, who
recently climbed to the top of the castle to accompany a visiting
New York newspaper columnist, Earl Wilson, who lost no time
in implanting a reverent kiss on the worn cold surface.

"But not for me," said the disdainful Irish scribe. "That's
for foreigners."

Another Irishman, showing marked indifference to, while yet
implying the efficacy of, the Blarney Stone itself, issued a brief
but classic statement when invited to make a pilgrimage from

England to his homeland and undertake the time-honored ritual. In a personal letter to the *Blarney Annual* he "indicated that it was not necessary for him to seek eloquence at Blarney." The author and playwright added by way of explanation:

"My natural gifts in that direction being sufficient, if not somewhat excessive."

He signed his name G. Bernard Shaw.

Irishmen wonder what the old mooter might have amounted to had he accepted the invitation of the committee. In Erin now it is a matter solely for sad conjecture.

. . *Och wisha, ullaloo, ullagone!*

Chapter Two

Blarney in Reverse

The word *blarney* itself in the Gaelic tongue is said by some scholars to mean "urn of flowers"; some say daisies, but the sweet perfume of its blossoms is that tasted by the tongue and not inhaled by the nostrils. Those who have licked these intoxicating odors find their vocal powers besieged with delight and carried away with joy and ecstasy. But these emotions now were absent from the lips of the Blarney Stone's neighboring godchildren.

Many of the thousand-odd residents of the small, historic place had already journied some weeks earlier to Cork to see the Hollywood cinema that had made their own beloved village the locale of its plot, and costarred the glorious palladium with Bing Crosby. It was a subject that would not die. It was entitled *Top O' the Morning*. There has not been a living Irishman who ever saw the film who was not taken aback by it. But to the proud Blarnearian it was a deadly blow.

Their eyes bulged in their loyal sockets when they saw it.

The affront was real and earnest. Local and even national honor and dignity were outraged. It was a matter of grave importance, a matter for the statesmen, for De Valera and O'Kelly and Acheson and Truman, for Washington and Dublin.

It was a most unfortunate period for the Americans.

Much of the aggravation, as usual, was caused by exaggeration, but no one felt that anything was exaggerated at the time. It was not only because of the pooka. The entire American

15

Republic was being blamed for the appearance of one American moving picture.

However unlikely it was deemed that war would be declared, the Americans nevertheless found themselves the target of snipers as they bore the brunt of Blarney's resentment.

Many of the pilgrims in the Season of the Pooka had come by train, but arrived on foot in the village square with bad tempers, and little patience for the joke about the railroad station which is located more than a mile away from the trains' advertised destination. Unprepared travelers have always been annoyed by this discovery, and the people of Blarney have a standard answer that makes the native laugh.

"Why," the testy newcomer demands, "is the station so far away from the village?"

"Indeed," replies the Blarnearian, " 'tis because they want it near the railway!"

And there was the American traveler who has his senses blunted altogither by this old Blarney wheeze of the tongue and the mind:

"Does the Blarney train run on schedule?" he asks.

"No, it runs on rails," replies the Blarnearian.

And that other Yankee fellow who asks if he can go to Dublin by Mallow.

"Why not go by train?" asks the innkeeper.

But these old stand-bys, always good for a hearty chuckle, did not seem funny any more in the Season of the Pooka, and unreasonable orders of free-spending Americans, for such things as portable television sets, one-day laundry service, bourbon whisky and Manhattan cocktails, usually provoking only a sense of pity, now were greeted with almost bristling intolerance.

"Blackmail dollars!" That was what Yankee greenbacks became in the unfortunate Season of the Pooka, having some apparent connection with the Marshall Plan and other United States aid to starving Europeans.

Some of the high and mighty American buggers actually inquired as to the location of the nearest Turkish baths. Once O'K., an innkeeper, would have patiently explained the nonexistence of such a luxury in the tiny village of Blarney, and suggested that to the best of his own limited knowledge there was no such thing to be found in all of Ireland, for that matter, but the pooka drains men of patience, and instead he fairly snapped their heads off their shoulders.

"Th' nearest one o' th' haythenish things is located in Constantinople!"

Blarney now was no longer the language of persiflage, but the mauling tongue.

The injury suffered from the American cinema was still fresh in mind, when one of the pooka's most capricious pranks brought to Blarney Village a state of "complete isolation." Complaints of impatient, rich American millionaires were clamorous and more than any patient innkeeper could contend with. There was no blarney in Blarney now.

The "isolation" began on a midsummer Saturday when Cork switched over to automatic service. All telephones in the county were cut off at 11 A.M. for an announced two-hour delay. Elaborate plans to celebrate the innovation of the dial and the demise of the crank involved the highest of dignitaries. At the high point of the official rites the Lord Mayor at 1 P.M. rang up the Bishop, everyone being supposed to congratulate everyone else. It was most embarrassing. His Lordship had time only to say hello when everything mechanical connected with a telephone system jammed.

It was Tuesday now and everything still was.

"When," demanded the harassed Americans, "can we call New York?"

"Chicago?"

"Milwaukee?"

O'K. shook his head in mock sympathy. "Niver in me life heard o' thim," he said.

"St. Paul?"

"Faith, I know where himself is," retorted O'K. sarcastically, "but ye can't ring there."

"Hell!"

"Begob," whispered the hard-put-to-it O'K., "here they are in hiven and wantin' to call hell!"

But aloud, he gleefully told of an experience by which the present emergency might be judged.

"When Dublin went automatic last year," he explained, "after th' openin' ceremonies not a sowl could telephone for *three weeks!* Th' Dublin mechanics were so ignorant altogither they understood not the meanin' o' a blissid button."

"Three weeks! Damn! But what are they doing about Cork and Blarney?"

"Oh, th' Corkagians, now, themselves can do nothin', but they called a mechanic from Dublin."

"Dublin! Hell, you say!"

"Don't fret. The Dublin mechanics *must* have had a lot of experience by this time."

When the exasperated Americans departed with their black moods, damning Ireland and ass carts and grumbling that the deplorable state of communications in Ireland could be compared only with those of the deplorable Philippines, the pooka put other uncharitable words in O'K.'s mouth.

"Good thing they're not here in the winter. Guess they'd be wanting the pavements heated. If those works ever jammed they'd slip down and break their necks. Flyin' over here in droves like migratin' chitchats. They treat th' ocean like 'tis a mill pond." Somehow, O'K. felt that this was something to resent.

They came into his pub asking for American bourbon. "Tom Burns" was one of the brands demanded by some of the well-fed, flashy divils.

"Fat burns too," O'K. was sometimes prone to reply.

O'K. was a massive and rubicund man, of a type common in Ireland, sunburned in his mother's womb. His hair was crisp, short and flaming. The fine crow's-feet of his eyes were red-hot on an anvil of a face where the sparks were always flying. There he hammered out the thoughts, confusions and passions from the homemade forge of his mind and many were there wrought for all to see.

With the evil pooka now stimulating his imagination, O'K. leaned his elbows on his bar and permitted his imagination to soar. The situation in his mind was funnier than the telephones. *It was winter in Blarney Village, and on the heated sidewalk Americans were going down like ninepins on unsuspected ice. The other side was rapidly getting red-hot after a Dublin "expert" had a crack at the works. Old ladies (American ladies) were leppin' like beings on a griddle, and startled old men (American men) were doing pas de chats. Roars of laughter from babies (Irish babies) in their prams.*

O'K. felt better now after his happy vision, and not at all guilty. It would serve them right!

"They want everything," he muttered, "even to a glass roof over Ireland to keep it dry!"

O'K. burst out laughing.

The inordinate demand for iced drinks fairly drove O'K. mad.

"Why!" exploded one American when told that his inn was iceless. "Blarney's even worse than Dublin. At least one can get ice there."

"But what ice!" laughed a companion. "I ordered some for a water pitcher at the Shelbourne and, ha ha, what do you think the hall porter brought me? Why, he paraded into my room carrying a twenty-five pound *block* of ice on a silver tray with a rusty carpenter's hammer!"

"Maybe he brought it for your head," suggested the malicious publican.

And then before the American could think he blurted, "Oh, no, to crack the ice with."

He did not realize what a fool he had made of himself until his countryman burst out laughing. That was the way O'K. lost a lot of business, but it was the Season of the Pooka. He did not care a damn!

"Bah!" or the equivalent thereof, retorted the American. "What's the use of being Irish if you can't be thick! I'm fed up with this donkey burgh, anyway. This place is as phony as my eleventh finger." Turning to O'K., he snapped out a question: "Can I take the train from Blarney to Dublin?"

O'K. scratched an itchy wrist on the red sandpaper of his chin somewhat reflectively.

" 'Tis not that I give one flat happy damn either way," he said finally, "but why not let the train take you?"

This insolence owes its very origin to Blarney itself, and first was uttered when the heavy, storied mail and passenger coaches of the Sassenachs shook the pleasant vales of the countryside in full career to their stages from Cork to Marrow, and on the rumbling, rutty way to Limerick and Dublintown.

O'K. had just brought the old wheeze of the centuries up to date from wood and horseflesh to steel and steam. Old or modern, it still was Blarney's own, as good today as when heat was used only for food and fireplace. Things change, but never the wit of Blarney. O'K.'s retort was new to the foreigner, suddenly new and terrifying. He could not compete with this ready, witty fellow, this dismaying Irish tongue. He went away mumbling.

The pooka was up to other deviltry, too.

The enchanted cows had been seen walking again up out of Blarney Lake, where they had not appeared for years before its

coming, and some of the disquieted old folk who believed in
such things now were grumbling that the little flint chips and
neolithic arrowheads that faeries use as weapons, had lost their
efficacy as remedies for disease of man and beast; that now
when they dipped them into drinking water, the colic of either
ailing human or ailing bull was affected not a bit one way or
another except as to their bladders from too much stretching
liquid; and there were spread abroad the unlikeliest of reports
that thirsty ghosts were milking the peasants' cows.

Some idiot had even cut down an Irish thorn, an evil and
unlucky deed in Ireland. Such always brings ill luck from the
faeries who live in its roots.

The enchanted cows never emerged except as omens of impending danger, and the fact that they had been seen by a
London gentleman who had no patience or belief in such things,
was considered conclusive proof that mischievous forces were at
large in the world. This man first had heard them sneeze. It
was a startling and unmistakable sound that came out of the
soft, creamed darkness, and one that many had heard before, for
no longer is the existence of the charmed milch cows doubted
by any reasonable man. The only question is as to their color.

The latest spectator of the magical phenomenon was a highly
conventional and realistic visitor from London, and intolerant
of all this sanguinary twaddle about Irish leprechauns and elves
and the "Secret Commonwealth" of the "Little People." It was
on a bright midnight that he looked spellbound from his window
of the "New Castle," the Scottish baronial mansion of the old
demesne, upon the rare sight of an entire herd of beautiful
and radiant creatures winding slowly up from the lake and
ruminating in smug bovine disdain, even as mortal cows will do.
Still, they were unlike any others he had ever seen, dispelling
such a luminous awe that the white garlic flowers and little
nameless weeds danced like beam-shot molecules over their
blankets of grass, and fell away in mollescent shadows as they

came radiantly on their way. Their herdswoman was a laughing, hunchbacked old crone who carried a fiery blackthorn staff. No, by God! She was not carrying it at all. It was walking, or rather hopping beside her, as though held by an unseen companion. And could he believe his eyes! There a lurid pail bobbed along in midair, supported by another eerie hand! By Jove! An invisible specter of a milkman!

The correct English gentleman wavered and trembled before the ghostly parade. Unbelieving exclamations tangled in his throat.

"Extraw'd'n'ry, extraw'd'n'ry," he managed weakly, and he tugged with desperation at a satin cord to shut out the awful revelation before him; but the hardware of Ireland is never repaired, and nothing happened, and so, helplessly, he had no other choice. He stared.

"By Jove!" he finally cried. "They cawn't be, now! But . . . but they are! They . . . they're faery cows!"

The old hag must have heard him, for she gargled a frightful cackle and she, her herd, the ghostly shillelagh, the milk pail, and whatever awesome thing had been carrying them, all reversed their paths and marched off together with the greatest indifference toward the lake. One by one, its royal purple waters swallowed them up and left not a ripple in the doing of it.

Next morning, pale and shaken by his experience, weak from tossing all night in a 500-year-old bed, and hoping to find that he had been dreaming, even though he had never closed his eyes, he hurried down to the lake, wildly looking everywhere in the dawn's sane light for any shred of evidence to dispel his concern.

"Even a calf," he muttered. "Things look strange in the distance at night. And I . . . I was tired." Hopefully he thought it might have been that fourth large helping of beef and kidney pie on which he had gorged. He knew that he was overdoing it at the time. Whatever foolishness the Irish might take stock in, their tables were loaded down, anyway. This particular English gentleman, like so many of his hungry countrymen, was actually a week-end refugee from his own austere London board, and a recipient of the kind hospitality of the baronet of Blarney.

Now his worried heavy-lidded eyes stabbed expectantly to right and left, searching for the sight of even one everyday bossie to allay his fears. The reassuring sound of just one simple, nonenchanted "moo" would have steadied his British nerves no end. But the *bawnafinny* was empty. He heard only the coy music of a skulking whitethroat enlivening the hedges and a pied wagtail twittering the foliage with song. Finally, a thousand yards away, he came upon a very, very old man as grizzled as the ailing laburnum he was inspecting near the bog. The Englishman halted in some alarm and embarrassment, too.

"By Jove!" he muttered fiercely to himself, "if this blighter turns out to be the invisible milkman, they'll put me in Bedlam for sure!" But being an impeccable man with the use of his tongue, he hastily corrected himself of the corruption.

"Er . . . er, that is to say Bethlem Royal." And Bethlem Royal being the oldest insane asylum in the world, we gather therein some idea of the distraught man's personal alarm.

And as for Bedlam—while it was being built in London in the year 1247 A.D., when the English levied the first punishment of being hanged, drawn and quartered, a "marvellous and strange earthquake" trembled Ireland, "and held near three months," and made Blarney Castle teeter on its precipice. But the earthquake did not shake Ireland any more than the news of the new and frightening form of execution devised by their enemies across the Irish Sea. While terror of it in England drove men stark, raving mad, and added new names to the population of lunatics and *ideots* of infamous Bedlam in England, Ireland counted the days before it would come to her shores. She did not have long to wait.

But this goes ahead to tortures which will come later on.

Now we are concerned only with one tortured Englishman, in particular.

"I . . . was looking," he explained awkwardly, "for those . . . those, well, I guess they were cows. White cows."

The ancient fellow rubbed the bark of the poisonous laburnum tree for an exasperating time before he answered.

"Isn't any white cows in th' park," he said slowly. "Anyway ye can niver get a white beast or a white cow to milk well. And them cows is good milkers. Not white cows."

"But I saw them! I jolly well did! Who . . . who, now, my good man, are you?"

"A Blarney woodsman for sixty years," the old forester said, "and me father, rest his soul in peace, before me."

"Upon my word, but now . . . last night. I . . . saw those, those things!"

"Oh! Those craytures." The woodsman laughed tolerantly. "So you saw them too. Takes a foine night for a good look, but no good now comes of it. 'Tis a sight that's shaken many a strong man, just as now I see it has Your Honor. It's played the puck with heroes, sir, and heroines too. Bet you yelled and spoilt the milkin'."

The Englishman shivered over the dire prophecy hidden in the forester's words.

"I thought I might have lost my mind. Those bloody—beg pardon, sanguinary white cows! But others have seen them, too," he said hopefully.

" 'Tis me own guess there's nothin' wrong with yer mind, sir. 'Tis Yer Honor's eyes that's bad, I see."

"My eyes!" exclaimed the Englishman. "Why, there's nothing the matter with my eyes. They're twenty-twenty!"

The Blarney retainer regarded the visitor narrowly.

" 'Tis only two meself is seein' with me own ould peepers," the old man said. "In me long lost youth, now, walkin' home from th' pubs, I did see double . . . but . . ."

"Nonsense," the Englishman said, "I'm perfectly sober. Twenty-twenty merely means perfect vision."

"Then, sir, 'tis color-blind ye be. For 'twas ye yerself that said th' lovely green craytures was bloody, makin' thim red, and then white, which they are not either!"

"Green cows! My God, man!"

"Aye, sir, green, green as th' shamrocks ye stand on now, just as all daycent, proper, correct and self-respectin' enchanted Irish cows should be!"

Nothing but a pooka and a pooka alone could be responsible for such an experience, and only the most demoniacal and vexatious and malignant of them all could have wrought the other distortions with which the ancient village was visited. Petty things assumed the oddest of shapes and values and man was prodigal and imprudent of his tongue.

Such was the state of mind, mouth, spirit and soul of Blarney Village's weary and crotchety populace one summer afternoon when a listless and mysterious stranger without warning appeared in their midst and brought new and unusual problems to trouble them.

Chapter Three

O, Blarney Castle, My Darlint!

O, Blarney Castle, my darlint!
Sure you're nothing at all but a stone
Wrapt in ivy—a nest for all varmint
Since the ould Lord Clancarty is gone.
Och! 'tis you that was once strong and ancient,
And ye kept all the Sassenachs down,
While fighting them battles that ain't yet
Forgotten by martial renown.
—From an old ballad

This Kentucky man, Kane, purposely called by a misnomer
in respect to that privacy due unrequited love, and because
of its attendant suffering, arrived in County Cork with a broken
heart and the picture of a girl in his pocket. It was a long-
looked-at photograph, and the girl had the speckled brown
eyes of a doe that has been frightened while drinking from a
pool. The depths in them stared in the deep cool mirror of a
spring and saw a handsome, longing man standing off a little
piece away. The expression of the girl was curious and contradictory. There were both yearning and fear; and the picture
showed on her face where Kane had dropped a tear when she
ran away.

The Kentucky man came walking into Blarney Village from
Cork City having taken the six-mile road that leads from rose-
bushed Blarney Lane through the world's greatest paradise of
beauty. But he had no eye for any of it, even though the route

he took was of such transcending and nostalgic floral glory that long ago it had inspired the composer of the famous old Irish song, "Where the Blarney Roses Grow."

> Can anybody tell me
>   Where the Blarney Roses Grow:
> It may be down in Limerick Town,
>   Or over in Mayo.
> It's somewhere in the Emerald Isle,
>   But this I want to know:
> Can anybody tell me
>   Where the Blarney Roses Grow?

Kane was detached and dusty and aimless, and any song would have jarred his mood, so it was just as well that day that the melody was not given him to hear.

Still, it was a musical clime of "soft mornin's." The poet Mangan had heard the notes singing.

> I walked entranced through a land of morn,
> The sun, with wondrous excess of light,
> Shone down and glanced o'er seas of corn
> And lustrous gardens to left and right!

The drought had been summer-long. Green Ireland was russet-splotched, and indeed 'twas a phenomenon for the eyes of man to see. The veins of the emerald were streaked with gold, and the fields of corn and the sward were parched under a wondering magenta fog.

The old custodian of an ass cart was halted on the wayside, and hailed the stranger with a great friendly "Morra, sir, and 'tis a foine day."

Kane made no response and trudged ahead. The Irishman squinted at the hiker and tried again.

"And 'tis th' furrst time in me life," he called out in a loud, wounded but hopeful voice, "that iver did I see Ireland lookin' fer a drop o' rain."

But Kane, if he heard the hospitable efforts of the old man, made no acknowledgment. He walked on down the road. His head was low and dejected. The Irishman watched him for a long time over hill and hollow. Finally he climbed back in his cart and flicked his ass with some celerity.

"Begob and may th' divil take th' English tripper!"

On Kane went through an emerald serenity ringed with fire-thorn and rioting blossoms, but blind to it and the green glory that is Ireland. A gull flying toward the River Lee plumed a poem in the sky. In the distance now there loomed a great pile of masonry, an ancient ruin of a castle, frosted and towered like a gigantic wedding cake, with pistachio hues lent by ivy and laurel, and fuchsia cotton candy clouds settling softly upon its turrets. A pale, white rainbow hung like a ghost in the mist of the River Martin where the sun came through. For the first time Kane showed some interest. He stopped abruptly on the road and stared hopefully at the spectacle of majesty before him, standing on a little bridge spanning a stream of platinum water where salmon finned an alchemy of gold. Scattered over the hills pink and white cottages rested like parti-colored coral beads upon the warm rolling throat of the land. But the castle alone held Kane's eyes. He swallowed and walked on toward it. There might have been a perceptible lengthening of his stride had anyone been there to see.

The quadrangular remains of yonder eventful ruins that had claimed Kane's gaze, once was the 15th century stronghold of the royal race of McCarty. Its 18-foot-thick walls free from sappers' mines, rising 120 feet from a rocky precipice over the Martin River in a narrow valley where the Comane and the Shournagh flow on to the Begorragh Mountains, and its great pile of sandstone blocks held together with ancient mortar mixed with bullock's blood and the bristles of swine, it once was reckoned the strongest of all the bulwarks of castle-studded Ireland, and its chieftains esteemed the most powerful in the land.

So powerful that they could insult Queen Elizabeth, mock the Crown and live to joke about it. The good Queen Bess received a figurative, varnished nose-thumbing from Lord Muskerry (McCarty) grinning out of an ogee-headed window of the old castle, as rare a sight as a foine day in Eire.

In 1602, Elizabeth's Deputy in Cork, the Lord President of Munster, Sir George Carew, believing him guilty of inviting Spain to invade Ireland, and also for other slippery traffic with the enemy, in which a fortune in doubloons, the employment of treachery and a bold plan to sweep the hated British back into the Irish Channel were allegedly involved, called upon the Irish Chief to "come in off his keeping" and surrender his stronghold.

Professing a "loyal and guiltless heart," McCarty "seemed very inclinable to the notion," and Queen Elizabeth was notified that the powerful Irish leader had bowed to her august authority. Ostensibly, this already had been achieved with his own avowal of devotion to the Crown, but now day after day he "put off the fulfillment of his promise" to deliver old Blarney to English trustees pending the disproval of the charges against him.

Finally, in disgust, Lord Carew notified his queen that in the process "it is perceived that he intends nothing but juggling and devices." Of "fair words and soft speech" there were plenty, but the princely owner of Blarney Castle continued to hold its possession for such an extended and exasperating time that finally Elizabeth exclaimed in anger of her glib and unwilling subject, "This is all blarney, what he says he never means!"

All of Cormac MacDermod Carty's trifling with Queen Elizabeth's royal patience occurred while he languished in her prison at Cork. The faithful members of his sept held his castle. So valuable was this Irish prisoner that the queen's deputy nervously issued many warnings to the gaoler to secure and watch his person with the greatest vigilance. One specific charge was to keep the Celtic Lord "in a handlock with his own servant, or some soldier of especial trust."

The gaoler's confident reply was this:

"If shackles of iron, walls of stone and force of men can make him sure, then shall my prisoner be forthcoming whensoever the state may be pleased to call him."

But the prisoner had no fears. He was waiting in confidence to test the prophecy of a witch. He had met her under extraordinary circumstances one sunny morning while he strolled the banks of the River Martin beneath the precipice of his castle, pondering the affairs of his troubled dominions. He wore his battle byrnie, a coat of linked mail made entirely of gold. It was a precious garment befitting a medieval king named Mc-Carty and he wore it in reckless bravery, for on its brilliant surface danced the rays of the sun and welcomed the attention of enemies to his person in combat. But now the dazzling raiment caught the eyes of a drowning woman who floundered for her life in the stream.

She was an old, old witch disguised as a peasant.

"Save me, great knight," she cried, "and I will make you the master of men!"

The old witch's mouth was full of water and with every word she spoke a tiny golden fish swam from her lips. In a trice, McCarty was out of his byrnie. He dived into the river and pulled the struggling creature to the shore.

True to her promise, the grateful witch pointed to the top of Blarney Castle and told her rescuer of the location of a marvelous magic stone.

"Go kiss it," she said, "and th' tongue in yer mouth will melt a heart o' stone. Gould 'twill become, gould as soft as th' speech o' birds, lovely birds altogither, and they will roost in yer mouth, and into yer throat they will sing their songs. Th' music o' yer words, once heard by man, man foriver cannot deny thim."

McCarty laughed at the silly babbling, but his sleep was troubled, and one night he decided to do as he had been told.

"Yer voice," the witch had said, "will become as soft as th' nose o' a cow that's just come in, nudgin' her calf o' th' same marnin's pain. And there will be a faery tongue in that head on yer foine Irish shoulders."

Forty-eight hours later Lord Muskerry had the temerity to escape during the night into the loyal arms of mantlemen waiting under a window to speed him to freedom! He eluded the most frenzied pursuit.

It was a furibund queen in London who received the stunning news and read in a flaming mood the alibis of her servants across the Irish Channel.

"Yesternight," began a report of the English Lord President, "the greatest mischance that hath fallen out in this province since I came into it happened, either by negligence or corruption, or both, which is the escape of Cormocke McDermod, being in irons and a guard to attend him . . . the power-fullest man of his own proper followers, and both a very strong country."

Queen Elizabeth raged in London, but her pride was to suffer yet another blow when she was forced to pardon her mocker!

"Not to forgive him might have bred new broyles, and protracted the warres of Mounster ad infinitum."

So was Cormac Dermod McCarty received back into Queen Elizabeth's troubled grace, restored to his estates and titles and at home again under the protection of old Blarney's walls and the guardian Stone of Destiny. He had been empowered with a great and mysterious eloquence which had enabled him to talk even the shackles from his limbs!

With shaking hand the queen read the report of a pledge her "power-fullest" Irish subject had freshly signed:

> Whereas the Lord Deputie had devised the forme of an oath for the Northern protectees he (McCarty) was content to sweare and subscribe to the same oath; and lastly himselfe with foure of the best barons of parliament in Mounster, were bound in 3,000 pounds for his future loyaltie and subjection, so that he was bound in heaven and in earth, before God, and before man, by law and by nature, and nothing but onely hell was remayning for his further assurance.

But hell itself could not long assure the English of the loyalty of any of the Irishry and especially that of the owner of the Blarney Stone that imparts a quality of rare impudence to the behavior of every man.

"Poised and ready to fight and die for this man were the powerful septs of Reardin, Murphy and Sweeney of Muskerry, and the O'Learies, O'Mahonies and O'Driscolls of Carbery," but with his family held as hostages by the English, McCarty preferred to use his golden tongue rather than the sword.

This especially charming Carty, called by the Sassenachs "the greatest man ever born among the Irishry" because of his aid in helping them overthrow the Desmonds, as the spirit, gold or political advantage moved him, sold out his arms first to the English and then to the Irish, profiting handsomely each time and always retaining the fierce affections of both. His death was the occasion of great and confusing international mourning.

The English, of this McCarty, whom they lauded fulsomely on occasion, upon his death described him as a "comely-shaped, bright-countenanced man, who possessed most white-washed edifices, fine-built castles of any of the descendants of the Eoghan More." He was further praised by the English for his "loyalty and civil disposition."

Of this McCarty, the Irish wrote, "We have no hesitation in saying that the word *blarney* has derived its peculiar significance from this loyal, rare, civil, comely-shaped, bright-countenanced man."

The peasantry said: "Faith, and this lovely man altogither is now rewarded in blissid glory by th' good St. Patrick who pairsonally sits in judgment on all o' th' Irish in hivin itself."

Even in his grave, the powers of his great gift still were working strong and blarneying a fitting epitaph.

So now it is easy to see how mistaken was Queen Elizabeth in her inference that the terms "blarney" and "liar" were synonymous.

But thus it was that some writers, following the queen's erroneous interpretation, persisted in the unfortunate and widespread assertion that *blarney* is an expression of "deceitful flattery, mere quibbling or insincere profession." This is heresy.

The nearest even Lord Muskerry's conduct may justly be compared is another conception with a fine shading, namely, that blarney is "pleasant talk intended to deceive without offending."

The McCarties ruled over a seigniory so vast that the human eye could find no horizon for it on the plains of County Cork, or in the mountains, or in the valleys and the dales that it once embraced, a demesne of villages, towns, castles, fairs, fat cattle, horses, woods and rich rivers of fish, churches, nunneries and abbeys and vassals, flocks, herds and game beyond census, and wildernesses and wolves without end, and a hound for every fox in Cork and a beagle for every boar, and *wilde fowles* so thick in the air that their wings made a curtain for the sun.

The wealth of this, the oldest family in Europe with the "tightest tree" traced to Noah, once was estimated at $500,000,000. Founded in the second century, and yielding an income of 200,000 pounds for 600 years, no trace of the fortune remains today.

Whither flew this great abundance when, despoiled of his dominions, Donogh, the last McCarty chieftain, fled Ireland to penniless exile in 1734, leaving behind the family's twenty-six castles and the accumulated returns of centuries? Rustic historians say the McCarties possessed cases of Phoenician jewels, golden armor, chests of Spanish doubloons, the heirlooms of Milesian kings, and golden ducats of such weight that all of the cannon of Cromwell were not as heavy. This treasure increases or decreases in value as it is described, depending upon the conservatism or the enthusiasm of the enumerator encountered. But the fact that great stores of gold were housed in Blarney Castle, whatever the amount, is historically incontestable.

Legend is that its secret is hidden by the waters of Blarney Lake, where it was consigned when the castle fell to Cromwell's men in the 17th century.

From the air Blarney Lake, one mile in circumference, is a great heart contained in thirty acres of purple blood. Its surface is quiet and its arteries are quiet too, 100 feet deep, fresh springs pumping through a blanket of human bones and golden Druidical snake eggs. On its bottom the herd of enchanted cows grazes on aquatic plant life growing through the other treasure chests of the McCarties, and leeches and pike and giant eels swim between their legs. Blarney Lake's deep waters hold the confidences of the ages, and a replenishing auricle, jealous of its troves, gushes its flood and fills the banks with secrecy.

Thus far has this been inviolate and well preserved by the heavy tonnage of its purple flood, but some day, as legend says, the McCarties will come into their own again. And a great day for the Irish it will be, for the McCarties will know exactly where to look for their long-lost gold. Three of their forebears were given the secret of the hiding place, and only on their deathbeds, one by one, have they passed it on to three others of succeeding generations, a secret pledged inviolate until the demesne is justly restored to their clan.

Tempting thought it is to the pilgrims that this staggering trove, or some part of it, lies beneath the surface of Blarney's purple spring-fed lake. But the wise pilgrim would not hesitate to swap it all, this relatively paltry sum, for the gift of the Blarney Stone.

It is this, a greater treasure, that they seek, one without compare; for with the true gift of Blarney, empires worth a thousand half billions wait for the asking by the honeyed tongue. And the very world itself begs to be given away, and the hearts of the fair are yearning to be cajoled.

Where lives the man who with persuasive fluency of speech, smooth and ready talk, golden and honeyed words, cannot win the earth, and heaven too!

All of these are the gifts of Blarney, and what greater ones could the fates bestow?

So commingled is this stone with the country's definite history and the disorderly pages of its fabulous past, that it has become to Ireland as green is to her fields, a rock with lore so entwined with the tumult of her destiny, her ballads and her folklore, that it has been immortalized as the palladium of the land.

And old indeed is the Blarney Stone. Older than the mists or antiquity's distant date when Noah prattled in swaddling clothes—that being about the time a certain fascinating Lady Ceasair led to the Irish shores a colony of fifty women and three men to populate the emerald isle, who were drowned by the flood before a single babe was born. Older even than *Ogygia,* which means very ancient, and was the name that Plutarch gave to Ireland; older than the days when Aristotle knew it as *Ierne,* or Pliny as *Hybernia* and other writers knew it as *Iberio.*

Older than the Irish people themselves "who drew their history from remote antiquity so that of other nations is new to them."

> When Greeks and Romans still wore tails,
> And banqueted on bugs and snails,
> Who ruled like kings in golden vales?
> The Irish!

Or, if you like this verse of Frank Dunn's poem better:

> When Greeks and Romans still wore tails,
> And lived in trees, ate bugs and snails,
> Who dwelt like kings in peaceful vales?
> The Dunns, O'Tooles and Sullivans.

The Blarney Stone is the nation's most sacred possession, and there is much to justify the fierce pride of the Blarnearian in his village's sacred exhibit. Bard, scholar, philosopher, churchman, historian and geologist down through the ages have heaped their praises upon the fatal block.

One of the most extravagant estimations of it was penned in all seriousness by John Hogan in 1842, who asked whether the Blarney Stone was not actually the very "centre of the world"!

> Thus strong the Blarney influence is shown,
> E'en upon those most distant from the stone;—
> The power, alike attractive, through the whole,
> Is found pervading—thus is but the pole.
> Astounding thought!—have we the centre here,
> Round which revolves the human hemisphere?—

> Nor has discovery yet the rival found,
> So, well may Blarney have its name renowned.

And the immortal Francis Sylvester Mahony rhapsodized about its glory in prose only slightly less puffatory. In writing of Sir Walter Scott's impending visit in 1825, Mahony's "Father Prout" delivered himself of this rodomontade, enough to turn the head of any Blarnearian, and make him a man of compelling importance if for no other reason than merely having been born in such an atmosphere:

> He shall fix his antiquarian eye and rivet his wondering gaze on the rude basaltic mass that crowns the battlements of the main tower; for though he may have seen the Chair at Scone, where the Caledonian kings were crowned; though he may have examined that Scotch pebble in Westminster Abbey, which the Cockneys, in the exercise of a delightful credulity, believe to be "Jacob's Pillow;" though he may have visited the misshapen pillars on Salisbury plain, and the Rock of Cashel, and the "Hag's Bed," and St. Kevin's petrified matelas at Glendalough, and many a cromlech of Druidical celebrity,—there is a stone yet unexplored, which he shall contemplate tomorrow, and place on record among his most profitable days that on which he shall have paid it homage:
>
> *Hunc, Macrine, diem numera meliore lapillo!*

When Sir Walter, the "Aristo of the North," finally did arrive at Blarney Castle, the convivial little old parish priest of Watergrosshill was in rare form:

> You behold, Sir Walter, in this block, [he said] the most valuable remnant of Ireland's ancient glory, and the most precious lot of her Phoenician inheritance! Possessed of this treasure, she may well be designated:
> "First flower of the earth and first gem of the sea"; for neither the musical stone of Memnon, that "so sweetly played in tune," nor the oracular stone at Delphi, nor the lapidary talisman of the Lydian Gyges, nor the colossal

granite shaped into a Sphinx in upper Egypt, nor Stone-
henge, nor the Pelasgic walls of Italy's Palaestrina, offer
so many attractions. The long-sought *lapis philosophorum,*
compared with this jewel, dwindles into insignificance;
nay, the savoury fragment which substituted for the infant
Jupiter, when Saturn had the mania of devouring his children; the Luxor obelisk; the treaty-stone of Limerick, with
all its historic endearments; the zodiacal monument of
Denderach, with all its astronomic importance; the Elgin
marbles with all their sculptured, the Arundelian with all
their lettered, riches—cannot for a moment stand in competition with the Blarney block. What stone in the world,
save this alone, can communicate to the tongue that suavity of speech, and that splendid affrontery, so necessary to
get through life?

The only great stones of history Mahony failed to mention
seem to be the Tablets of Moses; the Black Obelisk of Shal-
maneser II, found in the Mound of Nimrud; the Codex Sinaiticus
of the 4th century, containing all of the New Testament and
sold by the Soviet government to the British Museum in London; the Rock of Gibraltar; the Rosetta Stone; the Tablet of
the Deluge; the Moabite Stone; Akkadia's seven tablets relating
to creation that came from Mesopotamia, the cradle of the
human race; the Nineveh Tablets from Egypt's sculptured walls;
Code of Hammurabi unearthed at Susa, in Persia; Stone Mountain, Georgia, and the Ten Commandments.

In behalf of the usually thorough Mahony, however, may it
be stated that at least some of these cornerstones of history had
not yet been unearthed by archaeologist or accidental spade
when this "wayward child of genius" lived and wrote immortally
of his beloved Blarney Stone.

As to those that were known in his time and not compared,
Mahony undoubtedly considered them unworthy of mention in
the same company with the "gem of the sea."

Under the shadow of the Blarney Stone, the McCarties were capable of raising 3,000 fighting men at a call, and from Blarney Castle's machicolated battlements during the 15th and 17th centuries its defenders fought the besieging armies of Cromwell, Ireton, Fairfax, and those of King William who partially demolished it after the Battle of the Boyne. Old Blarney was the scourge and the bane of the English, an annoyance, a confusion, a damnation, a flinty spear in their flesh, a taunting and impudent fortress whose long impregnable bastions always threatened the rule of the Sassenachs.

Few structures in Europe are of greater historical importance than Blarney Castle, of Cormac McCarty, "Laider the Strong"; and yet, transcending even its own undeniable fame and the deeds of valor and heroism issuing from its turrets and emblazoned upon centuries-old annals, one incredible little piece of it, a chip of its tonnage, a veritable fragment of its bulk, because of marvelous powers and properties shared by no other in the world, is more important than all of the castles on earth combined and wherever they may be; and for many good reasons, here being one alone:

'Tis said: to all who kiss its face
Unbounded talent to cajole the race.

Kane stood by the side of the road alternately looking at the picture of the girl, staring at the castle, and feverishly making notes in a little morocco leather book. He replaced this in his pocket, and the old dullness returned to his eyes. He stared in the direction of the castle as though he did not see it.

It was a long time before Kane went on his way. He arrived in the square of Blarney Village at the season when Americans had begun to lose some of their former great popularity. They were feeling a bitter frost.

If the mysterious Kentucky man felt it, however, he never

so much as shivered once. Without a word, he registered at O'K.'s Snug Pub and promptly found a permanent table near the bar. Daily the uncommunicative American took his place there.

He had become a fixture at that corner table from the hour he walked into the inn in the manner of a man who had no destination. He paid no more attention to anyone than he had accorded the outraged owner of the ass cart on the distant hill.

His remarkable demeanor never changed. As always, hour after hour and day after day, he sat alone, drinking his gin-and-mix with ineffable dejection and staring at the photograph of a beautiful sad-eyed girl.

Chapter Four

Up, Kerry!

By Blarney's Towers I pause to ponder
What deep, dark curse our land lies under,
Chain'd 'neath the foreigner foe!
The homeless horde whose guileful knavery
Coil'd the festering links of slavery
Round hearts where pure pulses flow.
From sires, whose sons are crouching slaves,
Or wanderers wild, or outlaws gory;
Mail-clad sires, whose green flag waves
O'er blood-red fields of ancient story,
Where prone groan their offspring of woe.

Lonely and long that hour of weeping,
Hopeless, joyless, tearful-sleeping
In salt streams mine eyelids of care.
    —"Expulsion of the Saxon"
      O'Sullivan, the Red

An ancient Hibernian, whose face is the portrait of Ireland's sorrows, pounds his fist upon a table in O'K.'s Snug Pub. He gulps a glass of Paddy's and turns his head to look about him. It is a belligerent and suspicious gesture, for he has been a hunted man. It is a habit of his youth that has returned to-night, but it is a gesture as empty as the sockets where once he had eyes to see.

His gray little ould woman who had led him into the pub by the hand from a long twilight walk from their tiny little cottage on the River Martin, where they live fairly well on an old-age pension of four dollars a week, sits by his side. Her white moustaches are sudsy with Guinness. The ould man is drinking the stronger stuff in honor of an occasion. There is not enough money for both of them to have the same.

He drinks again quickly and chases the effects of his powerful alcohol with a powerful shake of his head. It is as gnarled and bumpy as a shillelagh and the stress within him is bursting at the shriveled old blue-white veins in his temples, making them young and full again with angry blood. He is no man to placate now, or to argue with. No one tries, or wants to try. All are in sympathy with his mood. From the moment he entered he commanded respectful salutes and greetings.

They are men in the rude work clothes of the farm, the highway, the greengrocer apron, the plain men of agricultural Ireland, the majority of it, the men of the soil and sweat, rugged men with honest, hairy muscles of toil.

They leave him alone in his rage, he and his quiet ould woman, and another ould man, his red hair gray, and four young men with youth in their bristles and ages of hate in their eyes, furious and darting eyes, and two of their sons with pink silk on their faces, biting their lips with hate in their teeth.

"Ireland's such a little island, just a little island," the ould man rasps. "Those six little counties . . . Faith, not enough dirrt to fill a gopher's hole . . . th' size o' a map!"

"Up, Kerry!" a young man shouts.

It is a "Remembrance Day."

"Damn Basil Brooke and his rotten sowl to hell!"

Shouts of "Up, Kerry" ring again through O'K.'s Snug Pub. It is the rallying cry of that inflammable area of Munster that had bred the boys who rose and helped the boys of County Cork to fight the Black and Tan. The "Bad Times" are here again tonight.

"Remembrance Days" are fasting days in Ireland, but they

are days of high feeling as well, and they bring threats and fighting too. The partition of Ulster is damned to hell, men swear eternal vengeance on all of Ireland's enemies, and some get drunk and go to gaol. Others in the pub are speaking of the number of houses that will be burned down this night in Ireland. "Remembrance Days" are days to remember. They do. Old ghosts walk again and angry Irish martyrs clamor to be heard. They are. Memories have not died. They have only slumbered fitfully.

Ireland of "the long memory."

The intensity of every extremist cause in the angry strife for Ireland's freedom has written chapters of patriotic fury in the ould man's face and dug deep trenches of warfare around his mouth. It is as hard now as the frost of the gray stubble around it as he remembers in the darkness of his years.

He is a De Valera man, a *Fianna Fail,* Soldier of Destiny. He and his kind, all, would declare war on Ulster and wrest Ireland's six northern counties from the British tyrants.

"But England, now . . ." his eldest son begins, " 'tis as deaf they be as a beetle to it."

"England! Fie, fie! Into th' say we'll be throwin' England. Rot England's sowl!"

"Six counties for one festerin' sowl! England left hers rottin' here. A foine trade, now, Ireland might make o' it some day."

"England niver had th' price o' her rotten sowl to buy it, but 'tis a bargain for th' sale! 'Tis sold so much its threads are bare as a Kinsale cloak!"

"Heh, heh! Thim as th' Spaniards brought!"

"Aye, and more! As ould and thin as th' shrouds o' nekkid Eve! Come th' day th' shoddy rag o' England's sowl will a-beggin' go for a ha'p'ny. England give thim counties us? 'Twould be that long me grave would be tired accommodatin' me corpse. But take it we could that in a day!"

"Ireland, not as big on th' map as th' knuckle o' ye little

thumb," says the ould man's son. He holds up a widespread hand to show what he means.

"Give me the little knuckle rather than *all* th' hand altogither!"

"What? What?" the blind man asks hesitantly, squinting to see.

"Niver mind," his son says. "Th' meanin' o' what was said sure ye can feel!"

"But remember th' referendum," someone suggests doubtfully.

"Referendum!" explodes "The Diplomat." "Yirra go on. Niver was there a fair referendum. British troops drove th' voters to th' polls with bayonets and forced them to vote th' British way. Suggestin' such, ye have not th' prejudice to make a good patriot!"

"Furrst, though, in me own opinion, we should declare war on Roosia."

"Roosia, man! Ye give Roosia th' importance o' Ulster! Begor and go away!"

"Still and all, America feels th' same way. America might pitch in with us."

"Roosia can come after Ulster, then. There's plenty o' time. America fightin' Roosia is too good for Roosia. England would be better to fight th' Roosians. England beats them and starves them; America beats them and feeds them."

"Up, Kerry!"

It is a cry that marshals terrible, disquieting echelons from another side of death, death that makes noises, death that is troubled with insomnia. The restless martyrs of Ireland are on parade.

The other men in the pub shout enthusiastically and flog their passions with more of Paddy's. It is popular what the ould man says. "Up, Kerry! On to Ulster!"

"Yirra! Listen, we could take it in a day!"

"Rot th' foul divils in hell!"

Memories were awake and rampant.

The ould man knows what he is talking about. He is a contemporary of the fiery Maude Gorme MacBride, the living heroine of Ireland's fight for freedom, the beautiful firebrand of Erin, who lives in Dublin now, the godmother of the nation. The ould man knows the inside of jails, too. His torches had gutted the handsome residences and castles of country squires, absentee landlords—absent in London. He had watched the flames of scores dance their joy upon the skies of violent Irish nights. He had found the way to an Englishman's heart with an Irish skean, a dirk being the only way, they say. A drinker toasts his famous blade.

" 'Tis th' sorrt of deeplomacy Ireland needs!"

"God's blissin's on his skean!"

The ould blind man remembered when he had lost his eyes. It was on March 22, 1926, when he was still a young man of sixty. Irish Free State troops and the Irregulars that day brought gunfire to old Blarney again. He was sniping at the Free State patrol advancing from the Muskerry Arms, an inn on the green, to the groves of Blarney, when a bullet splashed like boiling water in his face. He feared for his eyes for a moment because he was bleeding, but they were all right. He could still see. The world was purple and he could not be blind if he knew the world was purple. He rubbed a hand gratefully across his forehead and his forefinger found a vacant hole. The other eye felt as big as a cricket ball bulging under his touch. He fainted then, as he should have in the first place. His ould woman came in the night and found him in the brambles, and dragged him back home.

He had lost his sight to an Irishman. An Irishman had shot him in that civil war, and he was glad, when he knew that he would not die, that he could number a few Irish dead by his own hand. Some Irishmen should be shot. Those who prate about dealing diplomatically with the English or who fight in their wars. Once they had called him a diplomat, too. In fact, he was "The Diplomat." That was his name, just as a man might be named Jim.

His was the sort of diplomacy the English understood. He was quick and good with his blade. He could throw it whizzing, or insert it even quieter with his hand. An English heart was soft and gave well when touched that way. He had crawled a lot and wriggled silently and flat on his stomach to the sides of many a sleeping English soldier, and had talked him out of this world, with his kind of talking.

Ah, his hands are ennobled with the blood of many of Ireland's enemies. The gutter rats and dregs of British prisons set by Lloyd George against Irish throats. The British Prime Minister who loosed the packs of desperate, hardened killers of the London underworld, pardoned for a price, to kill some more. The Irish. The ould man has killed the Irish, too, some who fought for England and came home in their British Tommy suits on leave.

Toasts were drunk to De Valera and he was cheered wildly.

"Up, Kerry! What are we waitin' for? We can take Ulster in a day."

Ulster is important talk tonight.

"In Ulster," a drinker says, "they ask you what time it is; have you paid your rent? Serious they are in Northern Ireland. Hardworking, they boast, law-abiding people without a song in their hearts, business men. Ulster men are ulcer men."

"Fair enough. Pretty close spelling and pronunciation. That's it. That's all there is to it."

"Aye, the Southern Irishman is th' ornament to the gay spirit. Th' Southern Irishman doesn't give one damn!"

"Like good ould De Valera—he is as straight as the gun of a barrel."

"Fair enough, man! Ho, ho!"

All of this time celebrating men of the village and country-side and tourists by the score came and drank and went their respective ways without interest from Kane, who was in his accustomed corner imbibing gin-and-mix.

He sat with his brooding spine bent like a long bow, his mongrel-chestnut hair ragged from indifference, falling over his forehead. His face was big and lean, hacked out of a piece of mahogany with a blunt ax, and stained with the juices of wild winds. He had entered the bar with the gait of a man who had just come ashore from a small tramp ship that had conquered monsoons.

Maggy, the pretty bar maid, had trouble with her throat when first she saw him.

"Oh!" she said. "He's th' handsomest man who iver . . . iver set foot in Eire in a hundred years!"

Maggy, from that moment, never left his side when she could help it. She was still there, regarding him anxiously, and as always ready to serve him and attend his slightest whim.

O'K.'s Snug Pub was also favored that evening by the accidental patronage of two impeccable Englishmen, members of a delicately esoteric coterie of London, both on a gastronomical holiday, lured by bounteous Ireland's unrationed food, and on their first visit to the late dominion of their king. They had wandered in from the leafy lane for tea, and lived to regret their impulse. Now, in desperation over what they found transpiring about them, they were recklessly gulping whiskies, and observing that the establishment was far from being top-hole.

They were stylish, even dainty, London gentlemen of sorts, with impeccable Oxford accents, men whose manners and behavior presented clashing contrasts with the humble clothes of butcher, baker and *bouchaleen*. One of the two, whom his companion addressed as Billy, his face reddening from the abuse of his country heard on all sides, shuddered.

"Ugh!" he said. "Irish-looking bunch of bla'guards, aren't they, Chappie? This Ireland, this land of scholars and saints!"

Two new rustic customers entered the pub. One was hailed by a tipsy neighbor as he passed the table of the Englishmen.

"Morra, and how are ye at all?"

"Ah, my friend, so busy I am I have not even time to fight."

"If it 'tis that ye mean to insinuate somethin'," the other said thickly, "ye'll find me burrdened with no such restrictin' labors."

"Don't pay no heat to me," the newcomer said placatingly.

" 'Tis like a banana I guess ye are."

"Faith now, and how?"

" 'Twas green ye were borrn, and 'tis yellow ye've turrned."

The late-arriving farmer walked on past his tormentor to the bar.

"No livin' man can spit on me and rub it in too," he said. "Open the barn door and somethin' is bound to come out. Speakin' of asses and mules, they all have long ears and bound to flop sometime. Give me an inch of time to get half-high on a Paddy's or two and no longer will I be so busy that I cannot make yer own frightful mulish head a vegetable garden, yer ears cauliflowers and yer face a raspberry. The only fight that's iver been better than this one will be was the one between me and I."

"Me high regards to ye," said the provoker, "and for yer pleasure I'll be waitin'. And a sadder and wiser man ye'll be for fair, for ye're as clumsy as an octopus with seven left hands. Ye're like an old bull that's been standin' at stud eight to ten years—yer meat is stringy—like an old cow that's dry—yer meat is dried out."

"Ye bumptious, lopsided larrikin, ye hair's so red when I break a single strand ye'll bleed to death."

"And a hundred thousand welcomes to ye when ye try! A spalpeen who'll pull hair will also scratch with his fingernails. Troth, 'tis like a colleen ye'll fight me then? 'Tis a bottle o'

Paddy's ye'll need to be a man, so drink away! There's time a-plenty and waitin's chape."

The baited customer ignored the question for the nonce, and the two parted with growls, the one to fortify with powerful Paddy's, the other to await outside, his raging insides and fleshy bastions already prepared with the fiery ammunition of potatoes and grain shot from a big bore weapon, a bottle with powerful square shoulders.

Soon, that familiar drinker is sobbing his impotence to fight, having flailed his courage to the point of buckling knees and listless arms.

"Born a banana, he said I was, turned yellow, then rotten, and I cannot lift me fist."

"Aye, it 'tis better so," said the pacifist. "Better that the wind blows up th' back o' yer coat rather than through a hole in yer head. For once, in yer sad and lamentable, unfairtunate and disreputable drunkard's life, too much o' th' *hot stuff* has been yer friend and prevented a fearsome fight. It has made ye an octopus with seven left hands. And fair enough."

"It 'tis always that ye try to spoil th' fun o' men."

"But I go around no bush," said the pacifist, "and I will take ye to yer home if ye tell me where it 'tis."

"Me address is No. 1, Open Air."

"Fancy naming *this* province Blarney!" Chappie said.

"Always heard how beastly Ireland was. Never dreamt, though, it *could* be this wretched."

These were dangerous words for Ireland, even in these tranquil times, enough to make a listener jump out of the seat of his chair, and uttered close enough for Kane, had he been stone-deaf, to hear. But he did not lift a lash from the lid of a lowering eye.

The Englishmen cupped their words discreetly through their hands, but theirs were high tenor voices of a type not easily muffled or disguised.

"Such great false pride. They think they have been here since God was a little boy! How they like to fight and sing and smuggle arms, and feel like heroes!"

"Yes," said Chappie wearily, "but they must have grievances to do these bloody things. Unfortunately, *we* are the grievance."

"Ireland would sooner be under the sea than left without a tyrant to torment."

"Or to lose the opportunity for martyrdom. Pity we didn't wipe them out when we had the chance."

From the bar an Irish drinker shouted, "There are only two kinds of people in this whole complete entire worrld, the Irish and those who wish they were!"

"Control yourself, Billy," Chappie said.

Billy was not the first to entertain the drastic notion of Irish extermination. Queen Elizabeth's father, Henry VIII, who had no more love for Blarney than had his daughter, once had seriously considered the recommendation of his Deputy St. Leger, who held an important command in Ireland, for the "complete extinction" of those "barbarous people."

Furthermore, the monarch was itching to test the power of his new ordnance obtained from the Fleming, Hans Poppenruyter, the celebrated "Twelve Apostles" and other marvelous instruments of death, including 150 pieces of many calibers, destined finally to make rock castles so untenable by the "magnitude of iron" that already worried chieftains were talking about building their strongholds of the same metal.

St. Leger's report on conditions in Ireland must have made the fat monarch's beard curl:

There byn more then sixty countryes, called Regyons, in Ireland, inhabyted with the Kinge's Irishe enymyes: some region as bygge as halffe a shyre, and some a lytyll lesse; where reygneith more than sixty Chyfe Captaynes,

whereof some callyth themselffes Kynges, some Kinges
Peyres in their langage, some Prynceis, some Dukes, some
Arche dukes, that lyveyth onely by the swerde, and
obeyeth to no other temperall person, but onely to himself that is stronge, and every of the said captaynes
makeyth warre and peace for hymself, and holdeth by
swerde, and hath imperiall jurysdyction within his rome,
and obeyeth to noo other person, Englyshe ne Iryshe, as
except only to such persones as maye subdue hum by the
swerde.

The royal plan for the universal slaughter of these Irish
people, although gravely discussed, finally was concluded impossible "solely due to their amazing faculty of enduring calamities
and privations."

Another sudden curdling cry of "Up, Kerry!" made the Englishmen quiver.

"Easy, quiet, old thing," whispered Chappie nervously. "What
the bloody hell is that!"

The ould man and his admiring friends were fighting the wars
of '98, gossiping animatedly about the ancient campaigns of the
McCarty heroes on this very hallowed ground of Blarney.

That Cormac McCarty, now he was a fair and comely man,
and what a cliver divil, too. Right here in Blairney he had made
a blinkin' goose out o' Queen Elizabeth. Why she was the
laughin' stock o' th' worrld; ah, now was that a grreat day for
th' Irish! Sure, and he had kissed th' Blairney Stone.

The good ould women of Cork love to sing the songs of Ireland's woes. They will sing them to strangers they meet on the
county roads in the stridor of their age, but fire the lyrics with
the strife of youthful rage, and cry in the renditions until tears
fall down and scald their words.

They will sing them to all those who will listen. No excuse
is needed for them to burst into patriotic song. The excuse is
ever-present, a duty to the living and to the dead. The unborn

children of Ireland will learn the same songs, grow old and sing them in the same way, and not a spark of the fire will be lost in generations of memory that does not grow cold.

> Let me make the nation's ballads and I care not who makes its laws.
> —*Andrew Fletcher,* 1665-1716.

The little ould woman was talking to her pewter mug and mouthing the tragic poem of Biddy Strange Ring Drum, of Macroom, the classic lament for her true husband Mickey Mike, slain by a Cromwellian Sassenach in a poignant and heartbreaking tragedy of 18th Century Protestant Whiggery. The powerful keen that Biddy composed and chanted in 1765 while her handsome husband lay dear and dead for refusing to sell or loan his hound to an English sportsman. The hound came home and licked poor Biddy's hand, after her owner was tracked down by English soldiers and shot for daring to wish to keep that dog when a Sassenach wished her for himself. The deed was a personal favor to that English landowner and performed in cold blood after he had reported the effrontery.

The faithful heartbroken hound raced Biddy back to the scene of death, baying as she ran in the sunlight of a rare Irish day as hounds bay at the moon on nights of death.

Mickey Mike lay still in death, and his poor blood was jelly on the wound in his chest. Biddy stained her fingers in caressing it and her tears melted it again. She mourned for her beloved man, with her fingers caressing the mortal hole over his heart. The beagle cried and wrote the music in her throat for the lyrics Biddy Strange Ring Drum composed of heartbreak.

The English threw the body of her husband into a grave and took his dog away for that Sassenach who liked to hunt.

The blind ould woman shares the terrible grief and rage of Biddy Strange Ring Drum as she remembers: Mickey Mike's

tongue was out, and his fingernails, too, and on the yellow
gorse of May. Here is what Biddy cried up into that Irish sun
scorching away at her tears:

"No fingernails, no tongue,
All pulled out,
Thrown on the flowering
Gorse of May.
Stabbed by a pike
Poor Mickey Mike.
God! O, God, staining the gorse
With his good red blood,
Tortured on his dying day!
His dog will eat your guts
Like tripe . . . that dear ould dog
Of Mickey Mike.
He'll hound you down,
You Sassenach, and smell
Every track of your stinking feet
Until you're claimed by hell. . . .

The ould woman chuckles quietly when she finishes the verses
and her eyes are dancing under the tears in them with the light
of vengeance shining through, sweet vengeance fulfilled. For
Biddy and the beagle had hounded the very moving shadows the
Sassenach made wherever he went, across the heather and
the moor, the buck on stolen land, hounded his shadows by the
moon and by the sun, as inexorably as the curse of the bride
haunted the tripe of his guts and his uneasy heart. One night
the shadow of the Sassenach stood still by a tree in the moonlight. . . . It was for better reason then that Mickey Mike's
beagle bayed.

The sacred reverie of the blind hero's wife suddenly was
shattered by the roar of a great and mighty whoosh of wind.
It was as the noise of a cyclone with choking Harpies riding
the gale force. Without warning it rushed through the doors of

the pub, blowing into the room with screech and clutter, clanging shattering bells and whistles. Two tables near the door were overturned and the occupants zoomed like coveys of quail from splintering glasses and spattering stout. Two of the heavy-drinking patrons slipped on the floor and lay there in stunned fear. The suddenness and violence of great wind staggered the patrons' senses.

The ould blind hero recoiled instinctively as a melee of hail consisting of knapsacks, textbooks, pencils, fountain pens, gold compacts, rubber erasers and green passports fell upon his head and shoulders.

"Holy Mary, Mother of God! What on airth is it?" he cried.

"It 'tisn't nothin' on this airth!" exclaimed his wife, fighting off a rain of planetary weapons with her fists. " 'Tis from anither worrld altogither! And not Herself's. And me hair is blown all over th' cape!"

The shower of strange missiles now was succeeded by a tangle of bicycles, a dozen of them, producing the sounds of Dublin fire engines. They crashed into the pub, driven by a besom of destruction accompanied by shrieking devils, she-devils in pants and male devils in knickers. The devils laughed and giggled hysterically across a wake of wreckage, and hurled themselves against the bar with the force of meteorites.

O'K., the big proprietor, pouring a drink of Paddy's with his back turned to the juggernaut, was taken completely unawares. He dropped his bottle of precious spirits.

In his long career as a publican, O'K. had seen many strange sights and survived many disasters. He had lived bravely through earthquakes, conspiracies, rebellions, revolutions, fires, comets, plagues of influenza and the bloody flux. He had felt the hobnails of the English tyrant's heel, had seen without fear terrible eclipses of the sun and the moon, and had whistled at the phenomena when sun dogs and fog dogs appeared in the skies making false suns and spots and frightened the wits out of everyone except himself. He had stepped into the center of dust eddies and walked on haunted ground without fear of consequences. Here was something else again.

O'K. bellowed forth wildly and warded off the impact with his elbows, for without looking he knew what caused it. Any historical violence would have been welcome in comparison with this swooping disaster.

The hysterical cyclone subsided as quickly as it had started. It subsided with a "Whew! Oh, boy, am I thirsty!" A unisonous "Whew!" from everyone of the divils, a dozen of them, now with all twenty-four of their elbows firmly planted on the bar.

"Boy, oh, boy! What a race!" the divils shouted. "Hey, there, bartender! Give us a dozen ice-cold Coca Colas!"

O'K. goggled foolishly at the invaders.

"Bejabers!" he cried in disgust. "I woulda gone bail on it altogither! I could say them through th' back o' me skull. A flock o' newborn Yankees, th' craytures!"

This was a type of the breed that in O'K.'s considered and experienced opinion was the most deadly of all.

Which is exactly what they were, an exuberant group of American college students, sophomores, on a scholarly holiday to study the national monuments of Ireland.

O'K.'s customers were resentfully picking themselves up and dusting off their clothes. Maggy, whose skirts were blown over her head by the onrush, revealing the truth of reputed hidden glories, was blushing her shame away and adjusting the tables and chairs, glad that Kane had never even lifted his eyes.

O'K.'s great fists flexed defiantly on his hips.

"If anither American th' likes o' ye asks me for ice . . ." he began.

"Aw, come on! A man can dream, can't he?" demanded an authoritative, tall, youthful student spokesman as thin as a college hatband, with a scholarly ascetic Adam's apple.

"Now, mine host," he said in the tolerant manner of a world

traveler, "don't get your Irish up! Remember, we've had experience with this ice shortage before. Don't forget, we've been in Ireland all day!"

"None of that horrible hot Irish stout, now," begged an American girl whose pretty red lips puckered at the very thought, having been scalded earlier in Cobh. "Pretty please. It's so blah!"

With great effort to his muscles, O'K. bit his lips which were moving speechlessly, and pointed out some tables.

" 'Tis over there ye'll be findin' th' china shop," he said chillily. "Th' whole kit, shebang and kiboodle o' ye—hide, hair and horns!"

The tourists grinned, noisily stacked their wheels, picked up their scattered possessions, and threw themselves into chairs with war whoops of gratitude.

"Oh, boy, oh, boy, oh, boy, oh, boy!" they cried. "Bring on something wet!"

"My kingdom, my kingdom for a soda fountain!"

"Oh, brother, what wouldn't I give to wrap my tonsils around a good old Pennsyltucky super duper!"

"Stop! You old meanie!"

Maggy brought a favorite Irish mixture of warm stout and warm orange cola.

Slyly, O'K. watched his customers.

"Oh, brother!" one of them shouted to the girl next him. "More of these damned *room temperature* drinks! I wouldn't wish this bellywash on Paddy's pig!"

"When in Rome, now . . ." piped a shy little voice tucked somewhere under some books. Begor' there was a timid one!

"Borgias! Borgias!" another squealed after the first sip. "We *are* in Rome! Yip! Yip!"

She was looking around for a sign.

"What the criminentles is Gaelic for ladies' room?"

"Jumping catfish!" exclaimed a dumfounded connoisseur, the youth with the *cum laude* neck. "I'd rather swallow them!"

The degree of this youth's repugnance may be better understood when it is known how much he had hated the stories of collegiate goldfish swallowers who reigned before his time, and whom he considered had brought shocking and disgraceful publicity to his Alma Mater when they were campus giants and famed as piscatorial garglers.

O'K. grinned maliciously behind his bar. In the patriotic fervor of this "Remembrance Day," the mushrooming feud with Americans and the affront of the cinema that he considered had placed Blarnearians and the Blarney Stone in a comical light, had been all but forgotten. But now, how O'K. enjoyed the sight of their suffering, their mouths full of brew and pop, their cheeks ballooned with the good healthy liquid he had mixed with his own hands, constricting their unaccustomed gullets with rare torture.

"What on this great airth," he reasoned, "*could* be more comical than an American? Begor' 'tis even callin' their titties brothers, they are," he grunted contentedly. "Faith, not that a body could know the difference in their sweaters and britches poppin' out all over. Th' coverin' of a woman's nekkidness," he decided, "should make th' proper noise o' petticoats, not that o' pants full o' crickets. A barn's a barn without whitewash, but faith a woman's a man without paint."

But O'K.'s delicious triumph was short-lived. A feminine shriek of terrible horror froze him to his stout-splashed floor. It was the splitting, unearthly cry of a throttled banshee, high and prolonged like the noise of a charging American bicycle.

"Oh, my God! My God! Eeeeeeeeeeeeeeeekkkkkkkkk! Serpents! Reptiles! Eeek! Eeeek! Snakes! Snakes!" It was the American girl who simply loathed stout.

"Lady! Lady!" shouted the startled O'K. "What ... what ..."

"Eeeeeeekkkkk! Eeeeeeekkkkk! Vipers! Save me! There are *so* snakes in Ireland!"

O'K. crossed himself frantically, blustered a quick prayer to St. Patrick and ran around the side of his bar waving a shillelagh.

"Where, lady? In God's name, where?" he pleaded desperately.

The girl sat down quietly on the edge of her chair and gritted her teeth at the publican.

"In the Dublin Zoo!" she hissed. "And I guess that will wipe the grin off *that* character's face!"

Chapter Five

Juvenile Gentry, U. S. A.

O'K.'s bravery was hereditary. In a country where personal courage is as common as shamrocks, his family's had been notably distinguished. Every generation, including his own, had steadfastly and recklessly fought the British by fair means or foul, and always as mean as possible, either way. But more than three centuries ago, the O'K. line was set down as one apart. These forebears had been listed among the few Blarnearians who had not been frightened by the world's first bombing scare. This occurred in the year 1629, in the reign of Charles I.

Hundreds of flying "bombs," making the noise of aerial divils, crashed upon the roof tops and the fields of the countryside, ricocheted from the merlons of Blarney Castle's keep, and sent superstitious archers and peasants diving for the safety of dungeons and wells.

During this alarming attack, members of the O'K. family, as the publican had heard it from his grandparents before him, the way things are handed down in Ireland for centuries without a detail spared, stood calmly in their gardens watching the missiles plummet.

The attack was preceded by a marvelous descent upon the earth of a blanket of snowy down and a great fall of dirty wet feathers. The air was full of alarum as of wild apostate angels raging with hell turned upside down and spilled upon the earth. Cows ran into trees from fright, and the hens, chickens and geese flew like pigeons, some never to be seen again. And a number of pigs drowned themselves in their wallows.

But the O'K.'s stood their ground. Actually, there was nothing to be afraid of, at all. The aerial bedlam was caused by one of the strangest ornithological phenomena in the history of Europe and is duly recorded in its scientific annals. Possibly nothing approaching its magnitude ever happened before. And certainly never since. Thousands of angry stairs, a type of sea gull, were waging a duel to the death under the dripping mauve nimbus.

Wing-broken bodies, literally hundreds of them, exploded as the wounded birds struck the earth in a tattoo of noisy blood and quills.

When the mid-air battle subsided, the timid citizenry, the archers, the shepherds and other rustic folk crawled out of dungeons, wells and bowers and grinned sheepishly over their silly behavior.

The blood and feathers of the shattered bodies of the gulls in time were washed away by the generous rains of Ireland or eaten by the insects, but the memory of the O'K.'s conspicuous nonchalance in the face of that frightening hail lived on. It mattered not a whit that little danger had existed. It was their cool poise that won its due of admiration and acclaim. That is the stock whence sprang the publican.

But this night he shamefully admitted that he was indeed a poor custodian for the sterling heritage of his forebears. His striving mouth pursed with loss of utterance, his great hands, the size of lean shoat shoulders, shook, and his fists fell flat and devoid of knuckles to his sides.

O'K.'s perennial summer enemies, the inevitable American students, his ould natural adversaries come over to waste their parents' good money on education, had swooped down upon him again, not as dead gulls but as brash magpies, and found his tongue nonplused. They were up to their ould irreverent tricks and follies, disdaining popular Irish potables and even reflecting on the sainted name of Patrick.

It had been O'K.'s complacent understanding that St. Patrick had so thoroughly fixed the reptiles that it was impossible for one of the craytures ever to exist here even in an Irish cage, just as the good Lord had made it impossible for shamrocks to grow anywhere else except in the soil of this fortunate land.

"And here," he muttered, "I stand altogither without a worrd in me mouth." His chagrin was unbearable. "Thimselves should be sint to hell from their breakfast tables!

"If snakes there be in th' Dublin Zoo, De Valera should know about it. Himself would extairminate th' poisonous craytures, togither with thim profanin' divils as sneaked thim into Eire!"

The shocking intelligence, coming as it did from foreigners, was especially mortifying to the patriotic Gael. But that is the way American foreigners were. O'K. had found long before that they were a breed of discoverers. Every summer they discovered things about the Blarney Stone that no one in Blarney had ever heard about, living there as they did every blissid day o' th' year. And here these tourists were as fresh off the gangplank of the S.S. *Washington* at Cobh as a dozen eggs from a cackling hen. If they knew so much about Ireland, why did they have to come here at all!

They thought this, they thought that, they leaned this way, they leaned that way, they leaned forward, they leaned backward. O'K. wished that they would lean so far over, one way or the other, that they'd fall down, break their necks and get it all over with in one grand and glorious accident.

They were full of Ireland, full of themselves, full of blarney, full of riddles, and full of the very divil. They were a bigger nuisance than their bottles of orange cola were worth.

O'K. could draw the pattern of their stay in Blarney with his finger in the suds of his Guinness on the bar. Tomorrow they would have their noses into everything. Even the dead were not safe. They would swarm like souvenir ghouls over the ancient graves of Inniscarra, scrape the ashlins from epitaphs, fall into a few tombs and come up howling their discovery of great archaeological remains, and surreptitiously pack a few bones into their knapsacks. They would steal the skull of St. Patrick himself if they had the chance.

Later, in time for tea, they would descend, uninvited, upon the "ould man on the hill," and gawk through the halls of his big New Castle as if they had never seen a baronet or suit of medieval armor before, all the time looking about to see what sort of genuine Irish castle memento might be lifted out of a box of gold and ivory miniatures of medieval courtiers. When the ould baronet could finally rid himself of their company they would head pell-mell for the ould castle and crawl like scientific monkeys with their cameras over every inch of its surface where a foothold was possible.

Their final kissing of the poor helpless Blairney Stone would be a burlesquing ritual to make the Irish shudder. They would be down on their knees supplicating it. They would woo it as gamblers talk to dice. "Come on, baby, papa needs a kiss!" They would pray to it. The boys would try to hug it like a vairgin who could not defend her vairtue and all but rape th' poor ould block altogither. They would make a wench out o' her for sure and all. They would use it like mistletoe to kiss the girls. The girls would feign to swoon and moon. Their eyes would roll in their heads like dulcet dying calves. The look of nauseous lovesickness on their very faces, faith, 'twould make the very divil bilch. Pucker, pretty please, pucker, pucker, pucker. It would be such a clowning, vomitous, pusillanimous, asinine, giggling, smacking, disgusting, yelling, stomach-turning, gagging and sucking performance altogither that O'K. preferred to shut the egregious picture out of his supersensitive mind. The less he thought about this, the better.

The Americans already knew more about the enchanted moo

cows than ould Donovan the woodsman, and not a one of them had ever so much as set a foot in the *bawnafinny!*

Warily, Maggy cleared their tables of the sinfully wasted drinks, while O'K. glared ominously at his unwelcome guests, and his other patrons eyed them with sullenness as interlopers who had interrupted "The Diplomat's" great peroration. Always ill at ease in the presence of fine feathers, even though they know that fine feathers do not make fine birds but only fine-looking birds, the Irish rustics also felt self-conscious and sub-dued in the same room with these obvious members of the American juvenile gentry. The taciturn Kane was busy with his eyes on the photograph of the sad and beautiful girl and made occasional notes in a little loose-leaf book, but was oblivious to everything else. The Englishmen's voices were, fortunately for them, lost in the general hubbub that the newcomers had never stopped creating.

"Now," wildly declared one, after their tables were empty of everything except their own multitudinous possessions, "let's do our homework here!"

The suggestion was received with laughter, giggling, yabber-ing and hoorays. The boys nudged the girls in their ticklish ribs, the girls squealingly applied storms of powder to their faces and the gore of abattoirs to their lips, and all produced an array of guide books and assorted sheaves of paper, notes, pencils and other paraphernalia of learning that had a most hilarious effect upon their senses. O'K. gasped and groaned.

"Begor'," he exclaimed helplessly, " 'tis half their lives they'll spind here in me pub this summer!"

The students were quiet for a minute, but a minute only, as their eyes scanned the pages of references. The pretty Yankee girl who considered stout such an abominable beverage broke the peace with a squeal of rapture.

"The icehouse! The icehouse! Children, we *must* see the Blarney icehouse. It's so, so *very* old."

O'K. grunted again. The very mention of ice caused his temperature to rise. Furthermore, he had never known that Blarney possessed such a useless thing. Still, his ignorance hurt him.

"If 'tis to hell iver I go," moaned O'K. in his helplessness, "sure 'twill be ice-cold altogither."

Ice could burn like hell, anyway. St. Patrick had proved that to O'K.'s satisfaction by turning icicles into fire. If any doubts remained they had been dispelled by that abomination of Yankee tourists. But O'K. was soon to learn more, as the girl gushed on as though she were telling bedtime stories to the occupants of cradles.

"Dears, listen to this: 'On Ford's Avenue, described on old maps as the *Rocky Road,* stands the old ice storage house of Blarney Castle. It is a dome-shaped cavity, some thirty feet deep, sunk into the ground, lined and roofed over with brick. The opening is a square door, half bricked, half the natural rock of the hillside situated under the ceiling. Ice once was purchased from Swedish, Russian and Norwegian ships in Cork harbor during the winter months, and packed and stored there against the summer.'

"Boys and girls! Just imagine," exuded the reader, "how perfectly romantic! Just think, in those days you just had to ring for a bucket of ice and you'd have it before you were half into your armor!"

"Oh, how precious!" enthused another young thing. "How perfectly exciting, drinking ice-cold Coca Colas in armor!"

"Th' divil blow me till!" exploded O'K. "If that would make th' poison taste any better, I'll sell me pub for a bob!"

"And listen, listen, children! What a pity we won't be here in January. On January 6, all of the wells of Blarney overflow at midnight. That is SS. Peter and Paul's Day."

"You don't mean it, darling, actually! How enchanting can a place be?"

"Yes, and what's more, January 6 is 'Little Christmas' in Blarney. In these same holy wells the water changes into wine for an hour at midnight!"

"Ooooh, ooooooh, how positively eerie! But I'm sure if I were there it would be just my luck that the water would turn into horrible *stout!*"

"Why, you poor, cute *thing!*"

"Faith, and what's so funny about that?" O'K. asked his bristling self altogither.

The good St. Brigit, the Mary of the Gael, had turned Irish wells into ale whenever she willed.

"Ale o' stout, now, it 'tisn't any difference," mulled the publican. Somehow, the pattern of their talk, all of their suggestions, created a feeling of flippancy for the ould miracles not at all to his liking.

"And the Blarney Stone! Listen! This authority says it must have been brought here by the Crusaders."

"I don't believe it, not a word of it!" exclaimed the cute thing. "It arrived here, my book says, about the time Daniel was thrown into the lions' den. That was *thousands* and *thousands* and *thousands* of years before the Crusades!"

"With me own hands I could throw *thim* into th' lions' den," muttered O'K., "and watch thim ate alive! God's own troth! They are like th' rattlin' o' pears in a drum! As busy as bees in a tarbucket! Th' day will come, though. Ye take yer crock to water only so many times. It breaks! This worrld and th' next one."

"A simply *divine* theory," admitted her friend. "There are so, so very many, you know!"

"I simply can't wait to see the castle's 'Ladies' Bower,' where all of those handsome knights made love!"

"How fortunate those ladies were," sighed Cutie Pie. "Just think! Having the Blarney Stone right over their knights' heads, night and day always there ready to replenish their ardor whenever they became just a teeny weeny bit tired! Darling, it made them *so* dangerous! And what *must* it have done to the ladies!"

"It makes the *senses* reel! I simply can't wait to lip it myself!"

"Oh, and the darling theory about that faery mermaid, 'a being as fair as the eye could see, who played on a harp of gold.' Her throne was a moss-covered stone on the banks of the River Lee. That was the Blarney Stone. But when the Saxons killed a McCarty there his heart's blood spilled on it and dyed it red. The poor mermaid must have fallen in love with him because she kissed his blood."

"Kissing blood? Ugh! How gruesome!"

"No, it was the sweetest thing! *So* romantic! Her kiss endowed the throne with magic, so

> " 'They who kiss it, old or young,
>   Are gifted with the faery tongue.' "

"Why everything in Ireland is positively Pandoraish!"

"Can the saccharine persiflage, embryos," interrupted a positive sophomore of the masculine gender. "Your comedy is passable, but what do women know about blarney, anyway? Blarney's a *man's* game! Hard as stone. Flinty! Get it?" He applied a touch of antiphlogistine carefully to a pimple on his chin, took off his glasses and waved them like an authoritative finger.

"Why you studious lamb! You should be an author—I'd be your secretary, your galley slave. We got it all right! But *do* tell us more! But what makes you *gweat* big strong men so crazy you'll let yourselves be held head down by the heels over one hundred and twenty feet of thin air to kiss a stone? You wouldn't run such a risk to kiss a pretty girl!"

"Ah, but there are other pretty girls, but only *one* Blarney Stone," replied the expert.

"Why, you meanie!"

"Girls, furthermore, require no such effort. The Blarney Stone makes you work for its favors."

"Did you ever!"

"And in the long run the Blarney Stone is safer, too. Very discreet. It doesn't kiss and tell. Stony silence. Get it?" he asked eagerly. "Stony silence."

There was a complete conspiratorial hush.

"Brother, you *got* it!"

"Oh, well," the youth said resignedly, "you're at a loss for words. That can be corrected here! Still I say blarney's a man's game. That's the only poem ever written about a woman's kissing the Stone."

"So a woman gave it the blarney in the first place, smarty pants!"

"If I hear any more th' likes o' that non compass menace," said O'K. raging now behind his bar, "sure and I'll be losin' me vittles altogither!"

"The joke is on the women, though, the way things worked out," continued the bespectacled authority, "giving us men such excellence of blandishment, our winning ways, dontcha know! For 'of its virtues, that esteemed most rare, which gives full power to fascinate the fair!' 'The blarney, the blarney, oh, a perilous thing is the blarney!' "

"Oh, I simply adore perilous things!" exclaimed the cute thing giddily. "Please fascinate my virtue, you perilous old bookworm!"

"Seriously, now, I've made a long study of this fetish stone. As to its origin, I'm personally persuaded it was Jacob's Pillow at Beth-el."

"Jacob's head sounds so dull and Biblish, though. Not exalting like when knighthood was in flower. So patriarchal, you might say. Did *he* make it tick?"

"No, the Irish did," replied the profound young philosopher, mysteriously.

"I always thought it made *them* tick."

"Just the opposite, and it matters little where it came from. Your faery tales are very charming, but the truth is not in one of them!"

"You mean old iconoclast."

"The Blarney Stone never gave the Irish blarney, the Irish gave it to the stone. That's the secret of the Blarney Stone."

"Why, you learned old thing!"

"But wax serious, kids. The Blarney Stone was nothing but a stone until it was first kissed. Then it became a bank, a repository, as it were. All of the Irish are born full of blarney. It even runs out of their diapers."

"Ooooh!"

"I mean . . . er . . . uh . . ." he stammered, "it runs out of their mouths from the time they are born. When they kiss the Blarney Stone they simply deposit some of their heritage in the rock, itself, get it? They've imparted their blarney to the stone so often that now it is infused with it, overflowing with that precious ingredient. Now, when it is kissed it gives the blarney back with interest."

"But that's all so . . . so scientific."

"Sorry, I'm just being practical. And a good thing for the Irish it is, too, that it's true. They're natural-born scrappers with hair-trigger tempers. If they weren't born with that leavening blarney of theirs they'd be at each other's throats all the time, instead of just on Saturday nights. Now take the Irish at home . . ."

"*You* take 'em, kid!"

"You know what I mean, though. Their blarney is a safety valve! Why, you can see the soft soap twinkling in an Irishman's eyes!"

"Why, I should think it would burn!"

"It's not the kind of soap they wash their faces with, silly."

"Whew! You've got it all figured out."

"Yes, and even for those who don't believe a word of blarney magic, blarney's still good for them. It is harmlessly autosuggestive, and *does* provide good exercise."

"But gee! It does suddenly strike one as crazy that an old stone with an intrinsic value of, say only two bits, has suddenly been acquiring such fame."

"Oh, the stone *must* be magic to get away with it!"

"Boy, and how!" The student looked around for confirmation. Kane was close enough to brush his elbow. Impulsively, the student directed his appeal to him.

"It *does* give one the gift of gab, now doesn't it, Yank? It gives from whence it takes?"

Other men in O'K.'s Snug Pub in sheer compassion had attempted to open up friendly conversations with their homesick-looking fellow American, but none had succeeded. Always in the past Kane had behaved as though he had not heard their questions.

Poor, worried Maggy to whom he had never spoken a word, saw his big shoulders move restlessly.

"Listen to *this* for blarney," the college boy urged.

> "Oh, did ne'er hear of the blarney,
> That's found near the banks of Killarney?
> Believe it from me, no girl's heart is free
> Once she hears the sweet sound of the blarney."

Maggy's hands went to her widening mouth, both at the same time, as Kane slowly turned his head.

"Oh!" she whispered. "Oh! Oh!"

"What a miracle blarney is," the bookworm went on. "It makes girls fall at men's feet. They tremble and shiver all over when they hear its sound. How they long for it, too!

> "Oh! When will the day come, the dear happy day,
> That a maiden may hear all a lover can say,
> And he speaks out the words he whispers to me,
> My Aileen, Mavourneen, acushlamachree!"

Kane was staring at the young declaimer as though his heart would break. His lips were twitching uncertainly and his eyes were blinking rapidly. His forehead was twisted with anguish. After a moment he sprang from his chair and hurried out of the pub. Maggy ran after him as far as the door and stood sobbing into the hem of her apron.

"Look what ye've done to himself!" she cried.

"Gee! What did *I* do? He looked like he had tears in his eyes, though. Wouldn't think of a man who looked like that as even knowing *how* to cry!"

"It's *so* romantic," sighed the cute thing, "the handsome man *must* be in love."

"Aw," said the boy jealously, looking at the empty glasses on Kane's table, "maybe it was just a crying jag."

The stout-hating girl had a fascinating discovery in a Dublin guidebook to report.

"Listen! What a peculiar epitaph *this* is. It's Daniel O'Connell's, whoever he is. It says, 'My heart to Rome, my body to Ireland, my soul to heaven.' "

"My, my, but what if the poor man went to hell and messed up the whole elaborate arrangement?"

Suddenly in the pub there was the bellow as of an outraged lion roaring in the jungle.

"Dann'l in hell?"

Daniel O'Connell was Ireland's hero of church and state. It was he who led the priests from underground during the dark years of the forties. It was his work that lighted the candles in the churches after a period of darkness that threatened the extinction of the Faith, as it already had the wicks on the altars.

He is almost apotheosized in the national mind and memory of Catholic Ireland. He was the Great Emancipator or the "Liberator" of Catholicism. Over his tomb in Dublin has been erected a soaring monument of stone, purposely a few feet higher than that English shaft honoring the memory of Admiral Nelson.

He was schooled in law in France, where all Irish Catholics were forced to turn for learning, if they wanted it, because of English restrictions against them at home. But O'Connell's tongue was born in Ireland and he brought it back to his native land to use it as a sword. It could sting a witness from the very seat of testimony. It was a sharpness of brilliance such as no barrister of his time could equal.

In an estate litigation in Dublin in which a deponent swore that a deathbed will, which was being contested for others by the Emancipator, was signed while the testator still "had life in him," O'Connell bellowed: "You mean he had a fly in his mouth!"

O'Connell, that day, had a wasp in his own mouth. His mouth could also be the home of a bee with a honeyed sting, the bee that sucked the sweetened dew from an errant blackberry bush that sometimes grows atop Blarney Castle.

All of O'Connell's biographers revel in this great story of the quickness of his mind. Without previous knowledge of it all he *knew* somehow that the witness had put into the testator's mouth a living, buzzing fly, so *life,* even a fly's life, would indeed be in him. The witness fell to his knees and confessed.

That broguing, bellowing, brawling arch-Papist advocate, O! that Kerryman. He won his tongue from the Blarney Stone. The scion of Blarney kings and queens, from Munster he was, and he had kissed the Blarney Stone four full times, held by his heels in the daring that was in him, head down, face down, he kissed in the old-fashioned way before those sissy protective iron bars were implanted, at the risk of his life and for the sake of his Irish tongue. "The risk is worth the reward," said Daniel O'Connell, and he proved his statement true. From no other source save heaven could such eloquence and perception have come.

You must hear of his meeting with that Biddy Moriarity, that queen of Billingsgate, that old virago, that rattling hag of a Dublin termagent. O'Connell bested her in a set-to on the banks of the River Liffey in the greatest torrent of confusing geometrical sesquipedalia ever known to history.

It was all a put-up job, it 'twas.

Let that great writer, T. C. Luby, Esq., tell about it all. No one has ever reported that encounter in better prose. And here it 'tis, with asterisks:

> But at this period there dwelt in Dublin a dame who was fairly entitled to enter the lists with him (O'Connell) as a scold. * * * and she kept a huckster's stall. * * * The fame of her abusive volubility had attained the highest pitch. * * * Her brazen impudence. * * *

Here was how Daniel accomplished the "terrible Biddy's" overthrow:

> "What's the price of this walking stick, Mrs. What's-your-name?"
>
> "Moriarity, sir, is my name, and a good one it is; and what have you to say agen it? And one-and-six-pence's the price of the stick. Troth, it's chape as dirt, so it is."
>
> "One-and-sixpence! Whew! Why you are no better than an impostor to ask eighteen pence for what cost you two-pence!"
>
> "Twopence! Your grandmother! Do you mane to say that it's cheating the people I am? Impostor, indeed!"
>
> "Ay, impostor, and it's what I call you to your teeth!"
>
> "Come, cut your stick, you cantankerous jackanapes!"

"Keep a civil tongue in your head, you old *diagonal*," returned O'Connell in the calmest possible tone. The effect of this calmness on the excitable nerves of the fair lady was even more irritating than his abuse.

"Stop your jaw, you pug-nosed badger! Or by this and that I'll make you go quicker nor you came."

"Don't be in a passion, my old *radius*, anger will only wrinkle your beauty."

"By the hokey, if you say another word of impudence, I'll tan your dirty hide, you bastely common scrub! And sorry I'd be to spoil my fists upon your carcass." * * *

"Easy now; easy now, don't choke yourself with fine language. You old whisky-drinking *parallelogram!*"

"What's that you call me, you murderin' villain?"

"I call you," answered O'Connell, "a *parallelogram;* and a Dublin judge and jury will say that it's no libel to call you so."

"Oh, tare-an'-houns * * * that an honest woman like me should be called a parabellygrum to her face! I'm none of your parabellygrums, you rascally gallows-bird! You cowardly, sneaking, plate-licking blaguard!"

"Oh! Not you indeed!" retorted O'Connell. "Why, I suppose you'll deny you keep a *hypotenuse* in your house?"

"It's a lie for you, you bloody robber! I never had such a thing in my house, you swindling thief!"

"Why, sure your neighbors know very well that you keep not only a *hypotenuse,* but that you have two *diameters* locked up in your garret and that you go out to walk with them every Sunday, you heartless old *heptagon!*"

"Oh! Hear that, ye saints in glory! * * * May the divil fly away with you, you micher from Munster, and make celery-sauces of your rotten limbs, you mealy-mouthed tub of guts!"

"Ah!" persisted Biddy's archtormentor, "You can't deny

the charge, you miserable *submultiple* of a *duplicate ratio!*"

"Go," vociferated the half-frantic scold, "Go rinse your mouth in the Liffey, you nasty tickle-pitcher! After all the bad words you spake, it ought to be dirtier than your face, you dirty chicken of beelzebub."

"Rinse your own mouth, you wicked old *polygon!* To the deuce I pitch you, you blustering *intersection* of a stinking *superficies!* * * * You inimitable *periphery* * * * convicted *perpendicular* in petticoats. * * * There's a *contam*ination in your *circumference* * * * guilt to the extremities of your *corollaries* * * * you *rectilineal antecedent* and *equiangular* old hag! * * * You porter-swiping *similitude* of the *bisection* of a *vortex!*"

Albeit worsted, Biddy is game to the last. Suddenly snatching up a saucepan, she aims it at the head of our hero. But ere it flies from her hand, he very wisely contrives to beat a hasty retreat.

This same trenchant mind of the idol was turned to good effect against the English in a lifetime of skillful political agitation that his country's enemies found damned diabolical. It could be full of poison or sugared venom, as he willed. In his shrewd tactics Ireland found its first hope of centuries.

"There's not a single English Act of Parliament that I cannot drive through in a coach and four," he said. He, indeed, could sting his way through any buggy and harness the English could rig. He made English Acts a parade ground for the carriage horses of his mind. The solemn decrees of the English became stable doors for his prancing steeds, secured with paper locks that were gaping loopholes for their master's relentless eyes. But mostly he picked the locks as a criminal, because the legitimate keys he found were outlawed by the peers.

The thought of the nearly sainted Daniel O'Connell in hell

gave O'K.'s tongue a roaring revival. He lumbered at the heretical students with his shillelagh whizzing.

"I've losht me hair-trigger temper," he shouted. "Clare out o' me paceful pub, th' lot o' ye! 'Tis no shebeen, ye bullyraggin' divils!"

The cute thing shrieked, pushed back against her chair and fell in a clutter of heels and protests to the floor. Her companions stumbled to their feet. Their tables tilted and a tangled bedlam of tripping ensued.

"Get out? Why? . . . why? . . ." sputtered the collegiate.

"Why?" hollered O'K. "Ye ask why? Because ye're dhrunk and disairderly, that's why!"

The alarmed students hurriedly collected their belongings and rushed to their bicycles in a flurry of outcries of rage, and revenge was sweet upon the air. O'K. ground out some hard pieces of thought in the red mill of his mind and they came forth powdered to his satisfaction, making the senses sneeze around him.

"Out there in America 'tis monkeys ye have in yeselves' *zoos*," he rang out gloriously, "but a dozen o' the' apes are fugitives coddin' th' saints in Eire tonight."

"Boo!" exclaimed the cute thing, almost in tears. "You have no sense of humor! If you ever kissed the Blarney Stone, you'd poison it."

O'K. stiffened subconsciously but he ignored the wicked charge. His mind was busy on other angry things he could say. St. Patrick had turned the water on his fingers into fire; he drove demons out of farm animals; turned water into honey and snow into curd and butter. He had made the earth swallow up wizards, raised his foster father from the dead, and rid Ireland of all the reptiles except those in the Dublin Zoo.

"Patrick should have currsed th' monkeys, too!" he blurted without apparent meaning. The students looked at the wild man in more alarm than ever, and rushed from his sight.

O'K. followed the group to the doorway, waving his shillelagh belligerently. He watched them mount their wheels, and the dust whirled.

"Pedal away!" he shouted after them. "And may th' Lord have maircy on the poor cows o' Ireland!"

Chapter Six

The Blarney of the Gael

O'K. returned to his post amid the cheering of his customers and friends, and he preened for a moment behind the bar in fullness of his glory.

"Up, Kerry!" they shouted.

"Those spasms of people were gone before ye could say life. That Johnny Madfresh! He gave him down the banks!"

"Still, he'll kiss th' Blairney Stone so often it 'twill become a love affair."

"If thimselves had heard all me own ears did," O'K. thought, "faith, and a brawl there'd been."

A frown suddenly replaced the satisfaction that had wreathed his features.

"Turnin' down me foine Tanola and Beamish! And th' tittie said meself had no sinse o' humor," he mumbled. "May th' divil split her britches!"

Of all his great and manifold qualities, his sense of humor is most fiercely prided by the Gael, and none has been more justly earned.

Life was hard under the British heel, but Ireland survived as much by her national sense of humor and her impudence as by her courage and her arms. There was never any lack of courage, but her weapons were woefully inadequate. Her defensive power has ever been the history of bowmen versus musketeers and cannoneers, the "arrowe against wilde fire, rocks against yron."

A mischievous eloquence provided a balance of resistance that saved the nation from extermination and dolor. The Irish tongue proved as strong as armies marching. Tongues sharp enough to clip hedges at will, or charm the birds from the trees, and re-inforced with ready wit and golden voice, went to work on the baffled minds of the invaders. They found this national trait a formidable nuisance. Every man, woman and child in Ireland, the brood of a stone, shouldered it as an avenging sword in her thousand years of warfare against the hordes of foreigners who came to scourge and slaughter. It was the sting of a snake with serum on its point. Blarney was Ireland's secret weapon.

Even the powerful sea-scouring Danes and Norwegians, whom the Irish called Ostmen, arriving on their warships in 795 to ravage the churches, drive the priests to foreign shores, plunder the raths of the rich for gold, slaughter the people—and build cities—were met with this peculiar arm. Early in the game they were forced to treat with the powerful McCarty kings, although they found them ostensibly equipped only with pitiful weapons such as stones and spades. Still the Irish contrived to retain some semblance of self-government.

The hairy Scandinavian hordes ended 1,000 years of Irish security from foreign foes but held the city of Cork that they had built up from a marshland and established as a fortress, and much of the surrounding country, only by the grace of the persuasive King of Munster, one Dermod McCarty. The area was still in this half-dispensed possession of the pagan Ostmen at the time of the Anglo-Norman invasion, when King Henry II of England arrived with his troops, took over, and granted the whole of the area to Robert Fitz-Stephen and Milo de Cozan. By this time, the Irish ordnance was as pathetically inadequate as the Danes had found it.

Yet, the might of the McCarty rule still presented an ominous consideration for the new enemies. Henry II promptly sought to meet blarney with blarney and minimize its effects on resistance by playing the role of cupid. Seeking out the Irish king he presented him with a beautiful Norman wife, instructed to use her woman's wiles where the sword might fail, but even in this romance Celtic blarney ultimately prevailed.

The Danish dominion over Ireland, or large and important parts of it, was not actually broken for two and one-half centuries, but blarney held it in check until Brian Boroimhe succeeded for the first time in history in uniting the warring Irish kings who had been eternally engaged in internecine warfare over lost, strayed or stolen cows and sheep, and engaged in squabbles and contentions over boundaries and wives.

The rape of an Irish king's wife by a powerful neighbor who fled to England to enlist aid, set off a series of domestic battles and actually hastened the Norman invasion of Henry II. But bickerings over such comparatively minor things as a setting of goose eggs, for example, were responsible for most of the country's quarrels.

The great new leader brushed these differences aside and overthrew the Danes in the bloody battle of Clontarf on Good Friday, 1014. Boroimhe's or Boru's united Irish forces slaughtered 11,000 Danes, and ended their supremacy.

The English were not to be so quickly overthrown. The howling Ostmen had been mere week-end guests. The English had arrived to set up housekeeping—for 700 years.

The Irish from that moment on by divers means sought to be as unhospitable as possible. The unwilling hosts vied each with his countryman, to make the long stay uncomfortable.

They sang in defiance and insolence while riding to the gallows in dung carts, knowing that the hated English soon would not only burn them alive or hang them at Gallows Green but also that they would be disemboweled, drawn and quartered, and their heads spiked on the gates of the gaol.

They laughed and spat in the faces of their hanging judges and joked at the expense of their executioners at Cork's grisly, blood-bathed gallows bird facing the Pound and Lough Road in Cork. With the dry slobber of their lips they toasted prosperity to the Pope and popery and damned the Sassenach to hell with ribald distich while gibbeting into eternity.

> To the Lord President, son-of-a-whore,
> Glad I won't see 'im anymore O!
>
> Now there's a man who thinks 'ee's smart, O!
> But for 'im now I don't care a fart! O!

While this couplet lays it rather thickly on the line, Ireland's quick and beguiling tongue has won more victories over tyrants who could not match such eloquence, understand such discourse, nor keep pace with such fluency, than all of her "poor tools for fighting the Sassenachs, tho' mighty good for wilde fowles."

The author of the couplet, it must be admitted, was under somewhat of a disadvantage when he gave forth with his inspiration on the scaffold. But another Irishman, less handicapped, composed lines more to the point of this argument. It spread balm upon the wounds of Catholic Ireland and even partly avenged the despoilment of old Blarney Castle.

The Cromwellian Lord Broghill had caused to be engraved upon the gates of Brandon Bridge sentiments to advertise his contempt for Roman Catholics:

> Jew, Infidel or Atheist
> May enter here, but not a Papist.

An Irish versifier found the lines made to order for his wit. With his skean, an Irish dagger, he scratched out his answer in the dead of night lest he might pay for his audacity with his life, and escaped in the darkness. Next morning everyone, including the jubiliant Irish and the apoplectic Lord Broghill, could read these lines:

Who wrote these words composed them well,
The same are written on the gates of hell.

The easy baiting, the easy retort, excelling barbs of wit and repartee which the slower mind of the invader could never match —episodes such as these—stung and maddened the English and weakened their prestige and muddled their judgment.

While the Sassenachs announced that their sovereigns' birthdays were being "celebrated with joy," gunpowder manufactories exploded in the outskirts of Cork, and daring mobs of Irish "ruffians," sometimes as many as 1,000 in a band, armed with bludgeons and sticks, created panic. The English dragoons were called out in greater numbers to augment those carrying the mails. Secret societies of many names, two of the more famous of the 17th century being the White Boys or Levelers and the Wild Geese, joined in these "celebrations of joy," with many forms of violence and rioting; and of necessity an entire regiment of soldiers was required to escort them to the gallows where they were hanged, hooded with white shirts.

The jittery English garrison was thrown into complete confusion one happy birthday night when some of the Wild Geese, with a delicious sense of humor, ran through the city crying "Mad bull!"

While Ireland laughed the entire English army tumbled out of bed and for a week searched for these yelling criminals. With ruffled dignity they marched up and down, up and down, but not a one was apprehended.

Some demonstration of joy!

The Irish frequently saved some of the victims of the gallows after they had been hanged. Spiriting away the bodies that had not been beheaded or disemboweled, they secretly and energetically applied friction and "fumigation" and forced spoonfuls of hot soup and rum into the dead mouths. An interesting number responded and came to life.

Pregnant women condemned to death were spared by the English until their babies were born, and then, the infants snatched from their breasts, they were duly executed. Even for this short respite, many doomed girls besought the arms of their gaolers, and when pretty enough—for the risk to a keeper was great—were accommodated. When the desired results were not forthcoming from these emergency amours, the disappointed girls pleaded pregnancy anyway, were examined, and hastened to the gibbet within the same hour.

When detected in the act of fornication itself, the keeper was punished by having hot irons applied to his arms, and the girl was hanged without further delay to forestall her cunning treachery against the Crown from bearing fruit.

The remarkable escape of a Cork tailor, who had been left hanging for ten minutes at Gallows Green before being rescued by an actor and restored to life, produced a pleasant *divertissement* for the Irish. The tailor celebrated his miracle by getting drunk, and staggered into the theater where his kind deliverer was playing, to offer his thanks.

Thinking the weaving man was a wraith, mass panic broke out in the audience, consisting mostly of Cromwellians, and many were hurt in the rush for exits. The play did not go on that day, but the hilarious Irish had enjoyed a great show.

It was such naïve and pathetic amusements as these that made life at all bearable. They were the delight of the bard and his inspiration.

When an amusing beggar exposed what was described as a "remarkably thick leg" to a virtuous and horror-stricken spinster of Cromwellian leanings, it was the occasion for a holiday. The anti-English beggar enlivened the moods of countless Irishmen by repeating his rare performance whenever he could find a hapless Englishwoman unescorted on a lonely street. The sight of his enormity struck terror to their hearts and sent them shrieking toward home. Some of the victims were so affected by the monstrous immodesty, however, that they fainted, while the offender stole away to lie in wait for other unwary feminine souls of English virtue. The beggar became a national hero, and when finally apprehended by outraged English authorities who had been besieged by pale and sensitive spinsters, he was found guilty and his offending member sentenced to the torture of branding with a hot iron.

Ireland was rewarded with still another hilarious laugh at the expense of their oppressors, when a sympathetic gaoler, ordered to execute the penalty, applied a cold iron to the howling patriot's "remarkably thick leg."

But the English had their vengeance, too, and laughter that the Irish could not share, such as the amusing antics of condemned maniacs.

They hanged crazy men along with the sane, and when gibbering "ideots" became frightened at their executions and dived head first from the gallows, they were prodded back viciously by sharp pikes which made them literally jump into the noose, some with their bowels hanging from abdominal wounds, so glad were they to escape this pain on earth.

And as to the charges of tortures leveled by their English masters against the Irish in Blarney and County Cork, may it be said that no instruments for inflicting lingering torment are to be found in the Cork Museum, the official repository for all historically significant relics of Munster. While there is no doubt that the Irish did slaughter thousands of Protestants in the days of "inveterate prejudice" and passion, their temperament is not such as would cause them to employ diabolical forms of punishment. Not one scintilla of such evidence against the Irish, for instance, is to be found at Blarney. On the other hand, there are few old castles in England where the visitor will not see racks, thumb screws, great, ghastly pincers and irons for putting out eyes, and English museums display them as the most commonplace of exhibits. They were the usual things.

If torture there was in Irish dungeons as the English have claimed, then it was the exception and not the rule. Today, there is not even an Irish hangman in Ireland. When a condemned man is to be hanged at old Maryboro in that republic, a mercenary English hangman is imported for the occasion.

It is inconceivable that a nation possessing the benign heritage of the Blarney Stone could be guilty of wanton cruelty.

However, one admitted example of an Irish type of torture is found in *The Life of Florence McCarty* that begins in 1020 A.D. with Carthac, twenty-third in descent from Oilioll Olum, son of Eoghan the Splendid, and of Saiv, daughter of Conn of the Hundred Battles. This old book contains depositions from a number of persons captured and robbed by McCarty henchmen and generally ill-treated in an effort to persuade them to become Papists. One man writes in a fury about losing a cow and sheep and being kept for the night in a cold room in just his shirt— but valiantly refusing to turn Catholic, he was let go home the next day, all nervous and exhausted, to instantly lodge a complaint.

And Ireland mourned that black day in 1740 when the bodies of hundreds of poverty-stricken men, women and children after a hard frost were dumped on the same day into a large pit behind Shandon Church in Cork. They had died of starvation and exposure, and left no money to purchase their graves. Murderous inflation had struck the country and a three-pound loaf of bread had soared in price to an unprecedented sixpence.

The Irish on that date had worn the English yoke for more than five centuries and its weight was growing, in one of the most dismal periods of their history.

But in their darkest hours the protecting "pebble of destiny" was always there. Touchingly, the poet turned for solace to the Blarney Stone.

> But still the magic stone
> (Blessings on it!) is not flown . . .

It had helped the Irish confound the tyrant with confusion. Now they looked to it again. The time for deliverance was not yet, but the "palladium" was working its magic in the strangest of ways. It was forging weapons of freedom for the tongue and fashioning a noose to choke their torturers.

Forced by the invading Sassenachs to speak a language they hated, the Irish soon excelled in it. They mixed a despised vocabulary with honey from a stone, and steeped it with the sweet scents flowing from a magic urn.

It was a long time—more than 400 years after Henry VIII, throwing off the Pope's authority and styling himself the Supreme Head of the Church of England upon Earth, turned 10,000 friars and nuns out of the monasteries, beheaded Sir Thomas More and burned John Forest alive for denying his ecclesiastic overlordship, and decreed that only the English tongue could be spoken in Ireland—that a man arose in the land who could properly evaluate the results of that arrogance.

It was Oliver St. John Gogarty, the Dublin man of letters, who also unconsciously paid tribute to the Blarney Stone, when recently he leveled this classic barb on the airways across the Irish Channel in the general direction of the British House of Parliament:

"You stuck your bloody language down our throats and now we can strangle you with it!"

Certainly, O'K. had thoroughly strangled the obstreperous juvenile American gentry. That he was a bit hard on them is indisputable. They meant no harm in their exuberance. They had never heard of Daniel O'Connell, the Irish hero. How many Irishmen, for example, have heard of the immortal General Longstreet of Georgia? Better not let an ignorant visitor say anything against him in Dixie, either.

Chapter Seven

Souls of the Dead

Someone yells out a heart-tingling cry of "Up, Kerry!" once more, and O'K. beams.

"So quiet and paceful 'tis now," he murmurs. His customers are no longer inhibited by the embarrassing presence of the wealthy Americans, and Maggy and her employer are making up for lost time.

The little ould woman is dwadling with her own ideas about that powerful keen of Biddy Strange Ring Drum. She gums her thoughts in choppy ululation, no one paying her the slightest attention.

"It 'twould have been better," she says, "had that beagle beast have ate th' tripe o' Sassenach's guts. He got off too light."

Anxiously, she looks at her blind husband. Faith, and into what a state he was working himself. The morrow would find her hands full. Sure, and wasn't it a fortnight last Remembrance Day she had spent handling him back to normal!

"Up, Kerry!" The "Bad Times" live again, Ireland of the "long memory" flames, and arms flail against cruelties seven hundred years old.

The men's eyes are red and wild, and disbelief in the enormity of many things is in their faces. Cromwell is as new as the stubble of corn in the newly reaped fields, as new as the neighbor's cow that has just come in.

"Up, Kerry!"

The very location of O'K.'s Snug Pub is reminder enough.

It is but a mile from Blarney Castle, that was besieged in the last engagement of the Commonwealth War. The Sassenach hordes, the hated English, called the ravaging *Gaillibh Glassa* ("Blue Strangers" of "perfidious Albion"), bringing an abhorrence of popery, are before the gates again. The murdering jack-booted men of Cromwell who practiced the black art and walked on water in desecration of the deeds of Christ, with powers that the devil in hell gave to him, his ally, storm the flanking bawn of the McCarty citadel.

The faces of the Irishmen are raging and O'K.'s alcohol burns blue words through their teeth.

Now comes Cromwell back to Blarney again, sitting in judgment behind his imported ordnance of death, "hollow shot of cast yron stuffed with fireworks or wild fire, whereof the bigger sort for the same had screws of yron to receive a match to carry fire kindled, that the firework might be set on fire to break in small pieces the same hollow shot, whereof the smallest piece hitting any man would kill or spoil him."

Blarney is a good target. Practice is at hand for the culverins of new siege trains, the tortles, the short "gunnes," brought over from England with 12,000 horse and foot, nine battering pieces altogether and of large size.

Since gunpowder had been invented and later improved by Roger Bacon, the English Friar, and cannon first constructed by another ecclesiastic, the German Berthold Schwarz, of Freiburg, about 1313, which had enabled King Edward to turn the tide of battle at Cressy with only four pieces and gain victory, remarkable strides had been made.

Now Lord Broghill's artillery was arrayed before old Blarney Castle, and so refined by the Flemish and German craftsmen that Schwarz's cannon were as obsolete as spades. The once formidable brass cannon, the bombards and "Twelve Apostles" of Henry VIII were being dusted off for museums, and Lord Broghill stood all-powerful with siege trains equipped with mortar guns thirteen inches in diameter, Deming culverins, minions and other fearsome ordnance, battering pieces throwing 350-pound shells—all howling-great guns capable of belching stones and chains and fused fire pots to the tops of the highest stone castle battlements in Ireland, as they did even at Blarney.

The day of the stone castle was nearing its end. Earlier sieges with ordnance of iron had proved this, and Blarney was not to escape in the murderous march of military progress.

Cromwell has come to ask accounting of "innocent" Sassenach bloodshed in the Irish Rebellion of 1641, which the English called the "Hibernian St. Bartholomew." They allege the massacre by the Irish Catholics of 150,000 Protestants, to whom English kings had given more than 3,000,000 acres of land seized from the Gaels.

"They (the Irish)," said Guizot, "tried to avenge in a day ages of outrage and misery."

"Up, Kerry!"

The Old Thing is becoming more and more restive. He is squirming noticeably upon the area of the chair occupied by his small busy buttocks. It is close and hot in the smudge-choked pub, and the perfume of his excellent toilet water has lost its economy.

The celebrating Irish drinkers order their glasses replenished and more for the ould hero's table, all they want there, and toast Cromwell torment in his grave as to the dust, and gangrene as to his sowl in hell. These men are experts on all Cromwelliana and it was "the Brewer" he was called contemptuously, because that is what he was, a brewer. And when the Irish called him that, the way they said it made the trade sound bad indeed.

Somehow it carried the utterly damning implication that Cromwell brewed English lager instead of Irish stout.

The customers in O'K.'s Snug Pub were not lacking in knowledge of Irish history, even those who found reading difficult.

Some of their fathers and grandfathers also could not read. Many of their ancestors had suffered from an English decree prohibiting academic education in Ireland. Only the sons of the very wealthy or those who could borrow from English usurers, could afford to attend schools in France or receive even the most rudimentary teaching. To keep Ireland illiterate and in ignorance was a device of the invader to complete his subjugation of the people. To combat this, education, such as it was, went underground. Parents taught their children to the best of their knowledge, becoming modern *filid* and bards, giving of the effusive oral literature of the country, as had been done in days of yore. Learned priests also secretly taught the three R's, while also secretly teaching the catechism, and daily the cruelties of the oppressors were graphically told the youth of Ireland at their parents' knees, and adjectives were not spared, as the oppressions were seared upon the national memory.

The haughty Catholic-hating Lord Broghill is commissioned to take Blarney Castle.

Cromwell's glorious victories, accomplished with extreme cruelty, have already inundated Ireland in a sea of blood as though his intention is to make an inland passage for his fleet. At Drogheda he has made an abattoir and left its garrison of 2,400 men stacked with their wives, and their priests still clutching their crosses and holding them aloft as gory markers for the pile of death.

His son-in-law Ireton has vied with his sword to widen this matchless swath and swim his own armies to combat in the raging surf of blood.

Now Broghill rides the sanguinary tide. Holy medals snatched from the couplets of the dead, souvenirs for the folks back home, jangle the music of the battle charge in the knapsacks of his musketeers.

He swaggers confidently before the castle in the groves of Blarney. His hands are drenched with Irish blood from the recent battle of Knocknaclashy. Irish blood spilled cheaply with his cannon, but on that stormy day he raced his cannon balls with the sword in a butchering of Irishmen which lasted "for above three miles, and indeed it was bloody, for I gave orders to kill all. . . ."

"Our word," he said, "was 'prosperity'—theirs, 'St. James!' Our signal, white in hats; theirs, greene fearne."

His victory was foreordained. For when he encountered the Irish peasantry on the road who had come to watch the sanguinary battle that had been foretold would occur on that very spot, they told him sadly that "the English are to get the day."

"Like the Battle of Naseby," Lord Broghill reported to London, "from a fair day it rained hard during the fight, with thunder and lightning and afterwards cleared up again . . . my bravest horse being twice wounded became so fearful, that he was turned to coach."

McCarty had come out of the fastnesses of Kerry where his men flew to arms to help him lift the siege of Limerick. There Ireton's powerful forces were arrayed against it. Ireton sent Broghill forth to intercept and engage the Irishman.

"All of their foot and field officers charged on foot with pikes in their hands," wrote Broghill, "so that few got off, it being too farre from any bogs or woods, which they say they selected purposely that their men might have no confidence but in their courages—but we relied on a better strength than the arm of flesh, and when their strength failed them, ours did not fail us. Their priests all the way before them came to fight, encouraged them by speeches, but especially by sprinkling holy water on them, and by charms. . . ."

Broghill is especially proud of the Catholic "relicks and a peckfull of charms, and an infinite quantity taken from the dead . . . with a peculiar one on paper said to be the exact measure of our Lady's foot and written on it . . . 'Whoever wears this and repeats certain prayers shall be free from gunshots, sword and pike, respectively, as each desires:

" 'This orizon was found on the sepulchre of Christ, and was approved by the Council of Kent. Whosoever carries this orizon about him shall not perish in battle, water or in fire, and shall be free from the pestilence, and from all his enemies, both spiritual and corporal, and shall be eased from disease of his heart . . .'

"Certainly, they are a people strangely given over to destruction, who, though otherwise understanding enough, let themselves be so deluded by ridiculous things and more ridiculous persons. Had I been one of the charmed I would first have tryed mine on the priest which gave it."

Cromwell's artillery roars as Lord Broghill bends it against the walls of Blarney.

> Oliver Cromwell
> He did pommel
> And made a breach
> In its battlement.

Making these loud noises with the iron playthings is a disporting change for the invading dragoons, a diversion from the slaughter of the sword and the block and hatchet, and exquisite refinements of torture—which include the frying of Irish Catholic women on the soles of their feet, burning them alive or shooting them at pleasure, hanging mothers to the crosses of Christ, and making innovation of a handy noose for their babies, left strangled over their breasts with "new fashioned haltars" of hair. "If they were suffered to live," cried the bitter Archbishop of Armagt, "they would one day be rebelly Papists."

And now these Englishmen, sated with the blood of the sword, toy with the engines of death.

So they fired off the bullet like thunder, and it flew
   Through the air like a snake,
And they hit the high walls of the castle,
   Which like a young curlew did shake . . .

But not all of the murdered are of the Irish race, not all are
Irish babies tossed on dragoons' pikes, for the bowels of many
an Englishman, those who have been found guilty of the capital
crime of marriage to laughing colleens, dangling from crossarms
on the waysides, paint the crosses of Ireland the colors of frightful, stinking rainbows. Their entrails nailed there stay on and on
and dry and fly like ribbons in the wind.

They are good reminders to the English and further heighten
the "embittered mood of the half-conquered."

And now the English counter with their own atrocity charges
growing out of the massacres of Protestants at Portadown and
Shrule Bridge, the raping of Protestant virgins and Protestant
wives before the eyes of their families and their husbands, and
the burning or burial of horrified survivors alive; husbands
carved piecemeal before their screaming wives in the determina-
tion of the Irish to "erase every vestige of the English name
from their country." Only a century or so ago fifteen ass carts
of human bones were removed from the dungeons of Blarney
Castle. The English promptly declare they were the remains of
tortured Protestants, but death is old in Ireland. The Irish say
they are the remains of tortured Catholics.

Cromwell, whom the Irish believe to be the founder of Free-
masonry and therefore a dabbler in wizardry, does not need even
one of his square murtherers to take old Blarney. His general
now uses "dumb powder," which the Irish believe is silenced by
Cromwell's Masonic black magic.

Guns alone cannot take old Blarney. The witch doctors are
forced to cast a spell over the defenders, and mass hypnotism is

employed. This is an extreme measure, but long ago the British had learned that the Irish "always fight well behind a wall."

> And because that he was a Freemason, he
>   Mounted a Battering Ram,
> And he loaded it up with dumb powder,
>   Which in its mouth he did cram.
>
> The ould castle trimbled all over, as you'd
>   See a horse do in July
> When just near his tail, in his crupper, he's
>   Teased by a pesterin' fly.
>
> Black Cromwell he made a dark signal, for
>   In the black art he was deep,
> So, tho' the eyes of the people stood open
>   They found themselves fast asleep.

Dead or alive, Cromwell would fare badly this night in O'K.'s Snug Pub.

Not even the angry British who turned on his carcass in 1660, after it had been buried for two years, hanged it with that of his son-in-law Ireton and then buried his remains under the gallows of Tyburn, could match the hate of the Irish on this Remembrance hour. If his corpse were available, they would tear it to pieces and feed it to the swine, and Ireton's with it. But they manage well enough with what they have to work with, and consign his sowl to hell, where punishment lasts longer than in a hog trough, excretion by a hog being deemed too pleasant and evanescent a fate for the murderous "Brewer" of the Commonwealth War, anyway.

"Up, Kerry! To hell with Cromwell's sowl!"

"And let it stay there!"

"That it will!" responds "The Diplomat." "The Irish will see to that! The Irish in hell would fight th' very divil himself to keep him there, but if th' divil *did* somehow trick th' Irish and throw him out, th' sainted Gaels in heaven, St. Patrick, St. Brigit, and St. Columba, would cast him back again. As long as good Christian Irishmen live in both places Cromwell will live in hell!"

Chapter Eight

The Blarney Diplomat

The patrons laugh at the ould hero's charming mistake, and some reckless enthusiast singlehandedly buys another round. Money he bangs on the bar and poetry comes out of his husky throat:

> "May the God above send down a dove
> With wings as sharp as razors,
> To cut the throats of all bad folks
> Who speak ill against their Neighbors!

"Up, Kerry!" he shouts. "Pour away!"

"Up, Kerry, hell!" snaps Billy disgustedly. "Up, down!"

Chappie laughs, "Up, Down! I get it, Billy! You mean County Down." He was delighted with his quick comprehension. "Up, Down. Sort of upside down, you know. Damned clever of you, now!"

"They're a bloody thin-skinned lot."

"And bitter, I'd say."

"But they don't have to be so beastly and wretched about it."

"And to think Henry II bought Ireland from that English pope for a penny a house."

"It was a bloomer. He paid too much!"

"Right!"

"Ugh! Look at that horrid blind old Irish donkey!"

At this moment, the "blind old donkey's" mouth, sans dentures, is wide open, but it is not baying like an ass. It is hissing like a snake.

"Me God's doom! If sowls can rot, 'tis English sowls!"

"Hear that?" demands the horrified Britisher, half rising from his chair. "Dashed if I'll just sit here . . ."

Chappie touches his friend lightly on his hand.

"Careful, now, Billy, please!"

Chappie is a remarkably silly-looking fellow with tusky Anglican canines pushing over, outward and beyond his upper lip, framing ever-present projecting incisors. This serves to give him the appearance of a perpetual grinner. He grins even at the funerals of his best friends, and shocked attendants in London, unacquainted with him, more than once have unjustly thought the ushers guilty of allowing an idiot to enter the church and mar things. Chappie has sense enough now, anyway, to know it is time to be afraid.

Incoherent cries against the English and toasts to De Valera are splitting the hubbub.

"Alcohol," observes Chappie philosophically, "with the exceptions that prove the rule, affects the Irish race wildly, as 'fire water' inflames the American Indian. Strong drink sends both on the warpath."

The pace is telling now.

Billy shudders.

The pub crowd grows. Drinkers at the bar are passing brimming pewter mugs of stout over their shoulders to those behind them, stout, the drink of the poor—molasses-colored, whipped-cream suds, cheap. But the odor of Irish whisky is also trenchant in the room. And there is the telltale pungency of potheen, illegal potato spirits distilled in the mountain cottages of Kerry, that tastes like vodka and atomizes the senses.

Theirs are the cries of phrenetic impotence, for even in their alcoholic haze their minds tell them that the morrow again will find them in the fields, some of them hammering little stones into fertilizing dust to scatter over impoverished soil. They hurry to drink more while they can. They drink in candlelight, and the rays of an oil lamp chop the shadows of the frying wicks.

"When you wake up in the marnin' broke and sick from drink there's hell up on airth," a gulper shouts through a sloshing tongue.

"Never before thought of stout as a boisterous beverage," Chappie observes.

"It's boisterous only when inside an Irishman," replies Billy.

"Did you ever hear that the Irish are really the lost tribe of Israel? That they are really Jews?"

"I personally believe that the Jews are the lost tribe of the Irish, and damned lucky. This Irish race-boasting. They have a family crest, all right, a pig and a bull. A harp is a harrup."

"But they're everywhere. Go to the North Pole and I'll wager you'll find an Irishman sitting on it."

"An Irishman would dull the point."

Two other Irishmen are arguing over Gaelic and other lan-' guages. Strife is rampant in their faces.

"How many languages do *you* speak?" challenges one.

"I speak only two," the other cries haughtily, "good and bad."

The pacifist steps between them. The drinkers cry out protests.

"It 'tis *in the rats* they are," murmurs O'K., *in the rats* being the curious Irish equivalent of the D.T.'s, since the Irish alcoholic sees rats running up and down his arms, rather than pink elephants on the walls.

Two men of different political alliances, one accusing the other of being too moderate, the other countering with charges of fanaticism, have argued for an hour at a remote table away from all the rest. Sometimes their voices are raised in anger, a charge of "straddler" is heard, but the plot to take Ulster is too absorbing for the others to pay attention. Now the two contentious drinkers are on their feet with blazing oaths. The table turns over, a candle flies through the air dropping hot tallow on the floor, and stinging hapless necks.

A big man goes down under a blow, and comes up again with the bridge of his nose crushed in and blood gushing from a terrible injury. There is a rush to the scene, men rolling up their sleeves on the way. They return to the bar disappointed, rolling their sleeves down again.

" 'Tis some sort of a private argument," one explains sadly. "And ourselves not welcome into it."

"Aye, and what a pity," says another. "I offered to box, kick, knife or currse and neither could I do, for it 'tis a private fight, indeed."

"Still, though," says another morosely, "any fight is better than none at all."

"My word!" exclaims Chappie, hopefully, "maybe they'll have a public argument and exterminate themselves."

"Remember that saying about the Irish and beware: 'With all their wars they're happy; with all their songs they're sad.' "

Maggy flusters first aid, consisting of a wet bar towel that the victim applies to his wound. His assailant is crying remorsefully and damning his own sowl to hell for hitting his best friend. Arm-in-arm, they walk out of the pub together, leaving a trail of blood behind them.

"Shame!" a pacifist cries. "Christ's worrds were to turn th' other cheek."

"Fair enough," agrees the sobbing victor, "but th' larrikin hit me in th' nose. It 'tis th' difference between cheese and chalk. I'm out in th' open; no one can tell me what to do."

There is a Kerryman here and drunk, talking out of turn, he is. A visiting Galway man spanks his face as a mother would spank her baby. The Kerryman fairly coos. The Galway man starts to cry.

"Here I am," he says, "weepin' like a human bein'. God be mairciful to me, a sinner."

"He's so happy," O'K. grins, "he can sing to th' birds."

Still blubbering, the Galway man leaves the premises to cry at home alone.

"Go," says O'K. "To ye I said *cēad mile fāilte,* one hundred thousand welcomes, when ye came sober. Now I say when ye're drunk, may th' road rise up to greet ye, may th' wind be always against yer back. May th' Lord hold ye in th' hollow o' His hand. This is a very wholesome and holy pub, but how can a pub make a bob unless men get tight! Anyway, good-by, poor divil, and may th' worrld wonder at yer riches."

Somewhat remorsefully, O'K. gulps the contents of a pewter measuring cup.

"Th' furrst today," he sighs, "and badly needed."

A piercing whistle from a customer splits the bedlam of the establishment. O'K. jumps and wheels angrily.

"Is it at me ye whistle?" he demands of the offender, who crowds close enough for the publican to smell the fresh sweat of the fields.

"Yeself indeed," shouts the farmer. "Pour a pint o' stout."

"Am I a dog?" asks O'K. "Have I got a tail?"

"Ye ought to!" retorts the customer.

O'K. raises his great fist, but the pacifist is there again.

"Fie, men," he says, "and shtop altogither. This and that; this and that. Too much o' this makes nothin' o' that."

Reluctantly O'K. lowers his threatening arm and pours the whistler's stout.

"Had it not been for certain unfairtunate interference," he tells his customer, "yer deranged mind would of disappeared into th' blissid sleep o' foriver! Still, your hair is so red, I'm afraid if I broke one strand ye'd bleed to death. And speakin' o' bleedin' hair, faith 'twould be murder even to crush yer billycocker against yer skull. Ye'd bleed to death smellin' o' ginger."

"On to Ulster!"

"Faiiiiirrrrenuff! We'll go with you. We'll *all* go!" three generations cry.

"I would crawl," says "The Diplomat," "if it took th' hide off!" He blinks futilely at his eyes that are no longer there and searches with his hands all through his pockets for his old blade of diplomacy. Six bombs were hurled by Southern Irish sympathizers at the police barracks of Belfast and constables of that city in 1950, but he knows that his *dadagh* is better than any bomb.

"And 'tis no eyes that I'll be needin' to find the Limeys," he says. "I can smell them out even in a pigsty. Th' pigs smell better! Ye can always tell th' difference. Never in me life yet killed a pig by mistake."

"Yirra!"

"The Diplomat's" faithful little ould woman swills some more stout and looks at her husband with worship in her eyes. She thinks of some old things and laughs like a hen laying an egg. She knows everything about him, even what he says at confession.

Knowing this she thought he was dead and in hell altogither when he lay wounded in the furze. But it would have made no difference where he was. She would have found him.

Already this year the Admiralty has reported twelve acts of sabotage against British naval installations in Londonderry, Northern Ireland. Some patriot also threw sand into the steering gear of a submarine. If her ould man had been in on the plot the whole English fleet would now be sunk. He is a little ould man and can crawl through small holes and get into big places. He was no trouble at all, lugging him home wounded and dead weight.

There is a frightful grin of adoration on her face, making her wet moustaches droop and seem longer, and her empty gums are bony and raw. "The Diplomat" will not have to crawl to Ulster if she can help it. She pats him lovingly on the arm. She will lead him there or carry him on her back, and shoot some Englishmen into the bargain while he is busy with his dirk.

The ould woman has never been to "The Borders" and has no idea where they are, but her ould man has said they can be taken in a day. That is enough for her. She could shoot her quota of Presbyterians in Northern Ireland where they do not permit daycent Catholics to parade on St. Patrick's Day. She is glad that she can still squint a bead on a haythen Presbyterian with her left eye, dim as it is from the cataract. She cackles her gratitude, and grins her mouth into the suds of her pewter mug.

"Such crap!" exclaims the English dandy.

"I'll wager a guinea they wouldn't even eat an English muffin." Chappie laughs. "Easy Billy, control yourself." He wags a rebuking finger under his friend's disjointed nose. "They're just crocked to their red gills. Have a spot yourself." He clicks the other glass musically.

"Crocked? Tommyrot! It's just an inferiority complex. All Irishmen have it where the English are concerned. Nothing flatters them more than to be mistaken for English."

The patrons around the room now are thoroughly gripped by their passions and their cups, and some are demanding an immediate march on Ulster. New and classical epithets in the eloquent manner of Cork men are heaped upon the English as the proposal gains momentum.

Billy makes a gesture of exasperation with his wrist.

"Listen to that, Chappie! Remember, we're English. I'm going to talk to that old beggar!"

Chappie again touches his friend restrainingly.

"Fe, fi, fo, fum," he says.

"Damn that rot, Chappie, it makes me nervous!"

"Better be, Billy boy!"

"I can swing the old bellwether with a word."

"The wretches might swing us. We came here to eat. We can't very well eat with sore throats. This is the sort of place I'd say one should be, er, er, rather, would one say innocuous?"

"Listen, we're English, you know."

Billy swallows the remainder of his drink and is on his feet before his friend knows it.

"I've reached my—my Plimsoll!" he cries, and is up and away with a flourish.

The Englishman walks straightway to "The Diplomat's" table, mincing resolution and annoyance in his locomotion, curlicues of exasperation attending his hips, the honor of England in his keeping.

The silence of a dead man's chest is in the pub. Chappie hears his heart ticking.

His compatriot addresses "The Diplomat" in a quavering voice.

"Here, now, my good man," he begins without ado, "don't you think you're being damned rotten? What's biting you! And all this infernal bloodshed talk, this hate. England's been damned sporting, you know, in giving you your freedom, anyway. And I'll wager you're already sick of your bargain, at that!"

"The Diplomat" raises his ould head and blinks away incredulously and wrinkles his forehead as though he is trying to grow new eyes to see what his ears cannot believe. The other patrons stand momentarily helpless and gape. "The Diplomat" is searching clumsily again for his misplaced skean. In exasperation, he pats every pocket in his clothes.

"Whisht, lovey, he's a cock-a-doodle," the ould woman whispers. "Foine feathers don't make foine birds, but he has th' face o' a hangin' English buzzwig."

"Dim!" the ould man mutters.

"All of this is high feeling and little sense on your part," charges the Englishman in a quavering voice. "If you'd behave yourselves, England would still be your best friend! Might even permit you to come back in the fold if you behaved yourselves. We've always tried so hard to help you!"

This Billy is being carried away with the strength of an argument he sincerely believes himself, and even beginning to feel pity for the misguided old blind man. Now he is fired with a great inspiration.

"Listen, friend," he says chummily now, and eloquently too, "let bygones be bygones, let old wounds heal, let England help you! Stop all this Ulster rot! I warn you! England and Ireland *can* get together. They will, they must!"

"The Diplomat's" nostrils are pulsing like a mad stallion's. He is sniffing at the air now and still fumbling all over himself.

"My good man . . ."

"Listen," says "The Diplomat" suddenly, uttering his first word and emphatically snorting smell of toilet water out of his nose, "me good man, yeself, if such ye can be called. Is it possible, me foine buckeen, that ye are heavy with child?"

Billy's peacemaking effusion is stuttering and freezing on his lips. The word "brothers" is a big piece of ice in his mouth, but his face is a furnace, burning with terrible susceptibility.

"Heavy with . . . with . . . what?"

"With child," "The Diplomat" repeats. " 'Tis strange notions, cravin's and follies some women do get when their baskets are packed. And I do not be havin' to see or feel to know th' young one's already jumpin' inside o' ye."

"Really, now . . . look here, you . . ."

"When it happens what ye say yer sowl's welcome will be wore out in hell."

Chappie freezes in his chair as he sees a circle of big red-haired Irishmen closing slowly on the person of his friend. They come in tighter like an inexorable red rope. He thinks he will faint. He is afraid he will not. He tries to cry out a warning, but his friend has sensed his danger and is backing away, foolish-looking in his bewilderment and his manners.

"The Diplomat" halts the human noose with a wild shriek of triumph. He bangs one fist on his table and with another waves his blade aloft. It catches the lights of the room like a mirror and flashes them crazily around the room.

"I found it! I found me *dadagh!* All th' time it had slipped down in me drawers!"

Someone shouts, "Up, Kerry, use it! And may th' divil mend him!"

Billy's face is as white as a churn of milk and bubbly. His eyes pop at the blade and he sways on away crazily on cater-wampusing hips.

"The Diplomat" is feeling his way to his feet.

His ould woman is cackling into his ear.

"Lovey, I'll lead ye to his heart, and guide yer hand!" she says.

" 'Tis me nose will do *that, acushlamachree;* if I can smell me Englishman out of a pigsty, 'tis sure I can smell him out of a rosebush. Faith, this one's easier yet. He's a skunk in a garden. Out o' me way, woman. Give me room."

"Then th' luck o' God on ye, lovey!"

"The Diplomat's" bright blade picks up a beam of O'K.'s oil lamp and flashes it hypnotically across Billy's eyes. The ould blind man seems to know it. He turns his skean around and around and the uncanny rays play like a burning glass with the terror in Billy's face.

The steel shaft is a grim semaphore flashing the silent words of dread diplomacy, the only language an old assassin knows, announcing a conference where not a word will be spoken.

Everyone is watching so closely that their eyes are still. One of them says "Up, Kerry!" but in an awesome whisper. It is frightened and does not sound the same.

Chappie's open lips try to form a warning shout, his fingers clutching at them like frenzied deaf-and-dumb talking.

"The Diplomat's" feet, in heavy leather boots, are as soft as moccasins on the carpet of a forest where Sassenachs bivouacked in his youth. He remembers, lest ould acquaintance be forgot.

Billy is drooping like a flagging burgee in a weary wind.

For weeks O'K. basked and expanded vaingloriously as the admiring populace beamed their adulation upon him. The cliver divil had earned the sun that shone upon him now, making his great red face glow like a forge. The sun's rays came in through every crack of his pub and danced merry jigs upon the bottles behind his bar and on the varnished stout kegs placed like great fat cherries around the room and used for seats as much as for the atmosphere of good cheer and plenty they brought to mind, or the thurrst they prompted in a body's dry and raspin' throat.

Such a quick mind he had, a quick Cork mind it 'twas, as quick as a bob in a woman's hand. His stiffness with the rowdy Americans would have made him a hero, but the plaudits of the multitude were reserved for a deed involving an example of mental agility that had no equal even in a village where, 'tis said, newborn babes compliment the old midwives upon the glowing beauty of their youth before they learn to say mama.

A good Cork publican with his wits about him niver had to call the polis. But, faith, 'twas murdher this time O'K. stopped before it happened altogither, and just with a worrd it 'twas in th' nick o' time.

O'K. rushed from behind the bar and gently tapped the ould "Diplomat" on the shoulder. Then he whispered into his ear worrds to cheat th' divil of an English sowl. O'K. stood there grinning trenches in his face and the ould man burrst into laughter. His *dadagh* fell to the floor, laughing itself with the clatter it sang like a song. But the ould woman pounced upon it as quick as a badger with a beetle, and she pressed it into his hand.

"Here, lovey, holy Biddy! Hurry! Th' buzzwig's runnin'! Quick! He'll get away."

"Fie, foe!" the ould man laughed. "Did th' English iver hang a pregnant woman?"

"Begor' if he did only have eyes," they said in Blarney, "sure ye'd think they were twinklin'!"

Chapter Nine

"Th' Ould Man on th' Hill"

It was in a gay holiday mood and in gay holiday best, heavily shod and unnaturally stiff in their Sunday suits, that the first group of Blarnearians, cronies all, weeks before the coming of the pooka, set out from their village to view *Top O' the Morning* at the grand Savoy cinema on Patrick Street in the city of Cork. They looked forward with eagerness to seeing a great spectacle that would do honor to Blarney.

All of their names are known, but out of a sense of propriety, because men should let bygones be bygones, they shall be called by their initials, O'D., O'K., O'S., O'L., O'T., O'H., O'M., O'F., O'R., O'B., O'C., O'N., O'G., O'W., O'U. and O'O. They were more or less respectively: a garrulous carder, frequently and for the most obvious of reasons called "skewer head"; a reaper of corn; the owner of our wayside pub; a drawer of water and a hewer of wood; a groom for the last old hunter in the stables of the same demesne; a political worker; a victualer; a green grocer; a dairyman; a wool grader; a drayman; a miller; a highway laborer; a shearer; a herdsman.

The holiday, the beauty of the season, the treat in store at the Savoy, filled the excursionists with nature's own glorious mood. They were walking at a swinging gait up the Commons Road which leads into the city over the ancient Blackpool Bridge, and no thoroughfare in the world is framed with such natural beauty. It was spring, too early for many tourists, and no speeding American automobiles skidded around the curly corners with the narrow shave and the missed heartbeat and covered their well-brushed clothes with dust. It was a blue, shining morning and the gorse was butter-yellow and every bird in the county was singing.

Tinkers the travelers met around every corner—wild, laughing people with brown children. Their caravans were freshly painted for the spring in gay colors, and piebald ponies ambled about among them. Their season of hibernation was over, and now they were out for the point-to-points and the race meetings, stealing beers and poaching salmon and *so* enjoying life. Our delegation hailed them with hearty "morrows," and dodged erratic cyclists and donkeys, and patted driven herds of fat black angus cattle on their friendly rumps, filling the roadbed.

They breathed deeply of the new air of Ireland's springtime and were happy men.

A fluffy, freshly laundered Pekingese joins them at the junction of the private road that leads to New Blarney Castle, where the dog belonged. This dog is a Colthurst dog and a privileged character but he has made friends on his own and in his own way. The men know him well. He is a frequent visitor to the village, where he has a low collie girl friend. They laugh happily like schoolboys when they see him.

"Good ould Puff!" they cry.

"Imperious crayture, isn't he!" says O'K. admiringly.

The dog ignores their greetings, as he always does, but the men like his proudness. He is always supercilious that way. He tolerates no familiarity. He is not a tail-wagging dog. He leaps ahead of the men out into the fields and woods. They are luminous with carpets of bluebells, all laced with white flowers of garlic, all starred with primroses, all in the green shade, with the sun shining through new young leaves.

The beech leaves are tender and pleated, and they have bud cases, dark and sticky like gingerbread. They get caught in the dog's fur, and he eats a few. The men think this a funny sight and laugh at his antics over the glue in his mouth and on his fine white coat.

"Eee-ee-i, good ould Puff."

Still, Puff disdains his companions. He is yellow now like a dandelion clock, as he runs for a baby rabbit. The men stop and watch the chase. Puff is gaining foot. The rabbit is under his paws now, and squirming, but Puff lets it go free. The men laugh again and cheer Puff's magnanimity.

"Ha!" said O'K. "See that now! Ould Puff wouldn't hurt a thing—except a human being."

"Why not? 'Tis th' crayture's charm. 'Twas a foine grip he had on th' English governess' calf on Sathurday. Th' ould man on th' hill laughed th' sounds o' fits."

"Hope ould Puff didn't get himself poisoned now." O'U. grinned.

Old Puff finally had enough for the day. Without so much as a backward glance he trotted like a dyspeptic old leprechaun back toward the fine castle on the hill. The men yelled good-bys after the waddling yellow ball going back like a dirty gypsy to his plush home in the New Castle.

The men can see it now distantly above the noble ilexes, a great Scotch baronial mansion with a marked lack of symmetry, left unfinished in 1874 after the expenditure of $400,000. Much of this was squandered on brownstone imported from Scotland. Only half completed, it was left with a stunning character of its own, an airy incongruity, an element of surprise, rare in the usually heavily symmetrical designs of this type of pseudo-Gothic architecture. Unequally shaped windows, turrets, stone ornaments and other decorations with which the outside is embellished, loom against the startled skyline, grieving for their unborn twins.

The Castle is a great open stage, as it has always been, its tragedies and comedies providing the most exciting entertainment for the most avid of audiences. The cast of characters in this perennial stock company are the three members of the household, the "ould man," his niece and her ten-year-old daughter Adrian, who has the light of fantasy glowing in her face.

Little Adrian is writing a novel. It is about a Constable Fox. Her mother thought at first he was a gay bachelor, but now it transpires very suddenly at the end of the second chapter that he "has seven children and his wife's gone orf to France with her sista." The first line of the novel is this: "It was early in the morning and the world was still as an egg." The curious simile, and so apt, is thought rather promising.

One morning last spring when the hedges were all white with hawthorn, and the grass a shining, lively green, on Ford's Avenue there was a family of baby wrens, already out of their nest, making clueless attempts at flying. They were as round as golf balls, and very trusting. Adrian put up a notice warning cars to be careful. There *is* a lot of kindness up there in the New Castle.

The supporting cast is a small army of servants and retainers, and the great and the near-great who throng its halls, all unwittingly enacting a drama of history and life with no ending and no intermission since the time of that McCarty who was called "Laider the Strong."

Old Puff, who has starred in many performances there, disappears over the hill now to join the actors within the walls and take his cues from his beautiful mistress, she who could be the twin of the "White Lady," her tall, brunette ancestress, a graceful and willowy Swedish princess who married a rich Jefferyes with large holdings in the East India Company and the Bank of England, who lavished his bride with diamonds and pearls. She herself once performed on the stage of Blarney. Her lovely wraith has lived for two hundred years in a ruined tomb in the ivy-choked churchyard at Inniscarra, where she was buried with all of her jewels. She is beloved of everyone and emerges in luminous radiance on some moon-lonely and frosty-still nights and wanders forlornly among the crazy-angled tombstones. Before the 1914 war, when British troops were stationed at Ballincollig nearby, some soldiers of a Hussar regiment broke into her vault at night. In the darkness they could not find the coffin of the princess but her grave was laid bare, and so now the princess wanders sadly looking everywhere for a stone to cover it.

The cast of Blarney characters has included many another beautiful and famous European lady.

One, more famous than beautiful, was the Countess of Desmond, ancestress of the present owner, whose eyes are still fixed upon the pageantry of the castle. In shrewd estimation, she stares down all who enter the rich and glittering drawing room, one of the most expensive sets for the enduring play, her eyes dancing in an oil painting from the lights of an enormous Waterford glass chandelier.

The hardy old countess bases her claim to fame on her famous ride on horseback to visit Queen Elizabeth at Hampton Court. She rode her mare throughout England. She rode astride as a man would ride, accompanied by her son and daughter, who were also of advanced years but so feeble that they were unable to mount a horse and so were forced to ride alongside their mother in a coach.

In her latter years, the countess became a trifle eccentric and had built for herself a small house in an apple tree, but at the age of one hundred she had the misfortune to fall from the branches and sustained a broken leg. This soon mended, however, and she lived to be one hundred and ten.

There is little about life up there in the New Castle not known by the excursionists to the cinema. Secrets of the gentry are not long kept from their rustic neighbors.

They know that the kitchen maid has left and the cook has varicose veins, and jolly well nearly twenty of the gentry the same day to tea.

"Faith, I'd go bail that new, temporary butler fellow's ripe as ninety for sackin'," prophesied O'D., the carder. " 'Tis a walkin' sponge he is from too much swimmin' in th' ould man's cellar. Sure, that's one cellar now not flooded with Adam's ale! Squeeze him even as little as a man does his own wife and it's a demijohn o' impirted brandy ye'll be gettin' for yer trouble."

"Me wife's no trouble at all. 'Tis herself I'd rather squeeze and smell th' butler," laughed O'O. "One whiff o' him's a suppeen o' spirits in their pure state."

"Ho, but 'tis a young wife ye have, O'O., and full o' juice now, but wait! Comes th' day she's dry as a prune, 'tis th' butler that ye'll squeeze."

"Fie, man! Tis yer balmy mind that's gone dry," chuckled O'O. good-humoredly. "Let th' polis squeeze th' butler fellow, as they'll be doin' soon. Himself's wife's a shiner th' size o' a turf block."

"Why not. 'Tis from the gangsterish ways he picked up out there in America."

"Sure, 'tis th' gate and th' gaol for *that* one."

"The kitchen boy's a strong, willin' lad, with a grand voice, too, but it 'tisn't pork he can tell from a toad's kidney," spoke up O'G. "Ho! And hell there's been to pay for sure. Muddle th' ould man's lunch and didn't he think 'twas th' divil and all his young ones leppin' out o' th' sheets at him. Th' poor blind bugger o' a kitchen lad cooked th' dog meat and served it to th' sick bed in a stew. Begor' didn't th' ould man have a mouthful o' horse's entrail before he discovered th' mistake!"

"Yirra! 'Twas a holy wonder anither seizure o' his poorly heart didn't take him out o' this worrld altogither. Th' heart under that one's ribs kicks like a horse in his stable."

But the ould man is better now, just as he always is when "Sister" Brigit comes to nurse him. "Sister" Brigit is not a nun, but she has the name of a saint, and is as holy as an angel in heaven could be. She is tempted only when the divil comes to her during Lent in the form of a chocolate cake.

Brigit's mother named her well. St. Brigit, "the Mary of the Gael," healed the leper, gave sight to the blind, healed consumptives and restored the sanity of lunatics. "Sister" Brigit, there is no doubt, has saved the life of the ould man on the hill. Long it has been forgotten who first called Brigit "Sister," but now one and all do.

She is a joy to everyone, with a fine Irish sense of humor. She really is a poppet, eager for a good gossip and as merry as a cricket. And yet so good. Everyone in Blarney now knows about that cousin of hers who became a monk.

"A lovely man, altogether," she said. " 'Twas the greatest pity he had to leave the world."

The deprivation he minded most about the new life, she said, was having to give up smoking. "But," explained the good nurse, "didn't me cousin get over that in a very clever way, the dog . . . O."

The rule said *No smoking on any grounds* at *all,* this even to bar asthmatic and herb cigarettes, supposed to be remedial. But nurse's monk cousin is cute as a fox. He smuggles his pipe out to a big old oak tree, shins up it to a comfortable seat in the branches and there (on no grounds at all) he enjoys his smoke with an easy conscience and the same old zest.

She cannot always leave her other patients to be with the ould man, but she comes when she can and stays as a member of the family. She was at the Castle all last Christmas and her eyes were as big as Adrian's over the joys, mysteries and promises of the season. But when she went to the larder and saw it choked with dead turkeys, dead geese, dead woodcock and great bleeding sides of meat she almost burst into tears.

"Are these," she asked, "to help us celebrate the birth of Christ becomingly?"

And when Sister Brigit went into Cork and visited the market, where some of the butchers' stalls had dead pigs' heads in the centers crowned with holly and flanked by holy candles, she enquired of the startled owners, "Does God laugh or cry?" They did not know what to think of this strange little woman who brushed by in long white flannel skirts that swept the floor, and asked such a random question, and then strayed everywhere, sometimes squealing with the delight of a child over what she saw.

There were nice things in the market, too. Fruit stalls gleaming with oranges, apples, bananas, nuts, dates, and hung around with bunches of holly and chrysanthemums. And dairy stalls selling blue duck eggs and brown speckledy ones, and gold mounds of butter and little cream cheeses in muslin bags. And then the fish stalls, smelling to heaven and surrounded by tigerish cats, but so pretty with color—purple lobsters, blue and silver soles, freshly opened scallops shining in their shells, eels as black as onyx, and here and there a delicate pink tracery of shrimps.

Sister Brigit stared at the fascinating people in the market until some of them blushed uncomfortably under her gaze. The old women in their black shawls, with shrewd eyes pricing everything. All the busy housewives of Cork out for bargains with a string bag. And the beggars and old men who just sit, and the children with cheery-cherry noses sucking sweets and getting out of the way of barrows. And the innumerable dogs coming in furtively or slipping out with a stolen chop followed by rolling oaths.

And now there is an old woman with a concertina who sits by the fountain in the middle and plays "I'll Take You Home, Kathleen" and "Come Back to Erin."

"Oh, it is like the opera must be!" exclaimed Sister Brigit, who would never dare go to an opera. She was very wistful, though, about the opera thought that came to her mind.

And back home at the Castle again, flushed and excited from

her trip, she tells every scrap of it to Adrian, who listens as
to enchantment, although she has seen the market every week
of her life. Sister Brigit makes the market things gleam and
wink in the reflection of her telling, and seem like spun-glass
faeries and wax robins clinging airily to silver twigs.

There is a way Sister Brigit has of scraping the inside of a
vegetable marrow—stuffing it with minced goose, sage and
onions—cooking it slowly, and then eating it *red*-hot with a
claret sauce. That is the way the ould man likes it, and she is
preparing it for him with her own hands. When it is ready, she
will take it up to him and serve it to his mouth in bed.

"Sure, and this will blarney Sir George where he needs it in
the stummick," she says.

This has been such a busy day for Brigit. The cook has made
eight plum puddings—full of silver charms, and stirred by
everyone in the house to bring luck and grant their wishes.

"Faith, and why should we be doing this?" laughs Brigit,
"sure, but what's the Blarney Stone for and so close by! And
the Wishing Well, too."

But this is said all in fun and coddin', and Brigit helps Adrian
ice the cakes for all the parties, dark and rich and full of brandy
and bristling with Father Christmases and reindeer, and she
flutters about to count the great jars of mincemeat for the pies.
There will be endless parties, rather like Horseshow Week in
Dublin, and the Castle will be as noisy as a Hunt Ball, and
champagne will flow like the Shournagh River.

Christmas would not be Christmas without Sister Brigit in
the Castle. She fills it full of kindly Christmas thoughts, glowing
warm, like cakes baking.

The patient she nurses now is the leading man on the stage
of Blarney, a character in a long parade repeating the history
of those who came before him and lived and died under the
influences and spells of a fateful piece of limestone, a cornerstone of common destiny. These actors have not changed. The

only difference, from time immemorial, being the difference between a suit of golden armor or mail or the hauberk of a Norman, and a suit of clothes from Bond Street, sometimes the difference between the machine gun of the insurrectionist and the pike, sword and fire pots of Cromwell—or the growth of a bathroom from a medieval sitting tub.

This current leading man uses spoons and knives and forks, instead of eating with his fingers, and sleeps on a bed rather than in foot-deep rushes used by former owners of the demesne. He has an old-fashioned telephone and a vaulted billiard room and Lancaster automobiles. There are no hawk perches such as the McCarties placed on the great stages of the old castle, and not as many marrowbones for the hounds litter the floors of the new. But such small differences these things really are! A goblet of Waterford glass rather than a leather goblet, a sirloin steak instead of the dripping head of a "wilde" boar, a glass of champagne rather than quaff of Irish *usquebagh,* that so interesting Gaelic beverage, that golden fluid—*uisge,* water; *betha,* life; the "water of life"—as intoxicating as the eyes of a blue-eyed colleen with the gay hell of life flashing therein and courting happy sin.

On the stage of Blarney the deliciously mad traditions and the sometimes daft and always charming men and women of history, often bewildered mortals, come to life again in the company of their successors, who reside in the rays of mysterious forces and spells. The daily enactment of modern life at Blarney is but a mirror of the past. The Blarney Stone changes its shadows every minute of the day, but it is the shadow alone that changes. Its substance is always there.

The lives of peasant and peer are alike ephemeral, but their shadows, too, will always be upon the stage with the ghostly actors who have played their parts and gone before. Ghosts or living mortals, they are all but puppets of a stone.

Its present lord is the Protestant Sir George Oliver Colthurst,

Bart., seventy-year-old bachelor-owner of all the demesne, seventh baronet of his line, and to all of the villagers known as the "ould man on the hill," just as all of the past owners, his ancestors, have been known as the "ould men on the hill." He himself is a Harrow man, a graduate of Cambridge, and bears a striking resemblance to his younger friend, the Prince of Wales, that one who is now the Duke of Windsor. He is a descendant of those English adventurers the Irish call "land-grabbers," his family's first crown grant having been obtained about the time Columbus discovered America, in the reign of King Henry VII.

English kings lavished the rich land of Ireland, millions of acres, upon their loyal followers. In the so-called "Cromwellian Settlement" in 1658, nine years after the "Brewer" reduced the country in nine months with utmost cruelty, sold 20,000 Irishmen as slaves, and forced 40,000 more to flee into the foreign service to escape a similar fate, two-thirds of Ireland was divided among English supporters.

The medal-spangled chests of Sir George's ancestry were weighted with English honors. Oil paintings of ancestors wearing armor, lace collars and curled hair, showing them to have been cavaliers in the time of Charles I, dandies in mail, smirk and glower from the walls of the dining room beside the likenesses of succeeding gentlemen of strife and combat, professional soldiers all, in the service of many kings of many lands. One was King Jan Sobiesky, of Poland. They fought for others in the Low Countries, Sweden, India, and France. Over a landing of the grand staircase hangs a full, life-size portrait of King Charles XII of Sweden, in the attire described by Voltaire. This king's life once was saved in a battle with the Danes by Sir James Jefferyes, one of the founders of the Colthurst fortune. The king made the Jefferyes Swedish counts.

Now a frail and brittle old gentleman of less than average height but possessed of supreme dignity, severity of presence, and the manners of a courtier, Sir George has acquired some English medals himself. He also was decorated with the Croix de Guerre for his valiant conduct in World War I. When in London he often sees his friend, Winston Churchill.

Sir George was prevented from entering the Egyptian Civil Service by a hunting accident that left him with a slight limp, but he served with distinction the British Intelligence at Whitehall and later in France. This sometimes gives him the air of a crotchety country squire as he walks with some difficulty, especially after he has become stiff from sitting for too long a time at tea with the unending stream of guests who throng his drawing room, or from brooding under the pictures of cricket teams. He cannot hunt any more because of his injured hip, and his bad heart that requires frequent checking by a distinguished English specialist who flies over from London, when necessary, to see him. His great stables with stalls for fifty horses now are bare of all save the favorites, Ranti, Redwing and Belinda, old hunters, turned, so to speak, out to pasture. They are faithfully exercised by the grooms of the estate, and the magnificent, aging animals, rheumatic like their master, provoke a feeling of sadness somehow, when seen doing their last constitutionals, restrained on the winding Irish bog roads and cocking their ears for the cry of the huntsman's horn in the woods.

The old bachelor lives close at home these days with his niece Penelope Hamilton and Sister Brigit watching over him. Sometimes he affectionately calls his niece Pene*lope,* as in envelope, and she always calls him "Nunk," which is affectionate for uncle. His beloved little grandniece calls him "Nunk," just as her mother does, but he is Sir George to all others except a few close relatives who address him as "Georgie," and by the public he is accorded the deference reserved for a duke, an earl or even a king, presiding over an international social suzerainty.

As to the personal estimate of the man by the people of County Cork as a whole, one of the best examples was the summation of a native chauffeur who had driven his employer to the castle for a short visit. While waiting without the portals, he was served by the castle butler with a cup of tea and a crumpet, sent out to the car upon Sir George's personal instructions.

"Yirra!" exclaimed the surprised chauffeur. "And here it was I was thinking all this time Sir George was a bit o' a snob."

Today in the New Castle at Blarney fronting the medieval fortress of the McCarties, where the Blarney Stone keeps sentinel, his four-story stone residence overrun with the eternal Irish dogs, its rich Persian carpets threadbare in many places and covered with hounds' hair, he tosses them greasy bones from his Spanish mahogany banquet table and lives in genteel and somewhat shopworn feudal grandeur.

He would not have been living at all except for the "miracle of Sister Brigit."

His English heart specialist was in a plane over the Channel flying from London to his bedside.

" 'Twas a great and serious waste o' pounds," said O'L. "For Sister Brigit herself arrived in th' nick o' time. There she was, away ahead o' th' Limey, down on her knees by th' bed and prayin' to St. Brigit before th' three joyous, happy and continted nurses could pack their pairsonals. 'Twas *that* fast th' good woman worked. Five hours she prayed for th' ould man's body and sowl. She sprinkled his remains with enough holy water from her medicine bottles to give a bigger man a bath! A special medal blessed by th' Holy Father for th' sick, th' dyin' and th' dead (which is what he was all th' blissid time!) she pinned on his nightshirt and she prayed 'til blisters sprouted on her knees!"

Gradually, the ould man, who had not known Brigit at first, became more peaceful and finally, by evening, he was completely himself for the first time in months, and so charmed he was, too, to see his ould friend Brigit, still down on her knees praying away for his body and his sowl.

"Niver once did he have th' slightest idea," said O'L., "that 'twas from th' grave he came. Th' ould man had been a corpse and didn't know it!"

It is a miracle, anyway. Dear, sweet Sister Brigit.

The ould man did not need the great English doctor. When he came he was amazed. He shook his head a few times and flew back to London in some perplexity.

The next day the ould man is well enough to raise a blazing row over the way his omelette is cooked. This makes Brigit smile with joy.

Sir George's ombepon, coramine and adrenaline bottles, on which he has lived for weeks, are unopened on the medicine table. He is sitting up in bed coddin' a stone-deaf English guest who had just got herself a hearing box. It is not an unqualified success as an aid to hearing, but it is a new and fascinating toy for the ould man. The guest stares in consternation as she watches the delighted baronet "adjust" it. He has broken the mechanism three times. The unhappy Englishwoman now cannot hear thunder. But soon she will hear whispers, the ould man assures her. Three new hearing aids with batteries have arrived on approval from Cork. The ould man sits up against his pillows making experiments with a screw driver.

The anxious guest shakes her head in terror as the ould man bellows out encouragement as he takes the things apart. She walks trembling to the bedside when he warwhoops "success" at last and triumphantly beckons the wretched woman for another "fitting."

At his early bedtime Brigit found Sir George looking from his window toward the top of old Blarney Castle's rugged battlements. The crenelles of the parapet were lined with tourists who had paid good shillings to kiss the faithful talisman. "Sister" was glad to see so many. She counted the little black dots of human heads bobbing on the heights like they belonged to hurrying Americans.

"One, two, three, four . . . thirty-six! And this late, too!"
That would help some. Brigit knew that Sir George had been
forced to sell his family's ancient diamond heirlooms. Some
of them had been Colthurst and Jefferyes baubles treasured for
five centuries. Some of those diamonds, emeralds and pearls
had been wrested from the jeweled turban of Chief Tipoo Sahib,
slain by a Colthurst hero in a sword battle during the Indian
Mutiny.

The diamonds were magnificent to see, and had been worn
by the Colthurst "debs" for generations when they were taken
to be presented at Court. They came from the Golconda Mines
in India. Christie's in London sold them to Lady Alderly. Sir
George kept back only one brooch, a miniature of the ancestor
who originally acquired them, set in diamonds.

Brigit sees a frown of worry lingering over the ould man's
eyes. He has another great concern and is weighing the consequences to his line. An American syndicate has offered him a
fortune for a short lease of the Blarney Stone. A generation
ago Americans had tempted his father with a guarantee of
$500,000 to tour the famous slab "out there" for the foreigners
to kiss. The elder Sir George had rejected it. The Yankees now
came dangling a million.

Golden dollar signs were dancing before Sir George's eyes,
but his heart was heavy as he remembered his father's great
fears and forebodings.

Sister Brigit sighed and pulled the drapes as her employer
let his head fall wearily upon his pillow. She watched him until
he slept, and drifted out of the bedroom on the hem of her
skirts. She was wrinkling her brow earnestly. She thought that
she could help Sir George solve the terrible problem that plagued
him.

For a long time she had been pondering over a solution she
had figured out by herself. Now she started to pray.

"Dear St. Brigit . . ."

Chapter Ten

Decline of the Brave

Sir George is smoking like fury and eager to get out of bed. His Turkish cigarettes have clouded the bedroom and the gray smoke curls out into the halls around the angular nose of King Charles XII of Sweden (whom the Turks called "Head of Iron"), and hangs in the folds of the velvet drapes. His alarming fits of breathlessness have disappeared.

"Indeed, himself's rallyin' foine again," O'L. confided, "him that was dead and in hell altogither. Th' ould man gives credit where it 'tis due. That Protestant Dean o' Cork, puffin' a long face, came to see him fit for a foine, haythern funeral. He received a turrible, shockin' jolt. Th' ould man was devourin' a chop in his fingers, like a half-starved woodcutter, chipper as a chitchat. With th' very divil twinklin' in his eye and his twin brother in his thrroat, th' ould man pointed th' lamb bone at his chest. He told th' Dean he put his recovery down entirely to Sister Brigit's healin' Medal from Rome."

Physically, Sir George is nearly mended, but other worries are heavy on his mind.

It was easy enough to joke with the Protestant Dean of Cork, but beneath that secular banter was hidden a tormenting mishmash of worries that weighed his reason and tested his conscience and his courage. The ordeal was real, under the circumstances excruciating.

Down through the strife-torn generations, when men of Sir George's origin have enjoyed little popularity in Ireland, the public relations of the family have, largely, been traditionally cordial. His New Castle was spared the torch in the "bad times" or "The Troubles," when castles owned by men of similar lineage were gutted throughout the burgeoning republic. The men who set these fires shared the earlier sentiments of the rebellious O'Neill, the Earl of Turone, who aided the Spaniards against the English in the invasion of Ireland. In the year 1600 on a sally to reinforce his allies at the Port of Kinsale, having had a house pointed out to him and enquiring the identity of the inhabitant, he was told the owner was a certain Barret, a devout papist, and member of a family that had lived there for several centuries.

"No matter," replied O'Neill, "I hate the English *churl,* as if they came but yesterday."

Although *Burke's Peerage* and *Burke's Landed Gentry of Ireland* list the murders by Irish rebels of his ancestors, Col. John Colthurst in 1607 and, in 1641, the Colonel's son Christopher, at Macroom, and the slaying of Sir John Conway Colthurst, the second baronet, in a duel with Dominick Trant, an Irishman, in 1787, the family's business and social intercourse with the populace otherwise has been comparatively tranquil.

All of the alarming threats to burn the New Castle during "The Troubles" never materialized. What part the respect of the Irish for the Blarney Stone played, in addition to the moderate behavior of Sir George, is a matter worthy of some consideration.

Certainly, none of his predecessors had ever run the risk of permitting the Blarney Stone to leave Ireland. This was not because opportunities had been lacking. Even faraway Australia had made frantic bids for it, and international promoters with alluring proposals had clamored at the very doors of the castle for generations.

When Sir George's father rejected the fortune for allowing the stone to be shown for kissing purposes "out there in America" at one dollar a kiss, he too had been in financial straits at the time and possessed on his death of a mere $50,000. He had also resisted many offers to sell the castle at fabulous considerations to men who thought its purchase price would be recovered within a year by displaying the magic rock.

Newspapers had suggested that Sir George himself had refused similar offers, one particularly of a New York World's Fair group, because of "family pride." But there were graver and more far-reaching causes that made him spurn the chances, not only for luxurious solvency but also to restore the glory of the line. They were the same desperate reasons that gave his father torturing pause.

An editorial in the New York Times in 1938 stated that "Sir George Colthurst . . . has apparently no objection to making thousands of dollars every year from tourists who come to see or test the famous kissing stone, but he is unimpressed by $500,000 a year for exclusive rights . . . yet it could not have been a very resourceful syndicate, for the Los Angeles promoters really had Sir George in a spot. They should first have kissed the Blarney Stone and then made the proposition. The owner could not have rejected the offer without impugning the magical qualities of the stone."

The current Sir George knew better. The promoters had both him and his father on a spot in more ways than one. They had made them squirm, as his son was squirming now.

The present owner inherited Blarney through the marriage of his ancestor, Sir George Conway Colthurst, Bart., of Ardrum, County Cork, Member of Parliament for Kinsale, and High Sheriff of the county, to an heiress of the Jefferyes family in 1846, so the historic estate has been held by those of the Colthurst name for only a little more than a century, a short period indeed, as time goes in the annals of the magic stone which was acquired with the deed.

Sir George fought with resolution for an Anglo-Irish concilia-
tion even while the castles of his kind made angry bonfires all
over the land. Ears in Dublin were deaf to his pleadings. Time
marched on to independence, but people of Sir George's generation and background just did not recognize the change.

The question of nationalities as applied here presents certain
complications. When Ireland proclaimed itself a republic, a special provision was made in England, at the request of the Irish
Government, to prevent Irish residents in England being treated
as aliens. They could *call* themselves Irish, but could go on being treated as English people. As that applied to about a quarter
of the British population, it would have been most awkward
for Irish people if the British Government had not agreed.

In a way, the same applies to men like Sir George. He is
Irish more than English, one might say, but he has been brought
up in both countries, and so in both countries he is treated as
having dual nationality.

Whatever the owner of Blarney Castle may be as to "dual
technicalities" of nationality, he is a British subject and retains
his British passport.

No descendant of a "landgrabber" has ever been completely
popular in Ireland. Ireland's "long memory" does not take a
holiday, or play any favorites.

Of all the "landgrabbing," however, one of the most humili-
ating grants of all was that of 1,000 acres of good Irish soil
by Charles I to his clown and court jester, Archibald ("Archy")
Armstrong, an example of the indifferent profligacy with which
the monarchs flung around titles to choice pieces of their newly
acquired kingdom. In "Archy's" case the transfer of the deed
was particularly repulsive to the Irish, for he was known to them
as a bitter and shrewd enemy of their country, a "dull, stale
joker, pompous, insolent, pretentious, presumptuous and mischievous." This hated clown dispossessed the rightful Irish

owners who had owned the land for generations and brought his cheap wit to old Erin, and insulted the people with crude "jokes" of his composing.

Sir George himself has always been popular with the natives as a landlord. Yet with most landlords of his pedigree, the air stiffens in all personal contacts with the native Irish. On Christmas, Sir George dresses himself up as Santa Claus, gives an annual tenants' party in the New Castle and passes out presents to the children.

Breathing heavily after his perilous walk downstairs, blindfolded by his mask and cotton beard, tripped by great boots, muffled up in thick red flannel, every year he manages to lug on his back the big brown sacks of toys and candy.

His friends contend he does not grimace when his guests sing "The Wearing of the Green." "The Wearing of the Green" or "God Save the King," say his supporters, is all the same to Sir George when he has his friends around him.

The difference in religion, or just plain lack of interest on the part of absentee landlords, has made a terrible barrier in Ireland between the title holders and the people on the places. But the generations of retainers, both at Blarney and Ardrum, have been bound together more closely than is normal with the Colthurst family, through just such things as the Christmas parties and other considerate acts of friendliness on the part of the liege lords.

At the traditional Blarney Christmas parties jigs and songs go on, far into the evening. At intervals, lemonade and biscuits are brought in on silver trays by the butlers and served to the farm people.

At last, in answer to repeated requests, Sir George gets to his feet and sings "John Peel" or "The Old Bog Hole" and all present join in the chorus. After the applause, a rustic spokesman makes a courteous little speech of thanks on behalf of all the guests, to which the host usually replies by wishing everyone good night, good luck and a Happy New Year. Then he himself retires upstairs.

Now the smaller children are collected by their mothers, some still singing drowsily, others more than half asleep and blinking like baby owls. They are bundled into coats and boots and packed into prams, still clutching their precious toys and sweets and the last-minute gift of an orange.

The musicians of the band, engaged for the gala occasion, stay on to have supper with the servants, and some of the guests stay on too. Sounds of revelry still float upstairs when the clocks strike midnight. But an hour after that all is quiet. The last guest has gone home. The happy but exhausted household sleeps. The party is over. . . .

It was one of Sir George's ancestors, of the Jefferyes family (who acquired the great demesne of Blarney in 1703 during the reign of Queen Anne, a hasty transaction that for a song with only a few bars of music, but sweet because made with a minimum of tinkling gold coins), increased their Irish land holdings to 220,000 acres. Their other vast estates in the "golden age" of the English Jefferyes included Ballyandy, Ardrum and Ballybourney, all of which once were owned by the royal McCarties and seized by the English when the last of that fighting sept was exiled for adherence to the Stuart cause.

While Blarney was almost a gift to the Jefferyes, unlike Ballyandy, Ardrum and Ballybourney it was not a Crown grant. It was hasty only because its owner, a certain Englishman commoner, Sir Richard Payne, Lord Justice of Ireland, who had acquired the property in 1702 for 3,000 pounds from the Hollow Sword Blade Company, resold it in a panic in 1703 to Sir James Jefferyes, Governor of Cork, fearing that the McCarties would return from exile and be restored to their despoiled fortunes and titles. Some historians say the Governor of Cork acquired the 1401 acres, the village, the castle, the mills, the fairs, the customs "and all the land thereunto belonging," for

300 pounds, so great was the Lord Justice's fear of the dispossessed McCarties in faraway Spain.

The Jefferyes warrior who fought in many battles of Europe and saved the life of the King of Sweden—this Jefferyes is called "the bravest of the Jefferyes," because of his heroic military exploits, but the English accorded this honor to his father, whose courage in purchasing Blarney under the circumstances won their admiration.

The movement to restore the McCarty titles already afoot in England was zealously sponsored by powerful interests. The Earl of Sunderland, McCarty's Protestant father-in-law, among them, pictured Lord Clancarty as a faultless person, and King William was on the verge of succumbing to the organized clamor when a Protestant storm of protest broke over the land. Lord Clancarty's violent acts against the British, and inveterate hatred of Protestantism were reviewed in presentments to the king, which also forecast civil war in Ireland, to be fomented by scores now holding the forfeited acreage if the exile returned to dispossess them.

Donogh McCarty, the last of his name to hold title to Blarney, had been reared by his mother as a Protestant, tutored by the Archbishop of Canterbury and educated at Oxford. A Protestant he remained until the arrival in Ireland in 1689 of James II. With astonishing suddenness, he returned to the faith of his fathers, displayed great cruelty to the Protestants of Cork, and filled the dungeons of his castles at Macroom and Blarney with as many as he could round up.

Donogh led a party of retainers who lynched a poor butcher in Mallow. The butcher, whose horse had been stolen by one of McCarty's men, reported the theft, and the authorities ordered restitution. Instead Donogh and his servants tossed the man on a blanket, allowing his body to hit the ground with each fall, until the butcher died.

When King William overthrew the Stuarts, forcing McCarty

to flee Ireland, the widow of the murdered butcher was granted a valuable piece of property, still called "the lands of the Butcher of Conscience."

King William harkened to the roar of the tempest, denied the old dominions to the Irish lord but pardoned him, gave him a pension of one hundred dollars a month on his promise never again to fight Protestant succession, and forbade him ever again to set foot on Irish soil.

Donogh complied and spent his remaining years on a little island he purchased near Hamburg on the mouth of the River Elbe, passing his time profitably salvaging shipwrecks.

Now safe in possession of Blarney, and all threats vanished except the curse of legends, Sir James Jefferyes relaxed in the bosom of his new possession. The purchase had been a sweet song with lovely notes.

Still, Pyne had been highly pleased with his "bargain." He had lived in such terror of the McCarties since acquiring the property that he would have considered himself fortunate even had he been able to give it away.

"Terry Callaghan's Song" in *Father Prout's Reliques* gives a somewhat incorrect account of the manner in which Blarney was acquired by the Jefferyes in stating that it was a gift from Cromwell, but for all of its errors, it is nonetheless amusing, and also significant because most modern Irishmen believe to this day that this was how the castle fell into the hands of the adventuring Jefferyes.

> Then the gates he (Cromwell) burnt down to a cinder,
> And the roof he demolished likewise;
> O! the rafters they flamed out like tinder,
> And the buildin' *flared up* to the skies.
> And he gave the estate to the Jeffers,
> With the dairy, the cows and the hay:
> And they lived there in clover like heifers,
> As their ancestors do to this day.

It is in a comparative sense alone that the heirs of the "Jeffers" live today like heifers. Every succeeding generation has seen this glory of the fat land diminish with the shrinking boundaries of the great seigniory. The shrinkage has averaged, during the 162,500 days since the generous English Crown granted them the forfeited estates, approximately 1¼ acres per day. It takes a long time, apparently, even indulging the most luxurious of extravagances and vagaries, to lose a dominion the size of Graustark. In this case, it has covered the better part of a half millennium. Today, the demesne that once required a theoretical yoke of oxen two weeks and eight hours, without rest for water and feed, and violating the injunction regarding the Sabbath, to plow a single furrow from cornerstone to cornerstone of the connecting boundaries, has shriveled to a mere 1,400 acres, that is Blarney. It seems that a yoke of oxen should be able to plow a furrow even through the state of Connecticut in fourteen days and eight hours, but one must remember the mountains of the Jefferyes might have slowed the team down somewhat. Also the rivers and lakes. Gone with the wind are 218,600 Kelly-green acres, mountains and rivers that once formed the proud empire of those favorites of English kings. The majority of the losses have occurred during the most recent generations.

A variety of circumstances has contributed to this disaster that has befallen the landed Colthurst-Jefferyes. Not the least was the inordinate pride of older members of the famous line. To say nothing of the fascination for the tables of Monte Carlo, and the passion for the hazards of other dangerous games of chance. The Prince of Monaco has been a notorious creditor and profiteer, because of the gambling fever of some of them who sowed their wild oats in the nap of his fields of green felt.

After the McCarties were dispossessed from Blarney, the property was held by the Hollow Sword Blade Company. This manufacturer gave way to the musket, just as the adventuring soldiers of arms lived past the times of glory. The same forces that put the sword company out of the business put mail into moth balls, and the couturiers who hammered out the metal fashions, into bankruptcy. Their customers were finished, too.

Gone was the breed of grateful kings who tossed a quarter of a million acres of battle-won lands to the loyal knights who served them. The Colthursts and the Jefferyes were soldiers of fortune. At the end of a regime they found a general's reward was a small salary and a medal, not an empire adventured with his blood.

Styles had changed. The Jefferyes-Colthursts now found themselves in the roles of businessmen forced to undertake adventures of peace for which they had never been trained.

The Blarney linen industry founded by Sir James Jefferyes, together with other enterprises conducted by "Protestant artisans" shortly after acquiring the village, thrived for a while with thirteen mills in operation, but shortly failed. Blarney took on the appearance of a ghost town. The village houses were roofless. There was a general air of sad dilapidation, and the pretty shade trees in the pretty green were cut down to stumps for fire wood, and weeds and corn grew around them in the square where once bloomed a flower garden. Failure had brought ruin and decay from which the village was never entirely to recover.

Running a castle is expensive. Taxes are high. There are dozens of servants to pay and feed and house, maids, cooks, kitchen boys, charwomen, laundresses, butlers, chauffeurs, gardeners, grooms and woodsmen by the score; and many times worry could be read upon the faces of the grownups who live in Blarney Castle, just as one can read the same emotions upon the faces of those who live in more humble quarters and worry over a bob for an importunate butcher about his bill for stew meat.

During these emergencies it has always been comforting to

know that the old Stone down in the ruins was working every day of the year. When the British pound sterling was worth its weight in Yankee greenbacks there have been big attendance days when the Blarney Stone kissers have come in such numbers and have bought so many mementos from old Katy Ford that profits have been as high as five hundred dollars and more. No one in Blarney Castle is likely to starve so long as the faithful block remains. And no one has ever missed a meal for any reason save satiety or gustatory effeteness, but the sumptuous life of kings to which the New Castle is accustomed is difficult to maintain on present income.

The hospitality there is lavish. The castle is more often thronged with guests than not. Our pilgrims see motor cars coming and going in the direction of its medieval gates. Three of the departing cars are loaded with a castleful of cricketers.

Those on the Oxford side stayed at Blarney Castle—over here touring Ireland. Two of them are South Africans, Louis and Jack Wylie, and at breakfast Jack Wylie told the story of a self-made millionaire who lives near his house in Capetown, a man who puts all of his success in life down to kissing the Blarney Stone.

Seems that this character was born and bred in Ireland and for the first part of his life was dogged by ill luck. Finally, in despair, he made a pilgrimage to Blarney. He arrived broke and down and out. He spent his last shilling to get to the castle, kissed the Stone and immediately acquired a golden tongue, and a golden opportunity through it to emigrate to South Africa. He fell into a marvelous job on landing there, made money in other ways, and now not many years later owns £2,000,000 and a chain of luxury hotels. Jack Wylie could hardly wait to finish his breakfast and go up and kiss it himself.

For breakfast, the cricketers were served with exotic tropical fruit grown in abundance in the hothouse, which produces so many delicious nectarines the year round, for example, that many bushels are sold to Cork markets.

Sir George also derives some income from the River Lee that winds down through the Lee Valley, past Ardrum, and Inniscarra, past the ruined barracks of Ballincollig, and so reaches Cork. He owns the fishing rights of four miles of the river, from above Ardrum to a point below Inniscarra Bridge. He leases the salmon fishing, though retaining the right of one rod. He allows people to trout-fish, provided they first ask permission, and do not interfere with anyone fishing for salmon.

The head pool in his part of the river is known as "The Loggeens." Below this comes a stretch called "The Priests Inch," and below this a rocky pool called Scorna, in which some of the largest salmon caught in the Lee have been landed. Next comes "The Wood Hole," then "The Goose's Breast," below which a large rock juts out into the current. This rock has been known as "George's Rock" for some generations, and was so named after a previous Sir George Colthurst—a keen fisherman —who, through an injury to his leg, became unable to walk, and used to be carried to this rock, upon which he could sit and fish the pools above and below it. Below "George's Rock" comes a pool known as the "Blue Pool." Then a stretch of river belonging to Inniscarra House, which stands beside it, and below this some more fishing of Sir George's, where the river flows past the ruined Inniscarra churchyard toward a weir. Some distance below the weir, a stretch of open rough water is known as "The Weir Stream," and is supposed to be the cream of the fishing in the early part of the year. It is a pity that Sir George cannot enjoy his river any more because of his arthritic back and bad hip. But the lovely Lee works for him anyway, like the Blarney Stone, without salary, maintaining itself, making itself fruitful with fat salmon that do not have to be fed.

The crops of corn and other agricultural products, the estate's respectable lumber industry and its forestry division, together with one of the largest dairies in County Cork, make no profit, but all help somewhat with their bustle and energy to keep the family solvent. None of these is as reliable or as bountiful in its return as the ever-faithful Blarney Stone.

Yes, running a castle is expensive, especially with a lavish hand keeping decanters flowing with Irish whisky, gin, Scotch, vermouth, and the old wine cellar stocked with the vintages of good years. That is the way Blarney Castle hospitality is operated. It is the manor itself. Why, it is the Castle!

If the "cruel auctioneer" ever comes to Blarney, it will not be his first visit. He has been there before.

There would be no threat of his ever coming again if Sir George could bring himself to succumb to the temptation the Americans had brought to Blarney.

Sir George postponed final decision, just as did the cunctative McCarty dally in the process of "surrendering" his castle to Queen Elizabeth. His conduct was comparable in many ways to that of his predecessor, whom Croker caller the "Irish Pozzo di Borgo." He was "as loath to part with his stronghold as Russia to relinquish the Dardanelles, and kept protocolizing with soft promises and delusive delays. . . ."

The delay had been long and irksome. The American representative was pressing Sir George. His New York associates were pressing him. Now he made his hundredth impatient visit to the New Castle. In his pocket was a cablegram from the New York department store. Its text was this: TEMPUS FUGIT; QUO VADIS.

To the Yankee, it meant "Time flies; what gives?"

To Sir George, it meant "More grief, what annoyance!"

His was a most difficult and trying position. A million would tempt a rich man! More than anything else he feared that an affirmative decision on his part would result in complete disaster, a storm over Ireland, retaliation by his neighbors, possible condemnation of Blarney Castle by the Irish government and its seizure as a national monument. Still, he could not bring himself to say either yes or no. The very survival of his demesne was at stake, and possibly more.

The most elaborate of safeguards had been guaranteed by the Americans who came with their upsetting bona fide million. To protect it, armed guards, even Scotland Yard operatives, were to accompany it everywhere it went. Insurance for $1,000,000 was stipulated in the proposed contract through Lloyd's of London. A private stratocruiser of the American Overseas Airline, to be ceremoniously christened *The Flagship Blarney Stone,* was being readied to fly it from Shannon Airport to LaGuardia Field in New York, where it was to land on a green carpet of dyed sawdust, and there turned over to the New York Police Department. New York's "Finest" were the sponsors of the entire project in behalf of its PAL organization devoted to youth welfare work in the world's largest city. Other police departments throughout the nation would duplicate the New York pattern. It was to be exhibited at R.H. Macy & Company, the world's largest department store.

Everything about the plan, from the big rental of $1,000,000, the big private plane honoring its historic cargo with an appropriate name—everything was big. It was to have the biggest guard imaginable. All of New York's police with Irish names were to be its custodians, which meant that the Blarney Stone would have had the protection of about 10,000 police, which is the approximate strength of the department.

Honors and safeguards that might have been reserved for the Crown Jewels of England, the Magna Charta, the King of England, or the Pope himself, if ever he might conceivably leave the Vatican, had been worked out in great detail. After a six-month tour of American lips, it would be restored to its permanent location with no flagging of security precautions, and Sir George, richer by $1,000,000 without having had to turn a hand or risk a penny of capital, could go on collecting his shillings from the tourists.

He could have his stone and eat it, too, but he wondered whether it could be digested.

For a hundred years the faithful Blarney Stone has been minting shillings for the owners, but never quite enough to shore up the tottering walls of their treasuries. They were forced, however, to shore up the walls of the castle. During the middle of the 19th century, the number of trippers who came to touch their "happy tongues upon the stone and acquire gentle, insinuating speech" had increased to such an extent that damage was caused by the sheer weight of the traffic, and vandals and souvenir fanatics began to leave their marks, while tourists who could find no other way by which to immortalize their names carved them upon the rock walls and the ceilings of the castle. The initials of more persons are scratched into the sandstone of the McCarty stronghold than upon any other favorite mecca for travelers in Europe. More persons visit old Blarney than queue up at Shakespeare's home at Stratford-on-Avon.

The "gate money" of 1/ per head was started primarily to repair the castle and to preserve it in the authentic state of its ruin, but the income now was welcomed for other purposes.

Although thousands are admitted to Old Blarney Castle at reduced rates for school children and "Pilgrimages," and untold numbers kiss it without charge as guests of the owner who enter through the private gate, it is a lean year that admissions do not bring a net return of 1,500 pounds. Members of the Colthurst family, considering this as interest on capital, estimate the value of the stone at around 400,000 pounds, or more, since the profitable sale of postcards and souvenirs at the castle is figured separately, and could not exist without the main attraction. The Blarney Stone belongs to no union, does not deteriorate, draws no salary, does not grumble about working hours, and has not had a vacation since 1446. Every shilling it earns goes to the owner. Upkeep is of negligible cost. The old castle has no

Close-up of the actual Blarney Stone, showing the two upright iron rails held by the communicants to protect them from a 180-foot fall.

**LADY CHARLOTTE
FITZMAURICE**

NICHOLAS COLTHURST

SIR JAMES JEFFERYES

LADY LANESBOROUGH

Four of the many portraits hanging today on the walls of the New Castle.

janitor, no electric lights, no heating system, no plumbing, no sanitary conveniences, nothing to get out of order any more.

Before someone had the brilliant inspiration of "gate money," millions had been admitted free of charge down through the centuries. This loss represented revenue that could have saved the jeweled heirlooms and the mortgages.

A fresh million from out there in America, all at once, could recover everything in one fortunate stroke of the pen—if it could be made to prove fortunate.

There was no question about the Stone's reception "out there."

Even a piece of ordinary granite, spuriously advertised in San Francisco as a genuine chip off the old block, had attracted hundreds who paid one dollar each to kiss it, before Sir George's niece via trans-Atlantic telephone, had exposed it as a fake. The promoters left town, and a Catholic Church that had innocently permitted its name to be used in connection with the exhibition withdrew its sponsorship.

The exhibition of a piece of genuine domestic American flint hailed with great fanfare as the "real article" was exhibited for the homage of eloquence-hungry visitors to the Chicago World's Fair in 1893 under the billing of "The Blarney Stone." The entrepreneurs profited handsomely with their hoax.

The Americans apparently were Blarney-Stone hysterical.

The Federal Trade Commission in 1942 even took the blarney out of greeting cards. A manufacturer was restrained from the use of any "delusive, artful or adroit statement having the capacity or tendency to mislead purchasers or cause belief that fragments (of stone pasted on the cards) were actually taken from the real Blarney Stone."

Americans took the blarney seriously. They would go to any ridiculous extremes to kiss it, and seemed to be the most gullible people in the world. Those seeking a capacity for lingual circumambience have kissed "Blarney Stones" all over Ireland.

Timid would-be kissers who shy from the danger of bussing the lofty block in its turret location may easily have a less hazardous substitute "Blarney Stone" pointed out by any guide "sweetened with sixpence." Taxicab drivers have taken visitors from the United States to "Blarney Stones" in Dublin, Killarney, County Mayo, Cobh, County Down, Kildare and Tipperary. Unscrupulous mercenary guides have been known to steer busloads of tourists from the passenger ships at Cobh direct to the "original" Blarney Stone in the graveyard of Ross Abbey, the ancient and common burial ground of pagan and Christian alike, where the unsuspecting pilgrims have kissed a certain tombstone so often that it has been worn as though by the elements. Ross Abbey being more distantly located from the pier than nearby Blarney, this deception has proved lucrative to the perpetrators, and few of the victims seem to have suffered at all from the gentle hoodwinking. The road to Ross Abbey on the way to Killarney provides some of Ireland's most beautiful scenery. They get eyefuls of that picturesque countryside on the way, earfuls of blarney from the lecturers, and what they do not get in their mouths from the tombstone could not help such fools, anyway.

Wearily, but doggedly, Sir George labored and pondered for some solution or some compromise by which the alarming purpose might be served. Suddenly, now, he sat upright in his bed and nervously crushed out the end of his Turkish cigarette. A dangerous inspiration had come to him in the flash of genius.

Sir George was besieged with pressure to send the Blarney Stone out to America. Many members of his family assured him that the Irish storm would be averted if he sent a *small piece* of the Blarney Stone on tour. But still he was greatly worried.

Quickly he pulled a velvet cord under his canopy to summon Sister Brigit to his bedside.

Chapter Eleven

Maggy

Our excursionists know about most of these things. Details they do not know now they will learn later. They are part of their own lives, these events at Blarney Castle.

Blarney Castle dominates the thoughts of the villagers. They are not like those who live their lives through on the slopes of a high mountain and never see its summit, nor villagers in homes nestled at the foot of volcanoes, accepting the rumbling as they do the sunrise. Blarney is different.

Every morsel and shred of gossip about its daily life that comes their way they pounce upon, devouring it with an interest more consuming than the happenings in their own usually humdrum days can muster. What does not come their way, they go in search for. The life there is identified with every soul in the village as it had been with their ancestors into antiquity. They had learned of all that had happened centuries before, just as they had learned from their mothers how to cool potato soup by blowing upon it with their mouths.

Had these men of Blarney lived a generation earlier, they would have been treated as outlaws; the value of a horse one of them might have owned would have been limited to the equivalent of $14.25; they could not have inherited the property their forebears had worked for, or even leased an acre for more than thirty-one years. They would have been forbidden from holding any kind of public office, lending on a mortgage, practicing law, serving on a jury, holding a commission in the army, although with their blood they were building the British Empire as exiled soldiers in wars of English aggression in Europe and the East.

All of the owners of Blarney Castle since the McCarties had been driven out in their respective times had gone along with the accepted current of oppression and had been part and parcel of a hated and shameful system, yet somehow they do not feel enmity or envy for this dual old man on the hill who is an Englishman in Ireland. They are philosophical about his living there. His is but a fleeting guardianship of an Irish shrine,

Some night they know that they will hear the baying "hounds of the dead," and Blarney will have a new owner.

The cinema pilgrims thought of it as though it had happened yesterday—the tragic effects of a curse that had caused the death of the rich old knight, although it occurred in the 16th century. Sir James died suddenly after causing the ancient parish church of Garrycloyne to be dismantled, even though he had ordered the construction of a new and more imposing one on the site. Dire things happen to those who destroy a church for any reason.

The peasants came to mourn for him before they had been told that he had passed away. There is a legend in this family, on both the Jefferyes and the Colthurst sides, that when one of its members dies, a ghostly hunt is heard in full cry, ringing through the forests in the dead of night. The baying hounds brought the news of Sir James Jefferyes' death to every house in Blarney.

The last hunt was reported at Ardrum, also a family possession, in December, 1925, upon the night of the death of the late Sir George St. John Colthurst. Again mourners came to the estate before dawn, before anyone save the immediate grieving family knew of the bereavement. But the peasantry knew. They had heard the hunt, the hounds and the riders, the music of the pack, the thunder of galloping hooves and the cry of the huntsman's horn, and they did not have to be told.

These men will hear the baying of the "hounds of death" and they also know that the echoes of a ghostly horseman riding around the lake will change everything.

The Irish historian Croker tells of a pathetic meeting between a Colthurst and a McCarty many years after the ancient Gaelic family had been cast into exile in Spain. This Colthurst came upon an old man late one evening while strolling in the beautiful gardens of the forfeited estate. The stranger was sprawled upon the ground at the foot of an aged tree raising its branches toward the Blarney Stone. At first, the Colthurst stroller thought the old man was asleep, but the writer says his audible sobs "proclaimed the greatest affliction."

"Forgive me, sir," the old man begged, "my grief is idle, but to mourn is a relief to the desolate heart and humbled spirit. I am a McCarty, once the possessor of that castle, and now in ruins; and on this ground this tree was planted by my own hands, and I have returned to water its roots with my tears. Tomorrow I sail for Spain where I have been an exile and outlaw since the Revolution. I am an old man and tonight, probably for the last time, bid farewell to the place of my birth and the home of my forefathers."

The cinema travelers wonder over the "curse of the McCarties."

The ghostly horseman even now is being heard in the night galloping around the old squire's lake. The significance of the eerie ride is famed in the poetry of other days.

> At seven-year periods, by an awful charm,
> From out of the lake there rears a naked arm:
> In deadly stillness, of a nightly noon,
> When first the waters catch a waning moon,
> The hand thrice motions to the sombre skies!
> And thrice a shriek "Revenge!" terrific cries!
> Ere echo touches the unearthly sound,
> A ghastly figure bursting from a mound,

As gaunt a courser as he himself bestrides,
And round the lake he thrice tremendous rides!
The steed nigh out his silver shoes has wore,
And when quite gone the charm will be no more,
Wonders to follow! 'mong the glorious things,
Again proud Blarney has to hail her kings!

The men of Blarney sigh now in pity for the poor princess who died so far away from her homeland, "The White Lady Ghost," the lovely wraith, who looks so much like Missis Hamilton. They damn the British ghouls to very hell and again go on their way to the cinema, walking now in a melancholy rhythm.

Their thoughts of death had made them very sad. There were reminders of it everywhere in Ireland.

They pass their own six feet of earth reserved in the Catholic cemetery, and the ancient Iniscarra burial ground where the Colthursts and the Jefferyes sleep in a veritable clutter of death. Tombstones slant at sacrilegiously rakish angles. Skulls and human bones lie about, only half hidden in the grass, and the walls of the church crumble beside them. The place is still used occasionally as a burying ground, but has been so crowded during the last five hundred years that old graves have to be evacuated before there is room for a fresh coffin. When this is done, the disinterred skulls are tossed into the convenient grass and left there with their naked bones to blink into the unaccustomed sun.

On the site of this Protestant graveyard of Inniscarra was fought one of the great battles of Ireland between the hosts of the Sassenachs and the warriors of a Gaelic king. Near there may be seen today, standing in a farmer's cornfield, a startlingly solitary headstone. Locally it is known as "The Soldier's Grave." The lonely rock slab is the only marker in what once had been the last resting place of thousands of Irishmen interred there since the time of St. Patrick, when it was known as the cemetery of Gurth. The last tombstone remaining was erected for an

English soldier who got there by mistake. In addition to being a Protestant he also had slain a priest while the good father was saying mass and had fired another bullet through the monstrance of the Blessed Sacrament on the altar.

This English soldier was among those slain at the Battle of Inniscarra. The Irish who came later in the night and buried their own dead in a common grave could not tell in the darkness that this victim was a Sassenach, and mistakenly interred his body with those of their own heroes. But those Irish, dead for centuries, knew! They rose from their graves in protest against the offensive presence of an Englishman, gathered up their coffins and tombstones and fled the now plagued spot. The flight of the outraged cadres of burdened wraiths was across the Shournagh River, some of the more decrepit dropping their tombstones in their scurrying haste and feebleness. A number of these may still be seen in the Shournagh's river bed. The next morning, where once a populous community of the dead reposed there remained not a mound or marker except those of the Sassenach, and vacant holes pocked the area on every side. Across the river a new cemetery where no corpse had ever been buried before, blossomed with a forest of tombstones on the hillside.

"Dan O'Connor's Ride" tells of this thrilling ghostly flight from plague:

Right behind pouring up from the Shournagh's deep glen
Such a sight as no mortal had gazed upon never
For the graveyard of Gurth had crossed over the river.
And for nearly a mile over meadow and bawn
Over hedges and ditches and garden and lawn
Rushed a skeleton host with their bones shining white
And ghastly and grim in the mountain's pale light.
Some were dancing in circles with elfin delight,
Some were struggling in shrouds that encumbered their flight.
Some were bearing their tombstones like trophies in state,
And each skeleton breast bore its own coffin plate.

"Wonder now," said O'D. suddenly, "where we will be buryin' th' American Kane?"

The startling abruptness of the question made the other trippers jump. It was a subject that had never been brought out in the open before.

"Sure, and I'm afraid he's not long for this world altogither," replied O'K. sadly. "Himself hasn't ate for so long, howiver, 'twill be precious little ground his thin remains will need, anyway."

"Himself could be poured back into a gin bottle," suggested O'O. "Himself's a walkin' spirits. They need no grave!"

O'K. did not appreciate the pun. He rebuked O'O. sharply.

" 'Tis as good as th' dead ye talk about," he snapped. "But if himself's coffin was a gin bottle, 'twould be th' most expensive casket in Ireland what himself's drunk in me pub alone."

" 'Twould take more than one bottle to bury *himself* in," contributed O'D., "but th' remains will keep wheriver they're put, pickled as a swine's foot, they are."

"A repulsive, disgustin' and stommick-turnin' suggestion altogither, since ye mention crubeens, me favorite dish, O'D.," said O'K. severely.

" 'Tis your vinegar!"

O'K. blushed some more red into his face and said nothing. He shuddered as he remembered the dying look on the face of his best customer. It was most disturbing, but there was nothing he could do about it.

The handsome Kentucky man was sitting there in his wonted preoccupation, still with the death look, staring at the ever-present likeness in his terrible silent agony, his eyes dry and fixed with hurt, after O'K. had left the pub.

Maggy, the barmaid, was hovering her attention as always, buxom Maggy possessed of cheeks looking as if they had been resoundingly slapped only a moment before. But, truth is, her cheeks had always been so rosy. The old women in the village where rosy cheeks are not unusual, but where the radiance of Maggy's is a phenomenon, know the reason why.

"She was born so big all over," they will explain, "that the midwife did not know in th' light of th' peat fire that had nearly gone out, which end to spank. She just spanked th' wrong end. And what a fortunate mistake 'twas. 'Twould have been such a pity to have wasted it elsewhere."

Flirtatious men had told Maggy more than once that they could not tell whether she were pretty or not because her rosy cheeks gave them sun blindness. Maggy's blushes then were like the burst of dawn.

"Oh, ye blairneyer," she would laugh, and blush again when she caught their eyes on her hips and everyone would laugh some more and josh some more.

That O'O., and faith what a fresh divil he was, as fresh as a crock o' butter, he was, th' rogue.

"I'll bet they're not th' only red cheeks ye've got, eh, Maggy?" he had teased.

It had been said so often, too, that O'K. was throwing his good money away on candles when he had Maggy's cheeks to light the pub at night. Some of the O'Boys had feigned to believe the tale, and without warning, but by diabolical design, one dark and stormy evening quietly took their places beside every candle in the establishment, and snuffed them all out at once on a given signal from that divilish O'O.

The loudest O'O. ever heard his name called out, came that night in screams from Maggy's throat. It was like the voice of a sowl in hell. A bit o' a ram O'G. was, as many a vairtuous Cork vairgin had good or sad reason to know. And many are the examples to enumerate.

"O! O! O! O! O! O!" shrieked Maggy, as though the good girl indeed was dying.

A candle flickered and there was poor Maggy fighting for her virginal honor. O'G.'s arms were tightly held around her waist and his face, which now had some scratches, was close to her ears, but he did not seem to care. In fact, he was shouting triumphantly.

"Oboy, oboy, oboy!" he cried. "Begob 'tis true about her cheeks. I could see them in th' dark as plain as th' very day!"

"Pooh!" grunted O'W., somewhat enviously. "Nonsense!"

In the general mad rush for the candles after the bloodcurdling screams, he had tripped over a chair and fallen to the floor.

"Then how did I go right straight to th' pretty colleen?" demanded O'G. "I was all th' way across th' room! Her cheekbones glowed like two lighthouses, that's how I got there, ye shipwrecked old divil."

O'K. let Maggy off early that night and the drinks were on the happy O'G. "Oboy, oboy, oboy," he kept whispering into his suds, and smacking over the memory of stolen kisses. "Lighthouses of love! They even burned me lips!"

O'W. grunted disgustedly.

Maggy *was* pretty. Any cause the midwife might have had in infancy in making certain anatomical distinctions, long since had been corrected. Time had worked proportional wonders.

Only Kane seemed unappreciative, but Maggy did not mind.

Hour after hour, her gentle hands kept Kane's glass filled. And not for the money it brought the house—or tips, sacrilege! Maggy's very own eyes were slaty and red with her sympathy for the poor wretched American. Lofty and spiritual feelings swept over the young barmaid, those rare, extra-soaring elations brides are said sometimes to experience at the altar.

It was enough to tear the heart out of a body watching a grief that cannot get drunk on a quid of gin-and-mix a day!

Kathleen, the other barmaid in O'K.'s Snug Pub, lent her helpful hands, whenever she could outrun young Maggy to the table where Kane lived with his despair. In his case both thought of the excessive numbers of drinks they served him as a necessary evil.

Kathleen now came every day and worked without wages and late into the night, helping Maggy dust, scrub and polish. Soon O'K.'s pub was crystal-bright and shining like Holland. Both of the nervous girls kept up a bustling vigil for Kane's daily appearance.

"So quiet he is," said Kathleen. "Sing up, man! Arrah, what ails him? Makes a body wonder if he can talk."

Maggy jumped and a half-polished glass crashed to the floor.

"I'm hopin', plaise heaven, he can!" she exclaimed resentfully. "Aren't ye th' one now, scarin' a sowl to shivers!"

"If we could get him drunk just once . . ." whispered Kathleen, "we could tell for sure and all. That American woman!"

"Th' curse of God on her for it," hissed rosy Maggy, between pretty, angry teeth. "She should be bate over th' head."

"Bad cess to her. 'Tis th' same as murdher!"

"Any girl he'd call 'darlint' or *acushlamachree* . . ."

" 'Twould be nothin' fancy like that he'd have to be callin' meself," avowed Maggy. " 'Twould be faintin' now meself'd do, if he'd as much as called me 'Maggy,' plain's 'tis."

Kathleen sighed deeply and filled another jigger of gin.

"Why-iver, though," wondered Maggy, "did he come to Blairney? Yet, still, if he hadn't I'd of died."

"Pooh! If he hadn't a-come, you'd niver have of known it."

"I'd of died, just th' same," said Maggy.

"Me, too," blubbered Kathleen into a square of Irish linen.

The unhappy girl finally controlled her tears.

"Now, now," said Maggy, beginning to tune up herself.

"I'll give him up to ye," blubbered Kathleen. " 'Tis no chance that iver I would have. If he glimpsed ye once he'd be like all th' rest. I'll just be stayin' and watchin' with ye, Maggy, and harborin' no hopes o' me own. Yer flesh and blood . . ."

"Pooh!" retorted Maggy. "His eyes are not for flesh and blood. Divil a one I iver saw like him. Now ye'd think he'd say a word to a girl, not just motion." She ran a finger through a springy golden curl. "Still I'm afraid he won't, and afraid he will."

"Ye're not wishin' him dumb, now?" demanded Kit, bursting into tears.

Spontaneously Maggy embraced her friend.

"There, now, Kit. I don't wish him dumb, and yer givin' him up to me isn't meanin' at all that ye've lost a thing. He won't come to. He has no smile for me."

"Ah," said Kathleen sadly, "but maybe he'd come to if ye pinched him a little, or stuck a pin in him a little ways . . ."

"Where would I be stickin' it now? But, oh no," said Maggy quickly, "if himself as much as smiled at me, 'twould make me very heart blink!"

"But," protested the practical Kathleen, "he wouldn't be smilin' now, would he, bein' jabbed quick-like by a pin? Wouldn't that be makin' him jump?"

"Just th' same," said Maggy to her ex-rival. "Jumpin' or smilin' . . . Faith, I'm dhread o' th' day."

"But if he jumped and saw yer cheeks, they might bring him to. He hasn't spoke a blissid single word since he's been here. He's dyin' of stairvation too. And he wouldn't ate mate that a fork could cut it. So poorly he is and th' beard on him."

"Not so much as a spoonful of marrow has passed down his poor throat since he's been here. He's as limp and spiritless as a pair o' tripe."

"Men can last a long time fastin', though. Our Lord and Savior, Jaysus Christ, did for forty days, th' priest says, and then was even strong enough to whip th' divil afterwards. But just look at him!"

Maggy looked and for the first time in her life her cheeks paled. She grasped her friend's arm spasmodically, and put up a hand to muffle an outcry. She turned her head away, moaning, "O! O!" as loudly as when O'G. kissed her.

"You look, Kit, I can't. You take him. You can have him, Kit! God save us, he *is* Jaysus Christ, our Lord and Savior!"

Now Kathleen paled, too. Goggle-eyed, she stared at the girl, unable to shift her gaze.

"Ye, ye say . . . what!"

"Oh! Kathleen, Holy Mother of God! Look, look for yerself!" Maggy shut out the terrible vision behind her neck with her two trembling hands and rocked on her feet. "O, O, O, O!"

Slowly, with a firm grasp on Maggy's back for support, by degrees so deliberate that eternities came and went away, her eyes finally rested upon the man Kane. Kathleen blurted a wild exclamation and crossed herself in palsied terror.

"Yirra!" Kathleen cried. " 'Tis so! 'Tis so! Himself is!"

She felt the support of Maggy's body failing her as all of the strength drained out of her own knees. Both of the barmaids were reeling, when Kathleen shrieked again. Kane was motioning for another gin-and-mix.

"Wait! Maggy, wait!" whispered Kathleen." Himself looks like Him, that's all. But him . . . himself's . . . not Him!"

Fearfully, Maggy summoned quavering strength and lowered her hands.

"Look, Maggy, he isn't. 'Tis just that all thin men with foine silky whiskers do resimble th' Savior, I guess."

Dangerously, Maggy risked a peek in the direction of the customer and began sobbing quietly. But a minute later, the color returned to her famous cheeks and she started to walk over to the table.

"We've been so wrought up," she said to Kathleen. "What was th' matter with us! 'Twas a festination over nothin'. But," she said carefully, "you better come along, too, now."

Kane did not look up. As usual he tapped a forefinger on the rim of his empty glass to make his wants known, just as he had pointed to the bottles for his first drink. Maggy lingered longer than she ever had by his side, crying quietly.

"Glory be to God," she said fervently, "and glad I am it 'tisn't so! 'Twould niver do for me to fall in love with th' Lord and Savior feelin' as I do about himself."

For the first time since Kane had come to O'K.'s pub, he showed a slight flicker of interest in something besides the photograph and the glass. With a wan, but somewhat puzzled smile, he looked up at Maggy's constricted and loving face.

"Wha . . . wha . . . what's th . . . th . . . that, you sa . . . sa . . . said?"

The barmaids fell upon each other's shoulders and bawled out their happiness

"Th' Lord help us!"

Kane was staring at them queerly.

"Holy Mother of God," whispered Maggy, "what'll I be doin' with himself now!"

Chapter Twelve

Treasure of King McCarty

What *is* th' poor colleen plannin' to do with himself?" asked O'K. " 'Tis head over her heart and ears that she's in love with himself."

"Better she'd be throwin' himself head over his ears into th' lough," said the jealous O'O. sourly. "Sittin' th' half o' his life away in th' pub lookin' like his own tombstone."

"Thin 'tis hurryin' she'd better be," suggested O'H. "Soon there'll be not enough water in it to drown th' delicious taste o' a Paddy's."

"Pooh! 'Tis enough water in th' lough altogither to drown th' thurrst o' th' British Navy," exclaimed O'K., "and th' battle-ships along!"

"Not whin Missis Hamilton finishes. Hins and chickens'll be scratchin' for leeches on its very bottom!"

"Och, whisht, man! Would herself *drink* it dry?"

"Not by herself alone," replied O'H. mysteriously. " 'Tis th' Roosians that'll be helpin' *some,* they say."

"Begor'," retorted O'K. angrily, "pop th' Roosians' bladders and th' divil mend them! 'Tis water ye have on yer brain!"

" 'Tis yer *own* sinses that's swimmin', man. Missis Hamilton and th' Roosians will drink th' lough as dry's a rattlin' August gourd. Pop yer own offensive bladder!"

"Fie, boys," interrupted O'D., "ye'll soon be batin' yer heads togither."

"That soft one'd not be hurtin' *mine*," growled O'K. " 'Tis coddin' me for a fool, he is. A woman and a bunch o' Anti-Christs drinkin' dry a lough that'd float ivery quackin' duck in Ireland!"

"And also a sairtin' quackin' drake from a miserable goose roost," retorted O'H.

"Ye web-brained loon, a goose don't roost! No web-footed fowl does."

" 'Twas a simple mistake in me fowl," said O'H. tartly. " 'Twas a loon-goose I intended sayin', one that roosts on a keg o' stout. And when ye see th' pike in th' lough dead and dyin' and gaspin' for breath in a dry, gapin' valley . . ."

Five of the O'Boys finally separated the two angry friends after O'K. launched an apoplectic attack. The puffing, red-faced men glared at each other ominously for an hour afterwards, but peacemakers wisely sandwiched themselves between the combatants all the way to the Blackpool Bridge, lest hostilities flare again and spoil their Sunday appearances entirely. But O'K. and O'H. managed to rumble at each other with considerable satisfaction and grunted insults back and forth for quite a piece down the road.

As a matter of fact, O'H.'s fantastic report was entirely incorrect. Mrs. Hamilton *was* planning to try out a Russian experiment on Blarney Lake, but as for drinking even as much as a drop of it—Well, there was plenty of purer water more readily available in the New Castle spigots. Her Russian plan, anyway, called for a wet lake, not a dry one. O'H.'s pipeline into the castle had this time poured forth a distortion.

Many remarkable women have lived in Blarney Castle and have done many remarkable things with the castle, to the castle, and also the countryside about it. Missis Hamilton was now venturing upon an ultramodern undertaking that was to admit no hoary peer in all of its history.

The Jefferyes and the Colthurst ladies have had capacities for lavishness and startling caprice, which sometimes have been both original and ruinous. Lady Louisa Jane Colthurst, who designed and built the New Castle in 1874, could not be content with good durable Irish sandstone quarried on her own land, but imported brown rock by the tons from Scotland to decorate the windows and turrets with such recklessness that the structure was never completed. One of her ancestresses had set a precedent for costly whimsy that matched or outdid anything Ireland had ever seen up to that time.

The remarkable Lady Jefferyes, whose love for flowers and her exquisite taste in their arrangement and landscaping some centuries ago made the stage of Blarney a garden spot of Europe, was the wife of one of the rich founders of the family fortune. It was also she who dotted her lawns with an array of curious life-sized lead statues of Julius Caesar, Nicodemus, Pliny, Jove, Nebuchadnezzar, Hercules, Diodorus, Diocletian, Diogenes, Dionysius and Domitian. They were purchased from a neighboring castle in Kilkenny and were originally cast in the foundries of Germany for an eccentric French millionaire whose plan to ensconce them heroically as tombstones for the members of his family went awry when his priest could find no heavenly virtues in some of the pagan personalities and discouraged the whole idea. However, they are famed in bad poetry and good galleries, and the lyrics they inspired are as curious as the subjects themselves. Their disappearance is one of the great, unsolved mysteries in the annals of European art. It is believed that they ended up in melting pots and were used for war purposes, a not too inappropriate fate considering the careers of some of their number.

Concerning them, the poet hints of a most scandalous skeleton in a closet of the Jefferyes family and also gives us a possible clue, at least as to the *why* of their disposal:

> Oh! The muse shed a tear
> When the cruel auctioneer
> With a hammer in his hand, to sweet Blarney came!

Lady Jeffery's ghost
Left the Stygian coast,
And shriek'd the live-long for her grandson's shame.

The vandal's hammer fell,
And we know full well—
Who bought the castle furniture and fixtures, O!
And took off in a cart
('Twas enough to break one's heart!)
All the statues made of lead, and the pictures, O!

What this black sheep of a Jefferyes did to bring such financial havoc to the family is hushed by the lips of the dead. But what havoc it was to old Blarney:

Oh, ye pull'd at such a rate
At every wainscoting and grate,
Determined the old house to sack and garble, O!
That you didn't leave a splinter,
To keep out the could winter,
Except a limestone chimney-piece of marble, O!"

Still, the statues while they lasted and adorned the park caught the eye of the Cork poet Milliken, who became the poet laureate of old Blarney. What was intended as a satire on the ludicrous Irish versifying of the times, a style that had become the butt of English jokes by the serious authorship of much doggerel, became his accidental masterpiece, and he regretted to the day of his death that he ever wrote it at all. Horrified by the creative writing of his contemporaries, it was his intention to ridicule the authors of lines such as these that delighted and charmed the Irish readers:

What is grammar?
I say damn her.

Croker says this was a schoolboy's answer to a question of his teacher, one which thoroughly squelched the teacher and made Ireland roar.

With the appearance of the "Groves of Blarney," it became famous overnight and was hailed in London as the national poem of Ireland. In the mischievous classically linguistic hands of Francis Sylvester Mahony, who was the master of deviltry, modern and ancient tongues, it was appropriated as his own domain for fun and glory. He translated it into Italic, Doric, Gallic and Vulgate, announcing to the astounded world of letters that Milliken's creation had been plagiarized from the earliest writers. One of the verses, he asserted, had been copied from *Doomsday Book*. Mahony audaciously offered scholarly "proof" of his great literary find that eventually baffled the most erudite of men, and placed him in the class of the world's greatest humorists. Mahony distorted, rewrote, revised and revived at will the "Groves of Blarney," but here is the celebrated satire in its original form:

The groves of Blarney, they are so charming
Down by the purling of sweet silent streams,
Being banked with posies that spontaneous grow there,
Planted in order by the sweet rock close.
'Tis there the daisy and the sweet carnation,
The blooming pink and the rose so fair,
The daffydowndilly, likewise the lily,
All flowers that scent the fragrant air.

'Tis Lady Jeffers that owns this station,
Like Alexander or Queen Helen fair,
There's no commander in all the nation,
For emulation can with her compare.
Such walls surround her, that no nine-pounder
Could dare to plunder her place of strength;
But Oliver Cromwell did her pummel,
And made a breach in her battlement.

There's gravel walks there for speculation
And conversation in sweet solitude;
'Tis there the lover may hear the dove, or
The gentle plove in the afternoon;
And if a lady would be so engaging
As to walk alone in these shady bowers
'Tis there some courtier he may transport her
Into some fort or all underground.

For 'tis there's a cave where no daylight enters,
But cats and badgers forever bred;
Being mossed by nature that makes it sweeter
Than a coach and six or a feather bed.
'Tis there the lake is, well stored with perches
And comely eels in the verdant mud;
Besides the leeches, and groves of beeches
Standing in order for to guard the flood.

There's statues gracing this noble place in—
All heathen gods and nymphs so fair,
Bold Neptune, Plutarch and Nicodemus,
All standing naked in the open air!
So now to finish this brief narration,
Which my poor genius could not entwine;
But were I Homer, or Nebuchadnezzar,
'Tis every feature I would make it twine.

No less remarkable than the Lady Jefferyes who brought the
statues to Blarney was the Lady Colthurst who caused the fireplace of the Protestant Church of Blarney to be bricked up so
that worshipers have shivered there ever since. Her act was to
circumvent a noisy habit her husband had of poking up the fire
when he considered that the sermon had gone on long enough.

It was this determined Lady Colthurst who, hoping to better
the wavering family fortunes a couple of generations ago, braved
rustic superstition which respects the legendary presence of en-

chanted cows within the depths of Blarney Lake and also the prophecy that the rightful owners will some day return to reclaim it, by boldly announcing a plan to drain it to recover the lost McCarty riches. She desisted only when engineers of the time found the feat impracticable with equipment then available, and not because of the opposition of the peasantry.

No less brave is her descendant, Penelope Hamilton, who presides as castle hostess for her uncle and carries on the traditions of the great ladies of the past. Draining the lake is not in her plan. She is thinking of using a most intriguing and remarkable method that will be no trouble at all.

A Russian she met knows a man who is a water diviner and is an expert at it. It seems that he has experimented with different kinds of wood and finally discovered he could tell, not only the depth of a hidden spring, but also determine the type of water and actually what minerals it contained. He then made a plastic "twig" and discovered that this reacted even more accurately. It seems the thing bends a certain number of times for each metal, and in a separate rhythm for each. The Russian told her that with his own eyes he had seen it working, and that the interesting thing to him was that the twig seemed to put the same values on a metal as might a man. For instance, it would bend twice for lead, ten times for iron, and most of all—thirteen times—for gold.

The treasure is there to find, all right. A century ago a peasant boy fished up a silver signet ring from the depths with the curious McCarty coat of arms mounted with a bobtailed, horselike moose-deer with horns fashioned after the crooked branches of a yew. Copies of it were made and sold by a Cork jeweler. In Blarney, this is discussed as though it happened yesterday, and if it's more proof that a man'll be needin', for sure 'twas Missis Hamilton her very self only in 1950 who traced the course of the secret escape tunnel the castle warders used while Lord Broghill bombarded old Blarney for three days on end, not only because it was a military prize of the first magnitude. The English general also knew that the Clancarty wealth it hoarded would be a golden boon to the parliamentary government. England long since had discovered that it was expensive to fight the Irish. The O'Neill Rebellion of 1568 alone cost her £237,207,-3s,9d, as stated down to the last penny in the meticulous accounting of the times. This was over and above the taxes levied on the country, to say nothing of the loss of 3,500 English soldiers in putting down the bloody rising. Altogether, this comparatively short-lived campaign, based on the value of the pound of that day, drained her treasury of the equivalent of $10,000,-000—a staggering sum in England four centuries ago.

In England the provender for twenty horses cost but a few pennies, a hundred fighting men could be fed for a shilling, a sheep could be had for six of the meanest coins of the realm, as could a barrel of flour, and a fine fat ox brought the equivalent of a present-day American cheroot. But England, still saddled with the first national debt contracted during the reign of King Henry VI and increased through the years by expensive martial adventures abroad, had pawned the royal crown to the Dutch in the reign of King James for 300,000 pounds. It was only redeemed by Charles I by the Iron Ordnance in 1629, after four years of great national shame and humiliation.

Great scientific advancements had been made during the last century. Mills, invented in Germany, appeared in England. The secret of the Spanish needle, held by a London Negro who refused to divulge it, was solved by other artisans; pins had been invented, so ladies no longer had to use skewers; and stagecoaches appeared on the roads. Newspapers were first published in London, felt hats began to crown the heads of men, and violins were invented. All of these would seem to be the discoveries of a prosperous peace, but reckless expenditures for war and its modern requirements drained the royal treasury.

There are some historians who say that Cromwell, when appointed Lieutenant of Ireland in 1649, brought with him on his invasion only four "whole cannon" and five demicannon for his 12,000 horses and foot, and that only one shot was required to force the surrender of Blarney Castle.

The evidence of Lord Broghill's own inventory of the cannon used against Blarney Castle bears this out.

As late as May, 1677, there lay "aspoyleng" at the Fort Gate of Cork brass ordnance of Lord Broghill, brought from Blarney Castle, consisting of nine pieces, as follows:

"Mortar gun fixed in brass, basis 12¾ inches diameter, 1 unmounted. Demy culvering 10 foot, weight 33c(wt) per estimation, 1 unmounted. Minion scaled 7 foot, 1 unmounted; minion, 6 ft. 3 in., 1 unmounted; minion 6 ft. 11 in. wt 1460 lbs., 2 unmounted; minion 6 ft. 10 in., 1 unmounted."

In other words, Cromwell and Ireton considered dread Blarney so strong that they gave Broghill every great gun the English brought over for the slaughter, to bend against one castle, leaving themselves without a single piece of artillery for their own purposes.

Always had old Blarney successfully resisted every attack launched against her walls by the best a mighty army could offer, and prevailed against cunning treachery. Queen Elizabeth's deputies, unable to gain possession of the person of Cormac McCarty by any other means because of the great strength of his fortress, stooped to unthinkable subterfuge and the blackest dissimulation to take him, but this also failed.

This attempt was made in desperation after the chieftain had been called "a jugglying traytor," and the word "blarney" had become proverbial. The Lord President of Cork commissioned his military aide, Sir Charles Wilmot, with a sergeant and twenty foot to make a pretense or "a shew to hunt the buck" near Blarney Castle, and then giving the appearance of fatigue, to present themselves for refreshments near the gates of the *enceinte,* which means the castle's surrounding wall, and abuse the renowned hospitality of the Irish. When served they were to attempt the overthrow of the guards.

"Sir C. Wilmot," writes the 17th century priest of the Society of Jesus, Father Edmund Hogan, "asked for wine and usquebagh (whereof Irish gentlemen are seldom disfurnished). But the warders, whether out of jealous custom of the nation in general (which is not to admit strangers in their masters absence to come into their castles) neither Sir Charles (though he much importuned to see the roomey within) nor any of his company were permitted to go to the gate of the castle, nor hardly to look within the gate of the bawn."

So jealous were the Irish chieftains of their reputations as hosts that great rivalries were developed by neighbors vainly seeking to outdo each other in their liberality and the plenitude of their boards. Wagers as to the relative generosity of the native suzerains in such matters were made by sensitive followers, and spies, usually bards, were sent disguised as gamesters to visit the contending castles and report on the disputed conditions of lavishness.

One carrow, or gamester, acting to settle such an argument between Donald Roe McCarty, of Blarney, and Prince Fermanagh Maguire, lived in the castles of both for a year each before deciding in favor of the latter entirely on finding that Maguire, although his estates were smaller, retained more servants and provided during the tested year a greater tonnage of victuals.

Therefore, the very fact that Captain Wilmot was denied a welcome certainly must have been based on prior suspicions of hostile designs alone.

It is told that when this bard died of the effects of obesity after his gargantuan firsthand investigations, his body required the largest coffin ever made in Ireland; but this is said to be true of many Irishmen of enormous statue or girth, especially the famous fat man of Dublin, who is interred in a catacomb

recess the size of a cave large enough to hold the carcasses of
a yoke of oxen, and which is completely filled with his remains.
This remarkable fat man possessed of a pair of farthingale-like
hips required a special cutout table of most interesting proportions; that is, it was provided with a crescent four feet to its
deepest point, in which the diner's protuberant stomach crowded
in a tight fit, and also by generous-sized side leaves adjustable
to his buttocks.

However, the bard of Maguire and McCarty was never described in quite such elaborate detail, so it is not known to this
day whether the Dublin fat man, who died much later at a time
vital statistics were carefully recorded, exceeded his record, or
not.

However, the bard did prove that Irish hospitality left nothing to be desired as to victualing, and by his sacrifice pointed
up the reluctance with which Wilmot was turned away from
Blarney without so much as sniffing at the contents of a leather
goblet.

Thus foiled in their treachery, the English were forced to
wait until McCarty gave himself up voluntarily.

A bad omen it was for Blarney Castle later when another attempt was made to take it through a bully fighter. The best bully
fighters of the day were Irishmen, the most famous being the
celebrated DeCourcy—not exactly Irish, it is true—a Norman
Cork man who was so powerful and fearsome that a French
bully selected by Philip, the King of France, to meet the best
King John of England could offer, fled in terror at the very
sight of the giant and escaped into Spain, never being seen again.
Later, in a trial of his strength before the two kings now that
the argument between them as to the title of the Duchy of
Normandy had been settled without a blow in favor of England,
DeCourcy cut asunder with one blow of his sword a helmet full-
faced with mail. The blade sank so deeply into the block of
wood upon which the heavy metal was placed that no man, save

DeCourcy, could withdraw it. DeCourcy, who had been sentenced to life imprisonment in the Tower of London, from which he was released to adventure with his blood for the hated King John, was freed. The only reward he asked was the right to remain covered in King John's presence, that for him and his heirs after him. His request was granted and the privilege is retained by his descendants even until this day if any there be who care to avail themselves of it.

Now, say old manuscripts of the Royal Irish Academy, came the English sallying from Cork to suggest that McCarty surrender.

"Not without fighting for it," said the Lord of Blarney, and he proposed to leave the issue of the battle to single combat. The English selected one of their best men, and MacCarthy also chose his Bully, and both entered the field, each accompanied by a drummer and fifer.

The Irishman fought cautiously at first, to try the mettle of his opponent, whom he found a formidable enemy; whereupon he changed his manner of fighting, and attacked him vigorously, finally succeeding him and killing him and cutting off his head, which he carried on the point of his sword to the castle.

MacCarthy knew, by the triumphant music of fifer and drummer, that his man was victorious, but when he saw the head, he exclaimed, "This is a bad day's work!"

"How?" said his champion. "Would you rather see my head on the Englishman's sword?"

"No," said MacCarthy, "but they will revenge this."

Chapter Thirteen

Blarney's Golden Snake Eggs

L ORD Broghill had much to avenge, for the English memory reached far back too, even to the "Black Monday" of 1209 when the Irish spilled out of the mountains upon 500 Bristol people of Dublin picnicking on Easter Monday in Cullen's Woods and slaughtered them all, men, women and children. Shane O'Neill's rebellion was not so far away, nor the slaughter by the Irish of the large English garrison at the Castle of Arklow, in the year of the great famine, the burning of the towns of Leinster by Roy Oge O'Moore, and the ashes from 200 fires set by Owen Rowe throughout the countryside near Dublin had not been washed away by the rains, and Cromwell's losses of 2,000 foot before Clonmell were fresh in his mind. Broghill had much to avenge, but in old Blarney Castle reposed enough gold to ransom a crown.

Also, Broghill now coveted the castle as a place of residence.

In its golden age five-storied Blarney Castle was much greater in size than it is today, built in four great piles all joined together, flanked with strategic bulwarks. All that King William III left in his demolishment after the Battle of the Boyne in 1690 is the war-shaken but almost perfect keep, or tower, still standing in the embrace of ashlins and ivy today.

The very zeal with which Lord Broghill attacked Blarney may be some indication of the value he placed on the awaiting loot. But the loot did not wait! While he "fired of his bullets like thunder, that whizzed through the air like a snake, and made

163

the ould castle (no wonder) with all its foundations to shake,"
the warders of Clancarty's stronghold were not engaged in de-
fense alone. For three days and three nights, while longbowmen
resisted the siege with arrows and missiles dropped from anti-
quated medieval machicolations, the accumulated wealth of a
family rich for centuries was placed in strong oak chests and
bound with heavy chains, in the light of sputtering torches in
a strong room cut out of natural rock deep under the castle,
today the webbed home of poisonous blind spiders.

These chests contained no brass or other money coined in
England and forced into Irish circulation. This contemptible and
utterly damned dross was scorned with impunity by the powerful Irish chieftains and often rejected by less powerful subjects,
who were flogged or threatened with the gallows for the offense.

Two tunnels led from this dark vault to the outside world:
one to Ballincollig Chapel, which in other days would have
been treated as a sanctuary; and the second to Blarney Lake.
This latter tunnel was the one taken by the trusted warders of
Clancarty. One hundred and ten trips they made through the
dark underground passage during the seventy-two hours that
guns of Broghill roared against the walls of the old citadel. On
each trip one hundred of the strongest soldiers of the embattled
garrison carried nine heavy cases of treasure. Tons of gold and
silver were cast into the deep waters of Blarney Lake before
the castle yielded. On the last trip, when all of the soldiers
escaped through the same tunnel, one carried the heavy suit of
golden armor Laider the Strong had worn in so many battles
against the Sassenachs. This, too, was consigned to the waters
of the lake, together with seven small iron cases of jewels collected by McCarty queens and princesses for seven hundred
years.

Of all the many McCarty castles, Blarney being the strongest was chosen as the treasury of their kings.

The bard says that it required more than Cromwell's cannon to take Blarney. Here is that black Masonic magic again:

> Bad cess to that robber, ould Cromwell and to
>   All his long battering train,
> Who rowl'd over her like a porpoise, in two or
>   Three hookers from Spain;
> And because that he was a Freemason, he
>   Mounted a Battering Ram,
> And he loaded it up with dumb powder,
>   Which in at its mouth he did cram.
>
>
> It was now the poor boys of the castle, looked
>   Over the battlement wall,
> And they saw that riffian, ould Cromwell, a-
>   Feeding on powder and ball;
> And the fellow that married his daughter, with
>   A big grape shot in his jaw,
> 'Twas the bould I-er-ton they called him, and he
>   Was his brother-in-law.
> With his jack-boots he stepped on the
>   Water, and he march'd right over the lake,
> And his soldiers they all followed after as
>   A duck or a drake.

The strong, 18-foot-thick walls, and the valor of her archers, had held Blarney safe against the modern arms of the invader long enough for the frenzied guardians of its wealth to spirit it away. When Broghill finally stormed the walls and entered the keep, he found the evaporation of man and ducat complete. The poet writes about Cromwell's "looting," but there was nothing for the bitterly disappointed Parliamentary victors to loot. The prize had crawled away.

Bad luck to that robber, ould Crommil!
That plundered our beautiful fort;
We'll never forgive him, though some will—
Saxons! such as George Knapp and his sort.

But they tell us the day'll come, when Dannel
Will purge the whole country and drive
All the Sassenachs into the channel,
Nor leave a Cromwellian alive.

The cheated Broghill, however, had gained for himself a fine residence, and there he settled down to flay the enemy anew. Many of his letters, boasting of bloody victories over the Irish, were addressed from *Blairney*. He spelled it phonetically, as the Irish pronounced it then and still pronounce it today.

However regrettable it is to report, it must be told that the arrogant and cruel Lord Broghill won from his victory a prize even greater than the lost treasure of the McCarties. While in residence at Blarney he became a devotee of its eloquence and is known to have made a daily ritual of kissing the Stone; which required little effort on his part since his private apartment, "where once the trembling harps of joy were strung," was the "Earl's Chamber," a tapestry-lined room, the choicest in the castle, overlooking the Martin River and only a few steps from the talisman.

When he finally returned to England as the first Earl of Orrery, he was able through the gifts acquired from Ireland's magic palladium to win for his bride the most ravishingly beautiful girl in the kingdom. She was Lady Margaret Howard, daughter of Theophilus, Earl of Suffolk, who inspired the poet Sir John Suckling to pour out from his soul one of the greatest masterpieces of the English language. "The Bride" celebrates the wedding, and is written as the report of an enraptured rustic who had seen the grand nuptials on a visit to Charing Cross.

One of the best-known verses of the classic tells in rapt admiration of Lady Margaret's luscious mouth:

> Her feet beneath her petticoat,
> Like little mice stole in and out.
> But of her lips, the one was thin,
> But as for that one next her chin.
> Some bee had stung it newly.

Such irony it is, that this wonderful thing had to happen to Lord Broghill, the enemy of Ireland, but the Blarney Stone knows no favorites; and especially sad in this case because it consigned poor Maggy to such a lamentable fate.

> The maid: and thereby hangs a tale—
> For such a maid no Whitson-Ale
>   Could ever yet produce:
> No grape that's kindly ripe could be
> So round, so plump, so soft as she,
>   Nor half so full of juice.

The mistress of Blarney one blustery spring morning when the rains of Ireland fell under a blazing sun, and the winds dressed the saucy waves of the lake in little ermine coats, confirmed the old legend of the tunnel's existence, one Blarney never doubted in the first place, but it was satisfying to the villagers, somehow, to have a grand lady of Missis Hamilton's probity instead, perhaps, of having an old woodsman who told ghost stories and saw leprechauns (not that this would make a liar of a man, at all) do the finding of it.

Deep hidden in the rocks and water horehound near the lake there is a big cave, its back wall made of fallen rock, and near it in the park exists a dip or cavity where everyone had always said the tunnel had fallen in on top of itself. Missis Hamilton, when she decided to find out, uncoiled a long rope down in the old treasury room, fastened one end onto a jutting rock and followed the tunnel to this very dip. Now so far everything she had ever heard about the course of the tunnel had been proved up to this point. It did lead in the *direction* of the lake. Subsequent explorations revealed an opening at the other end of the tumble-down cave which led directly, just as legend had said, to the boggy shore.

All of this was very exciting, and somehow, in this setting of medievalism like the castle of Macbeth, one must applaud a decision to carry the search further with a divining rod in which the ancients believed; but now, one made of nylon plastic, well . . . would not witch hazel seem more in keeping with the atmosphere?

However it is dowsed, the peasants of Blarney will tremble if Missis Hamilton's new-fangled twig bends in the right place— thirteen times!

Possibly of even greater value than the McCarty treasure in the lake is an enormous clutch of golden snake eggs, about which we have heard before. In the Rock Close of Blarney the Druids once reigned and worshiped the mistletoe. From their retreat under the ancient ilexes, yews and oaks could be heard the shouts of "All heal!" as the priests cut the holy parasite with golden knives from the branches of the trees and slaughtered white bulls as sacrifices when this "gift from heaven" was found. It was a celestial panacea held in the greatest reverence.

In dark orgies of mysticism in their recesses, they watched writhing snakes squirm in masses of saliva froth, confusion and reptile sweat to produce the charmed "Anguineum" from the moisture of their energies. The "Anguineum" was a snake egg the size of an orange and as light as balsa wood, being so porous and buoyant that it could float in the rapids of a stream even when covered with a golden wrapping. When the snakes finally transformed their sputum into the egg, they hissed triumphantly and tossed it high into the air, where it landed in the cloak of a

The late Sir George Oliver Colthurst, Bart., the last "ould man on the hill." From a photograph in the uniform of a captain in the British Army Intelligence, World War I.

Old Blarney Castle and the 18th century mansion house.
From a color print.

Courtesy of Irish Tourist Association

*Blarney Castle today. The mansion house shown on the opposite
page has tumbled into decay.*

That little sprite, Adrian Hamilton, and Ould Puff. From a Christmas card, 1950.

Druid priest. This prophetic man emitted a wild Druidical exclamation of triumph, rapidly mounted a horse and galloped off with his treasure, the angry snakes in hot pursuit. Of course, this was before the time of St. Patrick. The hissing snakes chased the Druid until further pursuit was halted by Blarney's Martin River which empties into the treasure lake.

Imagine a Druid in full cry, galloping hell-bent for the lake, robes flying, a snake's egg held aloft, and after him a pack of outraged serpents spewing.

Never a dull moment at Blarney!

Pliny, the elder, wrote that he had laid his own two eyes on one of these fabulous eggs, and who are we to doubt him?

Chapter Fourteen

Ould Puff

O ur cinema-goers passed many majestic Irish wolfhounds on their journey, and many were the comments the happy pilgrims made about this proud and ancient breed of animal. One wolfhound, the size of a fawn, trotted by, all aglory in his size and superiority.

"All Irish," observed O'T., "th' very tallest dog in th' entire worrld."

"Bet a ha'pny ould Puff could handle him, though," said O'B. loyally.

"Why not," laughed O'T., "and I'd pity th' lion!"

They had not seen much of ould Puff of late and he had been sincerely missed by his friends in Blarney Village.

Ould Puff's reputation as a lion-killer had been achieved on the honorable field of battle, in an exploit of strategic heroism that would have done credit to the courage and the skill of the medieval King McCarty himself.

Blarney Castle life was a paradise for an ordinary Pekingese, but Puff was no ordinary Pekingese. He was an adventurer at heart. He loved to roam in strange and dangerous fields.

No estate in Ireland was possessed of more trees and foliage than Blarney Castle. Every month, new shipments arrived for the "plantations." There were so many trees, in fact, that only a few had been explored. It would take a dog's lifetime to get around to half of them.

There are beeches, various kinds of spruce, larch, fir, holly,

Irish thorn trees, never deliberately cut down in these parts, for fear of the ill luck this will bring from the faeries; horse and Spanish chestnuts, cypresses, laurels, ashes, willows, oaks, maples, many kinds of rhododendron, including the giant Tibetan kind which grows to thirty feet or more and has enormous crimson flowers, and a rare, early-flowering species, called Christmas Glory, which has been known to put forth its pale pink blossoms when there was snow upon the ground in December. In the Rock Close there is one tulip tree that only flowers once every seven years, of which there are a very few specimens in Ireland.

The morning that the gardener set out twelve new camellias and magnolias imported from Belgium, Puff did not so much as sniff his interest with his haughty, squinched-up nose. He was watching his mistress playing with her flowers.

She and Stafford, the gardener, were planting another spring bed with yellow, mauve and purple tulips, blue forget-me-nots, lilac primulas and miniature blue scillas. They were getting a bit foxed up on an elaborate American plan Missis Hamilton prefers, and there was a wrangle brewing because Stafford likes lines. He feigned deafness when told to lay them out in groups. Missis Hamilton sighed over his stubbornness and started to plant them herself. Finally, Stafford grumblingly pitched in to help her, giving a nasty laugh.

" 'Tis a foine salad that they'll make for th' rabbits, ma'am, and lucky ye'll be to see one bloom!"

Missis Hamilton merely smiled at ould Stafford. She might have pointed to the borders she had planted with her own hands, nice in their sophisticated way, mauve and yellow tulips rising from a mist of blue forget-me-nots, and banks of iris with their sculptured shapes and sword leaves, primulas as bright as the stars, creeping about the rocks in front, and miniature arbutus. Her gardens would challenge those of Blarney's golden age about which the poets trilled.

It was such a wonderful spring day. There was a reddish mist 'round some of the young trees that meant buds already, and under them the snowdrops and blue scillas seemed almost to dance in the sun. The tulip bulbs had shoots four inches high—so rich and green and sappy and full of life. A great blackbird was cawking just over the hedges and getting answered by a thrush. From where he is, he cannot see her, but Puff can. Does the thrush think she is a charming lady-blackbird? Or does he give a damn? Puff does not care one way or the other. He is restless and unhappy. In fact, he is miserably in love. Nothing cheers him.

Even the somber yews are covered in small buds of a lighter green. And the tennis court is white with daisies. They are tinged with pink and fold their petals over their faces at night. Everywhere the grass is growing rich and green and strong and the "Acto" mower, at last in trim, is whirring that intoxicating, wonderful smell of fresh mown grass.

The other Blarney dogs, Dunivan the collie, Rosko and Sally, are barking happily and rolling over each other in the grass. They never venture an inch beyond the boundaries of this lush dog heaven. The kittens, Silver, Lover's Knot and April Ann, are so smugly contented they are disgusting to Puff, who ignores them all completely. Just as he does Adrian's guinea pigs. At this writing they are Edward-Buttome, John Blarney, Bobby-Soxer, Pickwick, Snodgrass, Winkle and Tupman, some of them named on the morning she was reading Dickens, but nine babies born that day, all boys, are yet to be named and there are not enough male characters in *Pickwick Papers* to go around. It is that old rip of a father's fault there are so many, and Adrian is trying desperately to find some way to keep him from marrying his granddaughters. It is too late to save his daughters now.

In Puff's opinion, those guinea pigs caused more trouble than all of the creatures at Blarney Castle put together.

There was the time when all of those movie people, cameramen, directors and writers came to Blarney Castle to photograph it for the Bing Crosby movie, the identical one our friends from Blarney are now on their way to see. Adrian met them all at lunch. She was scrubbed as bright as a faery circle, as though she had just danced in one, so glowing and breathless, like a faery herself. The great director from London beamed his admiration upon her.

"My, my, Mrs. Hamilton," he said, "what a *beautiful* little daughter you have. She would make a Shirley Temple fortune in the films!"

Adrian's eyes were like the stars over Hollywood!

After lunch she and Puff went out to play in the gardens. They romped together through the weeds, chased each other across the hedges and waded through the streams. Adrian had never been quite as exhilarated. Being chosen to act in the movies was the most glorious news in the whole, wide world!

When she saw her mother and the wonderful moving picture man coming down a path together, she cried delightedly:

"Wait! Wait! I have something for you!"

Grubby and uncouth, Adrian emerged from under some bushes, a guinea pig under either arm, and in ecstatic gratitude for the compliment and the marvelous opportunity he had given her, she gave back to the movie mogul a dazzling grin and pressed *both* of her guinea pigs into his hands.

The startled power of the cinema firmament had obviously never seen a guinea pig before, let alone been given two to hold, and one could see that he was revising his opinion of the future actress. He never mentioned her stardom again.

Personally, Puff considers Dunivan, Rosko and Sally a blasted nuisance. He does not associate with any of them. He shuns them like the epizootic. At night, they are supposed to sleep in the great billiard room with the gun cases, fishing rods, croquet mallets, cricket bats, tennis rackets, riding whips, dueling swords, ancient armor and the innumerable tin deed boxes, but they all prefer to retire on the chintz-covered chairs and davenports in the drawing room. Puff has no interest in where they sleep. His personal bed is the velvet cover at the feet of his mistress.

He acts toward them as though he considers these dogs his mental, physical, spiritual and genealogical inferiors.

During the most recent excitement at Blarney Castle—a swarm of bees in the schoolroom—this time, the new governess was stung in almost twenty places and blaming everyone except the bees. Adrian was flying about the room in an ecstasy of excitement, with a butterfly net. She wanted to catch the queen and take her to a place of safety before "The Men" (hastily summoned) turned up to demolish the swarm with formaldehyde. All the dogs were going haywire with bees in their coats . . . acting very silly in comparison to Puff's behavior. He simply stood his ground and growled at the bees. Not a one dared come near him.

When he was scheduled for a haircut and a bath for his photograph with Adrian for a Christmas present to her friends and relations, the only way his mistress could get Puff to let her brush him was to have the groom feed him pieces of Turkish delight from the front, while she approached stealthily from the rear, armed with brush and scissors and poised for instant flight in the event of attack. Actually, he bit the groom by mistake. Puff had just as soon bite a maharajah, English earl, Jim Farley or any of the great ones who dropped in for tea or a chat after they kissed the Blarney Stone. One really needs a kind of Commando training to have dealings with Puff, plus all the tact and courtesy of the Chinese Court.

During Christmas it was freezing like old Nick. The frost made Puff mad. It pricked his paws. He came for a walk one morning and cursed under his breath all the way. Then down by the lake a duck was quacking. Puff thought it was laughing at him, and with a savage snarl he sprang off the bank at it, never thinking the ice would not bear his weight. His mistress got him out quite easily and luckily he was in such a fever of rage that he never felt the cold.

Puff has recently had some experience with the guinea pigs, too, and got himself innocently involved in a blazing row with the ould man. It was not at all to Puff's liking, or even his choosing, but he had just as soon bite the ould man as he would Winston Churchill when he dropped in for a brandy or so, although he never bit anyone unless first he was molested or accidentally stepped upon.

It was not the time during these trying days at Blarney Castle to get crossed up with the ould man. The Yankees were driving him mad about the Stone and he was like an old bear at the breakfast table.

That very morning he heard a hell of a row raging between the ould man and Missis Hamilton . . . over *milk,* of all things. The steward, having discovered ten T.B. cows at the farm, had told Missis Hamilton, who ordered all the milk to be boiled. She made her great mistake in letting him discover it for himself. With the first sip out of the glass he hit the carved mahogany ceiling with a roar, and then the fun began.

He immediately ordered his niece's instructions canceled, his raging argument being a) there were no sick cows on the farm, b) there is no such thing as T.B., c) you do not get it from milk, anyway, and d) boiled milk tastes like ditch water.

Missis Hamilton is holding to it, since it is only a few weeks until the cows are got rid of. Both she and Adrian agreed after he went upstairs that Nunk is a tiny bit unreasonable at times, though *very* sweet. Then Missis Hamilton proceeded to go to the kitchen and tell Mary to be sure to boil all the milk until further notice from her *alone.*

Sir George was in no mood that day to approach about such a serious matter as the rat. It was a dark mood. All others are pale gray compared to it. Even the sky was black and bulging with tear-filled clouds. And under it, wet Black Angus cattle gloomed—their backs to the rain.

All the livelong day he had been crankily mumbling something about "a little piece, maybe" of the Blarney Stone, and fussing and digging through a lot of old papers and studying yellowing press clippings about his famous possession.

It seems that several "little pieces" of the Blarney Stone, if the papers were to be believed, had already been broken from the old block. It might have been thought that that discovery would have simplified his problem, but instead they made him more uneasy than ever. Deliberately laying despoiling hands publicly on the Blarney Stone was not to his liking. If any pieces *had* been broken off, they had been stolen. There was a vast difference. If he put chisel and crowbar to it, how would the sensitive and sentimental Irish react? That was the question!

Also, a clipping from *The New York Times,* dated 1926, did nothing to improve his humor:

> Atlantic City, N. J. (Despatch) Following closely orders of the Governor to rid New Jersey of notorious roadhouses, State Police raided seven roadhouses simultaneously, squads going to every questionable resort between Harristown and Camden.
>
> At the Blarney Castle, a resort near Gloucester, James J. McGuigan was arrested and held in $500 bail for resisting arrest.

Another told of a wretched Irish-American, named Jeremiah Joseph Wright, leaving a "small piece" of the Blarney Stone to his delighted heirs. He also willed them among his personal effects "a real sod of Irish turf, a piece of the Treaty Stone of Limerick, a blackthorn walking stick and a choice collection of cigar holders." The cash legacies to Irish beneficiaries in Dublin were scarcely mentioned.

A New York Mayor named O'Brien had become ecstatic on being presented with a piece of *genuine* Blarney Stone carried in a case designed for precious jewels.

"I will treasure this souvenir," he orated in a barmy speech at City Hall, "with the hope that my future career, as in the past, will reflect glory on the native land of my father and mother."

Only one other genuine fragment had ever been traced to the United States, Mayor O'Brien was told. This caused great confusion among the politicians of the greatest city in the world. The *Times* said the news "spread like wildfire, and was hailed as an omen of success. But there was a fly in the ointment!"

"Suppose," they asked in horror, "our enemies get hold of the other piece?"

They must have gotten hold of an even larger piece, because O'Brien was defeated his next time up for election. The Irishman's opponent was an Italian-Jewish politician named Fiorello LaGuardia.

An American newspaperman brazenly wrote that he had stolen a large piece of the Blarney Stone at dusk when no one was looking. It was described as an "ultradaring" feat, "seemingly impossible," one that "electrified the world!"

"This newspaperman did something that was never accomplished before by any newspaperman, native or foreign—he kissed it and got away with a piece of it, which he is now exhibiting to hosts of envious friends!"

Adding insult to injury, the scribe not only stole a piece of the Blarney Stone but also ate his fill from a blackberry bush growing on top of the Castle, and vaingloriously set down the details of the crime. He stole a lot of free kisses, too, for the purpose, he stated, of taking some of them back to his friends in Portland, Oregon. He did not even pay his shilling admission fee. After kissing the stone about five dollars' worth, he picked up a rock, leaned out over the parapet and broke off a small loose piece jutting from the mother block. Just at that moment he heard the voices of members of an Australian regiment marching up to enjoy the ritual, and fled with his loot. Thus it seems that Ireland owes a great national debt to Australia. The Oregon rascal might have stolen *all* of the stone if left alone long enough. For a while he had seriously considered using a hammer and chisel on the stone and making a *real* haul.

The more Sir George investigated, the more distressed and uncertain he found himself. There was no end to the effronteries.

One American newspaper in an editoral asked whether the jolly theft had so marred the Blarney Stone that its good luck would run out of the scar, or hole, just as the bad luck runs out of a two-dollar bill torn as a precaution at one of the corners!

Americans took their blarney seriously, not with a grain of sandstone. Even the courts "out there" took no chances with it. They wanted their blarney, the whole blarney, and nothing but their blarney, so help them leprechaun.

There were two New York individuals, Michael Cohen and Frances Cohen, trading as the Meryle Publishing Company, who were restrained by the Federal Trade Commission of the United States from any sort of representation that the rock fragments pasted to their greeting cards were from the genuine stone itself.

The *Irish Independent* editor came across one of the Meryle Publishing greeting cards about a quarter of a century ago, and was highly impressed with it, however. He sent one of them to Sir George, and wrote an editorial about it. The card bore the legend: BEST OF LUCK, AND JUST A BIT O' BLARNEY STONE.

> Stuck to the tinfoil (wrote the *Independent*) which a pipe-smoking Teddy bear is carrying, is a small bit of stone—¼ the size of a postage stamp.
>
> The tinfoil further bears the printed legend: "A piece of *guaranteed, genuine* stone from the original Blarney

Castle,—*Dublin*, Ireland!" (The italics are mine as a commentary.)

The back of the greeting card shows a facsimile of a document, sworn at the American Consulate General in Dublin. It declares that the origin of "10 crates of crude limestone" is "Blarney, Co. Cork" and that the stone is quarried from the "seam of limestone, upon which Blarney Castle is built."

I forwarded my reader's greeting card to Sir George Colthurst, the owner of Blarney Castle, who refused a fortune to permit the original stone to go to the World's Fair in New York. He tells me that their greeting card stone comes from a quarry outside the Castle precincts, from which comes the stone, used for road-making in the district.

Thus, though not a chip of the Blarney Stone, it is truly a capital piece of business.

It did not prove so when the United States Government frowned upon it.

The greeting card publisher was not the only organization to quarry great quantities of stone from pits in the Blarney district. A Los Angeles group of showmen shipped many tons from Ireland via Liverpool, to California to build a replica of Blarney Castle!

A New York architect, who studied the castle at Blarney, estimated that it would require 2,500,000,000 pounds of sandstone, 4,200 gallons of bullock's blood, the bristles from the backs of a herd of 5,500 swine with which to mix the concrete, to duplicate the castle and dungeons as the structure stands today. The shipment of this much heavy cargo of blood, bristles and stone from Cobh to San Pedro would require a fleet of merchant vessels approximately as numerous as those flying the Panamanian, Salvadorian, Costa Rican and Madagascan flags.

A New York advertising agency imported large quantities of

County Cork run-of-the-mill rock to polish as ring settings, designed to spur the sale of packaged baby foods through premium tie-ups with box tops.

The more Sir George read, the angrier he became. All sorts of doubts were published about the palladium in his front yard.

More than a century ago, the Blarney parish priest, Father Horgan, wrote:

> The curious traveller will seek in vain for the real stone unless he allows himself to be lowered from the northern angle of the lofty castle, when he will discover it about twenty feet from the top, with this inscription: *Cormac McCarty, Fortis Me Fieri Fecit*, A.D. *1446.*

A gay and happy translation of this is:

> Cormac McCarty,
> Bould as bricks
> Built me in fourteen forty-six.

These old legends were quoted every once in a while to the owner's annoyance.

Was it possible that people were kissing the wrong Blarney Stone? The stone to which untold millions had paid homage, and for which so many had lost their lives in body-crushing falls from the parapet?

There was that statement by an English traveler, Sir Boyle Roche, about a century ago, and dragged out by the press as though it had been made yesterday, confusing everyone and tending to discredit the accepted shrine:

> No one could possibly kiss the real Blarney Stone unless he happened to be a bird, or an acrobat twelve feet long, and suspending himself by his feet from the summit of the Tower.

Another "authority" asserted that the original Blarney Stone was inscribed with the date "1703."

Richard Croker decades ago visited the castle, and on departing, wrote these disturbing lines:

> I regret to say that it (the Castle) has been wantonly mutilated during the past few years, and that the original Blarney Stone which was on the Northeast angle of the castle, and which I well remember as having a shamrock cut on it in high relief, has disappeared.

The heretical claims that the stone was actually an ordinary piece of rock quarried from the pits around the castle had been published too often for comfort.

There was no shamrock, there was no Latin verse, there were no dates on the currently accepted Blarney Stone, and no distinguishing marks of any sort except daubings of American women's varicolored lipstick.

The contract of the Americans called for the "original" Blarney Stone. Men willing to pay a million dollars would insist on getting the *real article*. God! What complications a thing like *this* could make. Sir George grunted disgustedly.

That was the moment Adrian picked to come flying into the drawing room to announce a) a big rat had broken into her guinea-pig house the night before and killed the incestuous old Rip; b) the groom had set a box trap; c) the rat had been caught!

"But Mummy! Mummy!" Adrian cried. "The rat looks so worried and he has such a nice white furry stomach! Can't we let it out somewhere on the bog?"

That new, unnamed gray kitten was sitting on Sir George's favorite footstool before the oak fire logs glowing on their andirons, just as she did whenever the ould man moved his feet long enough for her to take their place. She paid no attention whatever to the disapproving glare of the old Countess of Desmond hanging near the marble mantelpiece, made by the artist Adam, himself. This self-satisfied interloper, who was personally obnoxious to Puff, sat there like a queen all day staring into the fire with her eyes shut, and nothing could budge her. But she jumped now as though she were being chased by an army of giant killer-rats.

Missis Hamilton jumped, too. She had scarcely been listening to her daughter. She was reading an odd scrap of news from an Irish newspaper with headlines announcing a plague of octopi in the Channel, average octopus measuring seven feet. It said vast schools of them were menacing bathers, scaring fishermen and eating all the lobsters. In fact, they were scaring these lobsters and crabs so much that thousands were crawling in mad panic to the shore to escape the slimy tentacles. Disgusted and horrified, she was searching for further details in all the other papers, racing through tiny print announcing that some new sulphine drug was a definite cure for cancer, only to find dreary and frightening news about the hydrogen bomb, and Schumacher accusing the Russians of plotting to take Berlin. When, bang!

"What" roared the ould man. "Let it out? It's to be killed *at once!*"

He reached for the cord over the fireplace and gave it a furious jerk.

The butler came running. The ould man really blew up.

"Find the groom!" the ould man cried. "Have him kill that wretched rat *at once!*"

"Nunk . . ." Adrian began, but gave him one horrified look and raced from the room, as though from the presence of a murderer. Puff growled at the noise the ould man was making and followed gravely after the little girl.

When the groom arrived at the rat cage with a stick in his hand to carry out his master's instructions he scratched his head in puzzlement. The big rat was contentedly nibbling cheese, and on the cage he found a contradictory sign, as though scrawled hurriedly, on a sheet of tablet paper:

DO NOT TOUCH THIS RAT BY ORDER!

"Begor'," muttered the steward, "now by *whose* order? And who's feedin' a crayture like that *afther* 'tis caught?"

Shaking his head, he returned to the castle for advice.

A few minutes later the ould man, Adrian's mother and the groom, all in animated consultation, saw her furiously pedaling her bicycle, the rattrap under her arm, toward the bog. The ould man roared at her.

"Come back heah! I say. Bring that dratted rat back heah!"

The point of his ever-present blackthorn walking-cane punctuated the emphatic air.

Adrian never turned her head. She flew like the wind. Puff followed after her, galloping like a broken field runner, yipping severely now and then, ready to intercept any interference or bite the devil out of any scoundrel who might dare molest her or retard her errand of mercy.

Every bird that sang at Blarney came out of the hedges and the furze, the merry chiffchaff, the missel thrush, the song thrush and the redwing, and flew with them and over them like guardian angels to cover them with safety on their errand of mercy, chirping their encouragement.

Finally at the lakeside and ignoring the helpless ould man's roars, Adrian firmly put the cage down near some trees and opened it. Out shot the rat. From the adept way she handled that rattrap cage it became pretty obvious to her mother why no rats had been caught in the stables for so long a time, and why Adrian and Puff so often slipped down there in the mornings before anyone else was up.

Now, neither Adrian or Puff were one whit afraid of the ould man. Adrian loved him with all her heart, and Puff was willing to tolerate him around the castle so long as he behaved himself and kept off his tail. Puff was no one's cater-cousin, except for Missis Hamilton and Adrian, and even this relationship was contingent upon his ascerbic and dignified censorship.

But there is no telling what hell of a row was averted by the fortuitous appearance in the castle's drawing room of Sister Brigit. She was returning from mass as on the wings of a hurricane, borne aloft by her voluminous petticoats and her umbrella like any Constellation—four minutes from the chapel, a record. She was breathless and flushed. She hurried to the ould man's side. He was staring at her in amazement, the rat now completely forgotten. Never had he seen her in such a state of excitement.

"Sir George," she cried, "you don't have to break the Blarney Stone, afther all. 'Tis . . . 'tis already broken!"

Sir George sank into his big leather chair.

"Wha . . . what?" he managed saggingly.

"Yes . . . 'tis. 'Twas a vision! I saw it as clear as the very sun when it shines in Ireland! 'Tis broken half in two!"

Missis Hamilton ran over to Sister Brigit and grasped her hand.

"Sister! Sister! Wait! Do you know what you are saying? Are you *sure?*"

"As sure," said Brigit serenely, "as Cromwell's cannon broke it!"

Sir George's face took on a purple look. His eyes goggled over the strange words and his hands made futile, despairing motions over the arms of his chair.

"As . . . who . . . *who* broke it?" he sputtered incomprehendingly. "What th' . . . sanguinary . . ."

Brigit's face shone with high spiritual emotion.

"Cromwell! Sir George," she whispered, " 'twas a great gift, a revelation from St. Brigit! Faith, the stone is cracked straight down the middle like a churn bate over its head by th' plunger!"

Chapter Fifteen

The Great Matchmaker

That morning of Puff's historic visit to the Blarney Stone the pilgrims, in throng and clutter, had started forming with the first *chat! chat!* of a dawn-singing stonechat. The Irish call the bird the black cap. A black cap would have been a fitting hood for the gloomy Pekingese who took his place in line with the paying customers.

Ould Puff no longer could hold up his head at the castle, where his shame was known and advertised, and the compassion of his friends, grieving loyally with him, only increased the anguish of a lovelorn heart.

They read the story behind his hot, salty eyes and shook their heads. "Poor fellah," they would say. The commiseration was more than Puff could bear. He sought the company of strangers who could not guess his secret sorrow and tear his very soul with sympathy. Certainly, he had chosen the right place for strangers.

"They're coming early this saison," observed old Katy Ford, the lifetime custodian of the old Blarney Castle gate. She had not even had time to rub the sleep out of her eyes to open up for business.

The queue of pilgrims, in Scotch kilts and American-type haircuts and every manner of clothes, extended far back from the footbridge and turnstile across the old disused tramway and to the general post office and the ball alley before old Katy arrived to shepherd them. The citizens of eighteen nations were represented that day.

There were many women in the crowd and hundreds who had no idea of the ordeal they would face on the heights.

The fact that the Blarney Stone of today is difficult to kiss is considered an added inducement, because the experience leaves the visitor with the feeling that he has risked his life, which indeed he has. Still, many have come to kiss the Blarney Stone, looked in terror upon the acrobatic maneuvering of other kissers and have fled the premises without so much as a peck. Many women who have ventured to the heights to kiss it have modestly retreated, because it is impossible for a female wearing a dress to accomplish her objective without revealing generous portions of her anatomy. On busy days many are the witnesses who stand and watch and wait for just such exhibitions atop the castle. Some determined women weigh down their skirts with stones as they lie upon their backs and wriggle into the necessary position.

The questions she will be asked would drive anyone except Katy stark, raving mad.

Still 'twas God's truth this summer that a poor sowl like herself was not even supposed to sleep. Never had so many tourists been seen at Blarney as during this rush of the Holy Year. And no one was better qualified to know.

Katy Ford has been caretaker of the Old Castle since she inherited the job from her mother, who died at the age of 103, in 1909. This old Mrs. Ford was the wife of Ford, the head woodman, whose family have served the Colthursts for many generations. They have inhabited the West Lodge Gatehouse since it was built, and Mike Ford, Katy's brother, was head woodman in his turn, until he died some years ago. It is on account of this family that the west avenue has always been known as "Ford's Avenue." His widow and her family, and also Katy, still live here.

Old Mrs. Ford used to sell postcards and mementos at the entrance to the Old Castle, and Katy, assisted by her nieces, has kept up the practice, and does a brisk trade with tourists. She always wears a black dress and black hat, and has a black silk scarf wound round her neck, and has never changed, or aged in appearance since the oldest residents' memory of her from childhood.

One by one, the visitors moved forward, paid over their shillings and passed through the revolving entrance to mystery and eloquence. The gate clicked a merry song of prosperity. Ould Puff inched along after their heels in hangdog fashion, his head low and dejected, his eyes blinking back the tears he could not restrain.

Katy Ford dropped a handful of coins when she saw the dog. "Yirra! 'Tis ould Puff!" she cried, and burst out laughing. "Faith, ye poor crayture, and did ye bring yer shilling now?"

Old Katy had seen many strange sights at Blarney, but never before had she beheld the spectacle of an untended dog politely queueing up with the cash customers of the Blarney Stone. And of all the dogs in creation, the impayrious ould Puff!

Ould Puff gave the keeper a forlorn and hapless look and passed on through the turnstile, unable to find anything funny in the joke. He waddled ahead, sagging under the weight of his heavy heart, with the lonesome air of a dog who suffers alone.

For a year this aristocratic animal had visited his lowly collie girl friend in Blarney Village. Puff adored this monster of a female so that his eyes when he saw her swam in that same liquid ingredient that causes those of does to dote. She rewarded her lovesick little snowball of a swain with snarls. Her own heart was torn between a giant mastiff and an Irish terrier.

Puff's rivals were great, uncouth and predatory beasts whose law was the law of the jungle, and Cushy herself was inferior socially, living in a thatched cottage as she did, but Puff would gladly have given her a castle and made of her a queen. In fact, he would have abdicated a throne to win her heart! He had barked these ancient protests so often to Cushy that his throat was sore.

Puff was not afraid of the monsters trampling in the garden of paradise. He would sooner have chewed their ears off than sniff at a stump, but unrequited love gives the spurned swain peculiar doubts and anxieties. His disordered mind hesitates even to contemplate any actions save of the most delicate sort, lest he crudely offend his indifferent darling, losing that which he has never gained. Inactive through morbid caution, or rash with deeds, he is a pitiable spectacle either way, and the unbelievable thing that has happened to him runs the course of tears alone. Nothing save the ordered grief of time can assuage the flow, and rot the sting. Desperate plans incubate in such minds, but rarely hatch.

With man and beast, it is all the same. Ould Puff was wallowing in a vale of tears and running true to form.

Puff, brokenhearted, mewed at her like a hurt, wet kitten locked out in the cold. She snapped at him, called him names and set him back on his heels when he would not take a snapping no for an answer. He was dogged in the extreme.

He waddled with every rising sun down the hill to pay his court anew, bringing with him revived and irrepressible hope where love is concerned, that which rises eternal in the breast of Peke or potentate.

The villagers laughed over the comparative size of the two mismated animals as Puff made overtures to the siren, with dog-hurt tears brimming his eyes. Acushlamachree was her name, a big name for a big collie. "Pulse of my heart" her name meant, and all of that and more she was to the miserable swain from the great castle on the hill. But when Puff made a sally of love Cushy, as she was called for short, sent him back home with snarles and often had her mouth full of the suitor's splendid coat.

After these tragic rebuffs, Puff slowed down when he had retreated a short distance and watched his lady love for a terrible and tragic moment with that doggone, woebegone look that makes a sad dog the saddest-looking creature in the world and more heart-touching than a pretty woman crying.

No matter how beautiful Missis Hamilton made his white coat with fine English toilet soap, Cushy sniffed at Puff in contempt and disdain.

At home he shunned the castle household and morning, when he went to keep a lonely vigil on the hill for a mere sight of his beloved, found his satin bed damp from his night of silent crying. In the daytime he sniffed like an old woman with a cold, and his nose was hot from the fever within his heart. Everyone was quite worried about him.

" 'Tis worms th' crayture has," suggested the groom, touching his finger to Puff's dripping nostrils. Puff bit his finger sharply, and the groom gave an angry, painful cry. He did not try any further diagnosis and scowled darkly at the dog, still wisely keeping his distance. Puff asked help of no one, and certainly nothing in his manner invited any groom to stick his dirty finger in his nose. He had had trouble with that groom before at bath time, and with this experience to guide him the groom had received no less than he deserved.

In front of Puff that morning of his visit to the old castle was a tall woman patron of abundant proportions. In her hands she fiercely clutched two large rocks, and beneath her arms she pressed a long roll of tent canvas, a hamper-sized patent leather pocketbook, and an overnight-bag-sized shoe box packed with a picnic lunch of fried chicken, deviled eggs, cold biscuits, chocolate layer cake, jelly sandwiches, dill pickles, stuffed olives, and a thermos jug of buttermilk. She was middle-aged, and might best be described as a "middle" woman. There was so much middle about her.

She was dressed in a riot of black-eyed Susans growing in a garden of flowered voile cut in a glued-down princess line. The seams of the garment were saved from disaster by mysterious hidden sentinels armed with steel shafts.

She wore a large parasol of a maline hat. It was edged with rickrack, and was adorned by a big froufrou ribbon.

Her name was Miss Apgie Japgess. She was a determined crusader by hobby, and a social service investigator by profession.

Now she had stopped squarely in the middle of the queue and was shouting back over her shoulder at Katy Ford, as though prompted by an afterthought.

"Are you downright *sure* this is *the* Blarney Stone?" she demanded. Her voice was high and piercing, much thinner than her figure, and much like her face. It was like a loud whistle such as a man will make to stop a speeding taxi in the rain. Puff growled.

"Sure, and 'tis the Blairney Stone, ma'am," replied the astounded Katy. "This *is* Blairney Castle!"

"Humph! Well it'd *better* be," whistled the customer. "I've kissed every rock in Ireland, tombstones and monuments, from Dublin to Killarney, looking for it!"

"You've come to th' right place this time, lady," said a Texas-looking man right behind her. "It sho ain't th' Rock of Geebraltar!"

The woman gave him a haughty appraisal with an "how dare you!" look in her eyes and a suspicious sniffing about her nose, which was naturally equipped for expertness in that habit. It was long, capable, and busy on the eternal scent of outrage. She was confident that this tall, angular, drawling man had been drinking. Her nostrils spread fat and thin like a fast accordion.

"Humph!" she whistled again, and her nose twitched and wriggled its repugnance.

Puff, impatient to get going, sniffed dyspeptically at the woman's ankles and jabbed his nose against her struggling nylons. This time the woman shrieked the "How dare you?" that had formerly been restrained to the look in her eyes. Her darkest suspicions were confirmed. The scoundrel behind her was not only a drunkard and a cad, but a masher, as well.

She was obviously a "How dare you!" type, of a common genre, found often enough in the rosters of those American women's organizations devoted to the embroidery of scarlet letters. She blurted "How dare you!" for good reason, or none at all.

"Stop *tickling* me!" she snapped. "How *dare* you!"

The Texas man grinned genially and produced a pint bottle from his hips.

"I'm plumb sho you're kiddin' th' pants offen me, lady, but . . ." he said taking a swig.

"Your . . . what? How dare you!" the woman interrupted.

"But, as I was sayin' beggin' yo' pahdon, as fer as goosin' you's concerned, my hands ain't growed big enough fer no sech!"

"Then keep them to yourself!"

The Texan's wind-tanned forehead wrinkled the beginning of a frown around his eyes, but he swept it away with a genial broom.

"Reckon as how you ain't got nothin' to fret yoreself about, ma'am," he laughed. Sorghum flowed the Rio Grande through the words on his lips. He washed off some of the syrup with another pull at his bottle.

"Have a snort, ma'am? It's white mule. Durn this heah Irish Paddy's. Sho like my corn squeezin's. I lugged me a keg all th' ways frum Del Rio."

"How dare you! Better you'd lugged Coca Cola! I'm a Purity Leaguer! We girls are teetotalers!"

"Ma'am," roared the Texan, "that total adds up to tea as fur's I'm concerned, and that's pizen as a gila monster whar I come frum. This heah white mule's so pow'ful if I throwed th' bottle agin that old castle it would kick it plumb to hell and gone. I mean th' castle. Th' mule'd trot right back to his durned stable, good as new. Yessireebob!"

The super-Amazon shuddered violently.

"How dare you!—I mean just think of your *liver!*"

"I do! I'm a two-bottle man, ma'am. My great grandpaw was a two-gun man. He settled down in Del Rio when Jedge Bean was Law west of th' Pecos and speakin' of livers, that was a long time ago, when a whole beef liver was wuth a nickel. White mule ain't hurt none of his ancestors' livers ever since."

"A nickel! Why they must cost five dollars now!"

"On th' hoof, ma'am. That's why I can kiss th' Blarney Stone. Liver has been mighty good to me. But it sho takes a lot of cow liver to travel this fur. My great-grandpaw, now, he coulda come here, too. He didn't fool 'round with no nickel livers. He was in th' undertakin' and hardware business combined. Sold coffins and six-shooters. Couldn't go broke. First metallic burials in America. Metallic burials, get it?"

"Ugh!"

"No, ma'am, white mule never hurt my grandpaw's liver, neither, but he et a big mess of it fair his evenin' meal th' night he died."

"Indigestion, I presume, from gluttony."

"In a way, yessum. A sneakin' pirootin' sheep herder shot him thru th' liver, but it warn't his'n. It was that he et."

"Deliver me!"

"Haw! Haw! Ma'am, you sho went and stuck out *yore* liver *that* time! But you kin keep it."

"How dare you! I mean what did you say?"

"I said out on th' range we don't aim our six-shooters at a blamed coyote 'til th' critter's travelin' forty miles a hour. I'm too happy today to take advantage of nobody's liver. I'm on a kissin' holiday."

Miss Japgess gasped, shivered and shied.

"Now don't you start anything!"

"Haw! Haw! Why, ma'am, I ain't laughed so much since we licked th' hoof and mouth disease! I come heah to kiss myself a rock. Pretty soon I'm goin' to plunk my kisser smack-dab on that thar Blarney Stone and I kin talk a blue streak!"

"Deliver me!" repeated the woman.

"Ma'am, you sho don't ketch on. But, ma'am," the cattleman said apologetically, "a man cain't be blamed for a leetle curiosity, and here I been standin' plunk flat-footed with wonderin' 'bout somepin.' Beggin' yore humble pahdon, it's 'bout them two articles yer clutchin' in yore hands. Mind tellin' me, confidential like, ma'am, just prezackly whut they is?"

"Any fool can see they're rocks!"

"Rocks to Blarney Castle, now . . . hmmm. Seems to me it's sorter like . . . well, like totin' coals to Newcastle. What they's fer, ma'am?"

"To anchor my skirts down when I kiss the Stone, that's what," she replied emphatically.

"Lawsy me! Think they're big enough?"

The super-Amazon ignored him.

"I'm taking *no* chances," she said. "And I'd never in this world wear slacks!"

"Cain't say as I blame ye. But, who's a-goin' to hold yore legs, ma'am?"

"How dare you! No man is going to hold *my* legs!"

"You say *man,* ma'am?"

"I flew over here *strictly* to kiss the Blarney Stone," Miss Japgess said haughtily.

"You mean to say you *flew* over?"

"Certainly! What's so funny about *that?*"

"Oh, nothin', ma'am. Guess I'd said th' same if you told me it was a battleship."

"How dare you! I mean . . ."

"What fur you goin' to kiss it, ma'am?"

"Every girl can dream," replied Miss Japgess airily.

"You mean, you aim to git all gabbed up and talk some pore cowhand into lassoin' you?" the dumbfounded cattleman asked in amazement.

Charitably, he wondered privately how much rope would be required for such a performance as he calculated the bulging dimensions crowding the sandstone walls of McCarty's castle. He gave up and permitted the white mule to take another kick at his liver.

"You put everything so crudely," Miss Japgess said, sniffing with intolerance at the aroma wafting from the rear. "How dare . . . you . . . you liver salesman!"

"Bet you could sell off a lot, and never miss it, ma'am," the Texan said drily. "Furthermore, you brought this on yoreself. Yore orneriness started it!"

"How . . . how . . ."

Miss Japgess' body was twitching all over. She seemed to be doing a cakewalk.

Another piercing whistle interrupted her outburst. This time she wheeled and glared her full wrath upon the Texan.

"I tell you once more, once and for all—stop tickling my ankles! I . . . I'll call the gendarmes!"

The Texan slapped his saddle-conditioned hips with the re-port of a Wild West six-shooter.

"Ma'am, ma'am, you tickle *me!* That ain't me, ma'am. I ain't aimin' to brand you! If you look down you'll see it's a dad-blamed feist of a poodle smellin' at yore feet!"

With heroic muscular effort, the harassed Miss Japgess bent forward over her middle section, jutted out her neck and stared downward. She snapped back to erectness again with a whistling squeal, as though she had seen a mouse.

"That dreadful dog!" she cried, blindly kicking a side of leather at Puff's nose. "Scat! Shoo!"

Puff did neither. He growled and stood his ground. No one was going to bully him, not even a whistling volcano erupting over him. He had bitten policemen for less. He had his eye on the exact spot of a section of calf where he would take a fine grip, when she stopped her kicking with a terrified shriek.

"That fancy feist sho don't sound kittenish and chicken-hearted to me, ma'am. He's fixin' to reduce yore size!"

"Stop him! Stop him!"

The Texan chuckled and whistled a greeting to Puff.

"Easy thar, little dogie, you might be bitin' off more'n you kin chew!"

Puff could not understand the strange language that this man spoke. He had never heard anything like it in Ireland, or on his visits to England, either, but he sensed something friendly about the sound of his voice and declared an armed truce pending the woman's good behavior. This ensued, nervously, while his adversary maneuvered flesh, bone and muscle of body and soul through the narrow passages designed for battle-trim warriors, up the steep flights of newel steps.

At one point where it seemed the effort was hopeless and Miss Japgess' bulk rocked dangerously and uncertain, Tex waxed courageous sentiments to the fore. He girded his loins and his tongue with the stamina of his two-gun fathers.

"Spiten all you've said to me, ma'am, down in Texas sweet, typical Southern womanhood's placed on a exalted pedestal. Th' fair ladies of Texas, praiseworthy Christians as they are, a credit and a legacy to their sex and a inspiration to the cowboys and the oilmen . . . for their deah memory's sake, I'll push you up this heah danged wall if it busts a gut!

"Whew! Ma'am," puffed the Texan as he pushed her from the rear.

Poor Miss Japgess now was in such dire straits that she could not be particular *where* the cowboy put his hands. She blushed like a maiden, but squirmed and squeezed ahead with commendable resolution. Her hips were gray with the dust of the ages scraped from the towered walls, her parasol hat teetered at a drunken angle, and a dangling ribbon over the bridge of her nose made her cross-eyed as she strove futilely to blow it away with the breath of her mouth; but grimly she maintained a hold on her belongings in the precious interest of virtue, modesty and the inner woman. And all of these were great indeed.

"Them Irishmen shore didn't make this blamed castle fur no aveydewpaw!" Tex groaned. "It'll be one hell of a note if you get stuck; th' folks on th' roof will starve to death. They'll have to take this castle apart stone by stone! My pore white mule's about give out."

The Purity Leaguer now was too tired and helpless to retort. Puff grunted along under her legs, keeping out of the way of her feet as they achieved level after level in the dark, quarried halls. Puff growled threateningly, but spared the tortured pilgrim a sample of his contempt. Too, it was hard to bite with a broken heart.

By the time they had reached their goal the gasping woman, still determinedly clutching her two rocks and the canvas roll that she intended spreading on the battlement floor to save her dress at the kissing ritual, had melted somewhat toward the obliging Texan. She had also melted some of her weight. Generously, it watered the black-eyed Susans on her voile.

The cowboy looked back down the tortuous stairs into a sea of faces, red from exertions and frustrations. The pilgrims behind braced themselves perilously against the walls. The feat

Miss Japgess had accomplished clearly was remarkable. Her safe descent would constitute a miraculous achievement.

"Providential thing you brung along rations, ma'am. 'Pears like you're goin' to be up heah a pow'ful long spell. If there's a double block and tackle in Ireland, it'll take it to git you down."

"Oh me, oh my!" Miss Japgess said weakly.

The trio of climbers emerged, bedeviled and shaken, into the sunlight of a beautiful day. A large crowd of pilgrims thronged the battlements, and scores, delayed by the laborious ascent of the Purity Leaguer, poured out in grumbling torrents after her. They gave her resentful stares, but soon their tempers were calmed by the glorious view spreading before them.

Far off, a hundred miles away in the west, they beheld the magnificent Kerry Mountains rising out of the blue mists of history. The mystery of distant skies lay upon their peaks and bathed them with whispering secrets of their dew. It was a purple dew, atomized by rankling shafts of the sun, a sight that only Ireland can provide for the eyes of man to see. Ireland mixes the pigments of nature and splashes them in patterns without compare. The peaks of Sugarloaf, Renna Bubble, Malachonish and Glounthounagum came washed, newborn, out of the yesterdays of creation, and swaddled in the raiment that is made of rainbows.

Cork City is hidden by folds of hills, and 'tis a pity, for "lovely is the Lee," the river and the city about which Spenser wrote:

> The pleasant Lee, that like an island fayre,
> Encloseth Corke with his divided flood.

A half of a thousand years ago it was like this, and is today.

But for the tourists' eyes compensations galore blaze and flame a patterned paradise. The groves of Blarney's blossoms feed the senses with the food of jealous gods, when man has climbed this little height to see them grow in rings of verdigris. And the sparkling lake is a sapphire in the palm of beauty's plenty.

The tourists feel it, as all must do, and the blind will, too.

They rush to the parapets and stand in the hush of a prayer that is painted upon the hills and vales of Ireland by the One to whom all prayers are said.

Too bad ould Puff cannot see this glory. He needs it for his broken heart. But he is such a little fellow. The stones of the merlons hide his view. He waddles in his sorrow and his eyes see only the dust of the parapet.

Miss Japgess placed her possessions safely within a 500-year-old crenel of the castellation and followed Tex over to a merlon for the view and the recuperation of her lungs. She spanked at her hips and made the dust fly from her deep flower beds.

Tex was flashing envious eyes upon the scenery.

"Onliest sight ever I seed," sighed the cowboy, "that's pur-tier'n Texas." It was a grudging and painful, but honest admission of the Lone Star stater that made his loyal heart ache.

Miss Japgess hit her dress again and Tex snapped his eyes in the direction of the report—her hips. He blurted a half-finished inspiration.

"Only Texas is a durned sight bigger!"

"Why, you . . . you . . ."

Tex laughed cheerfully.

"Aw, don't take it th' hard way, ma'am. They ain't quite *that* bad." He pulled himself away from the parapet. "We better git goin'. It's time for you to kiss that Blarney Stone, and git yoreself *de*-livered."

"Why, how . . . I mean, what do you *mean?*"

"If you ain't gonna allow yore legs to be held, it's shore, guaranteed, genuwine suicide. If that hole's big enough for you to go through it, it's good night nurse, liver and all. You're a goner!"

Miss Japgess stared worriedly at the dangerous aperture. She hesitated for a moment, hurried over to her two stones, food and canvas cached in the crenel, and returned to Tex's side to join him in the line of kissers. They would not have long to wait. Five of the would-be communicants, paling at the risky procedure being demonstrated ahead of them, stepped aside.

"Guess havin' a man aholt of yore ankles is that fate worse'n death?" suggested Tex.

His companion made no reply. Instead, a shrill cry issued from her throat and she pointed a trembling finger at a ball of snow rolling exploratorily toward the Blarney Stone. The ball of snow possessed a nose, a pushed-in Chinese nose, now very busy smelling out the gutters of the old castle. The snowball was ould Puff. He was approaching the magic slab in a dog-legged manner that foretokens only one procedure.

"Stop him! Stop him!" shouted Miss Japgess. "You know what *that's* leading up to!"

"Hey, bub," cried Tex, "control yore carcass! That ain't no saplin'."

"Scat! Shoo!"

Puff growled, and sidled and sortied toward the target of the sloping tunnel in the battlement wall leading to the Blarney Stone.

"If he does," exclaimed Miss Japgess, "I won't go near it!" Puff was getting hot. "What will he do?"

"Wish I knew," said Tex miserably. "But I've come blamed nigh six thousand miles to kiss that piece of rubble, and spiten hell and high water, I'll kiss it wet or dry!"

Puff shifted closer still.

"What *can* I do?" asked the woman helplessly.

Tex closed his eyes.

"Ma'am," he said, "if I was you, I'd pray for rain."

Chapter Sixteen

The Stone of Love

The nose of Miss Apgie Japgess, fresh on the juiciest scent of sin, had never worked with more enthusiasm than the pulsing snoot of ould Puff at the shrine of eloquence. His nostrils and his mind were enveloped by a joyous redolence such as never dog before him had respired. It was a fragrance of mystery that curled into his very senses, that was sucked in by his soul, that oxygen infused by Aprodite into the womb where Eros breathed and dreamed of love.

Man, woman and child must lie upon their backs, hold the two upright iron bars with their hands and raise themselves upward to reach the Blarney Stone. But Puff stood erect upon his hind legs to gain its surface—a feat any dog can do, but one, and only one, ever has.

He stabbed his nose at the slab in a tattoo of the magic air before it that made no noise. The effusion of a great power emanating from that source of glory, that spring which flowed before the god of love was born, frightened the recipient with the gift about to be bestowed.

"Oh, dear me!" groaned the fascinated Purity Leaguer. But she did not understand what was going on. The sentient aura of the Blarney Stone staggered Puff with a terrible, heady promise. Slowly and reverently now he pushed his nose forward for the first and final contact.

Miss Japgess saw him hesitate within the reach of precious enchantment. She jabbed Tex with her elbow and whistled a

THE MYSTERIOUS ROCK CLOSE OF BLARNEY

One of the great natural beauty spots of Europe. Roofed by the branches of 3,000-year-old ilexes and yews, it was a shelter for the ancient Druids while they made human sacrifices in their cromlech.

The Witch who lives in the stone pillar in Blarney's Rock Close. See her face?

squeal of relief. Tex blurted an "A-a-a-a-amen!" to his prayer and opened his eyes.

"Look! Look!" whistled Miss Japgess. "We're saved. That dog's not smelling the Blarney Stone, why . . . why . . . did you ever! . . . he's *kissing* it!"

Indeed he was. Puff's lips were firmly upon the surface of that font which feeds the tongues of joy.

A rapture such as never thrilled the soul of beast, also galvanized and electrified the flesh of the furry communicant. Puff pulled back from the force of a wattage that twisted him into knots. His body curled skyward, somersaulted in a convulsive arc of hair and hide and landed on the parapet in satiny notes of music. Puff stood on trembling legs. His head shook in surprise and amazement. But now, a new light came shining forth from his eyes, shackles fell away from his heart. The little dog lifted his throat into Irish skies and gave the mating call of a lion.

He stopped and cocked his ear toward the west where Blarney Village lies, where a thatched cottage of the poor nestles within an endive dale. Clear and loud came an answer to his courting cry. It was a peal of stunned delight, and rippled like the harps of angels.

Puff raised his little head again as the dread King of the Beasts would raise his own in fearsome jungle roar, but that sound which now echoed o'er the groves of Blarney was the barking of a happy dog, such as was never heard this side of heaven. It was a fluted note of golden beauty in *sestinuto* that throbbed the skies, and the birds hushed their wings and listened in the furze.

Puff shook himself in a spasm of confidence. He lifted his head again and a paean of love's old story rode the air waves in a chariot of aureoles.

Puff bounded down the stairs of McCarty's Castle. He was a bombshell of fleecy snow.

Tongues that kiss the Blarney Stone do not make harsh noises. The birds of Blarney have kissed it, all, and the song of the Blarney sparrow is like the mockingbird. From the faraway Mediterranean and the sands of Arabia they fly to caress it with their beaks.

There is the Blarney faery tale of the homely, hoarse and brokenhearted little bird who one night found a cinder in a witch's eye. He removed it with his beak and fanned the inflammation with his wings and cooled it until the redness had gone away.

"Go at dawn to the top of yonder castle," said the witch, "and peck your gizzard full of grit from that one low stone that meets the rising sun. The lungs of eagles then will fill your chest, and your song will fly with your heart and can win an oriole, or you can charm a swan. Your notes will be the feathers of a peacock, the sounds of the earth will hush and the skies will listen where'er you sing."

The little bird could not believe his ears. He was of a species that had never before sung a song. The noises he made resembled the harsh and rasping throatings of a goatsucker, but when he had filled his gizzard full of grit from the Blarney Stone, he filled his breast with the strumming of the lyre. This bird became known as the nightingale, and all of his kind after him. Because the cinder was removed at night and the reward was given in the interest of romance, the charm restricts its use to the mating season and the sweetest hours of love under the stars. A tiny little hole, one as though made by the beak of a bird, may be found in the Blarney Stone by those aesthetic souls who take the trouble to look for it. It is known as "The Nightingale's Fountain," for when it rains, this little indentation, the size of a faery's thimble, brims a beakful of water that sparkles like a diamond in the moonlight.

'Tis said that even the hunting falcons of the McCarties, that roosted on perches by their beds, after wetting their beaks therein warbled like the gentle lark.

But birds that sing also have claws to scratch and beaks to peck for worms, and pity the rival of a male nightingale that invades his songful nest. Feathers are sure to fly.

And dogs that bark a melody also have teeth to chew their bones. A mouth that sings can also bite, and pity the rival of such a creature that trespasses and smells his tree of life. Fur is sure to fly in this garden of love and be swallowed, and the skin that anchors it.

Cushy, luscious Cushy, as luscious as her nickname, as eager as a bride on her wedding night, soft and svelte, as sensuous as Angora wool, was coiffeured with the vanity of her own tongue for the rendezvous. She was a plum-eyed beauty, wooed and won by silver echoes that chained a willing heart. From afar Puff saw her waiting as he careened over hill and dale. Our pedigreed lover came recklessly out of the east heralding the blessed rapture of his soul for the world to know. Demurely, Cushy listened to the floating call, and trembled with the promise in its ecstasy. The big maiden excitedly strove to walk around her front paws.

Tex and Miss Japgess leaned over a parapet wall and watched Puff race and tumble through bramble hedge.

"Yippi-iyay!" shouted the cowboy. "Lookit him run! Th' feist's got th' convulsions and fits!"

"Rabies!" said Miss Japgess temporally.

But other ears of Blarney dogdom heard the ringing trill of the Pekingese. One was a low-bred wolfhound. The other was a mongrel Irish terrier. Awakened from sound sleep, in a cottage on the wrong side of the abandoned tramway tracks, they opened their evil eyes and cocked their battle-nicked ears. They rose upon their haunches and listened in surprise. Their faces, hardened and vulgar, smirked contemptuously as they recognized the sound. There was no mistaking the breeding that could produce such cultivated tones. They were of the plush, red-coated hunt-club horn and yoicks, with a tenor all their own. It must be that sissy Chinese aristocrat from the castle on the hill.

The curs growled and snarled their hate and bared the fangs of maddened wolves. Now through frothing mouths they barked the challenge of the killer pack. They were off in a ruckus of mange, fleas and unmuzzled fury. The stentor of their rage curdled Cushy's blood. And great was her fear for the safety of her true love.

The malignant pair charged to the arena that is Blarney's green. Puff was bounding a corner of the village square. He slid to a halt. The music of his throat stopped in the shattering crescendo of a cathedral organ rendering the turmoil of hell.

Puff was a David without a slingshot, a lap-fighter, pampered with chocolate nougats, facing *two* Goliaths, trained on the jawbones of bulls.

Dimly from his instincts came the forgotten battle wiles of the Mandarins whose wisdom had been imparted to his ancestors, and out of the mists of the Mings he might have remembered a parable of stratagem and expedience. Reverend Master Kung say:

"When soldier lose honorable sword, fight foe with firecracker, also bang him over head with honorable porcelain vase."

Our hero's only training for combat had been limited to the governess' calf, the groom's fingers, and the butler's ankles. He would have required a stepladder to reach a single hair of the wolfhound's throat. One of the great teeth of the terrier would have made Puff a set of uppers. But nothing daunted him now.

The castle gladiator used the weapons at hand. With a yell of courage he charged the uncouth beasts and bit the wolfhound on a foot. He wheeled and feinted in an infernal crouching position to snap a stinging bite on the terrier's knees. He ran under the bridgelike stomach of the wolfhound and pinched the very devil out of his baffled adversary's tail.

The wolfhound howled like a banshee, the crayture; and the bewildered terrier, unaccustomed to the unorthodox tactics of a candy-fed pet, wavered uncertainly as Puff made a slashing assault, prancing on his hind legs like a trained performer in a dog and pony show.

He was an inspired and deadly foe, a pom-pom powder puff versus brute slasher force. Puff scuffed and cuffed his lunging antagonists, feinting with the grace of a duelist as the sword teeth flashed close to his throat.

Puff delivered a sharp incision of his canines in the terrier's stomach, and in a flash launched a confusing crouching attack. He chewed at the terrier's paws, whirled the unexpected, wheeled the impossible, spun the disconcerting and danced the warpath from one to the other, unerringly nicking both with each mad sally. Puff was in the broiling skirmish to win eternal glory. His enemies howled in pain, and blood from several wounds dyed the snow of his own throat, but Puff was master of the affray. His mouth was full of low-brow fur. The wolfhound, attempting to end Puff's life in one ferocious charge, stumbled and fell to the ground. In a trice, the quick-witted Puff leaped upon his back and adroitly stayed there for a deadly moment even after the skyscraper of a giant got to his feet. Puff was riding high, biting the backbone of resistance and sewing it up with needles, when the dog let out a frightful yelp, turned tail and showed how fast a wolfhound could run for home.

The terrier, deserted on the field of battle, his senses already reeling from the spectacle of this dainty snowball demon using a wolfhound as a saddle horse, turned in craven flight from a foe that could have come from no other place than the Celestial City or hell itself. The whining jackal slunk. The spoil of war was Puff's.

Cushy trotted over and circled the victorious little Puff with switching coyness in her hips. Fatuously, she groveled before her master. She crawled around him with her face tucked between her paws, with the eye nearest him cocked at an angle that fawned her slavery and her worship.

Puff accorded her one imperious and disdainful glance, ran under her stomach and waddled regally castleward. His face was a mass of blood. He was bitten behind an ear and wounded in a paw. But he was all a-swagger. His honor was satisfied. Cushy followed at a servile distance.

Missis Hamilton gathered Puff lovingly in her arms. He had been missing all day. Now Puff is stiff and smells of Dettol, the antiseptic used in the British Isles for everything except snakebite and hydrophobia, but he sleeps on satin at the foot of his mistress' bed snoring in Chinese. On his face is the most smug expression. Even his dreams tell him that a low but beautiful collie, an Amazon of a maiden, bigger than ten litters of Pekes, waits and whimpers for him outside the castle walls. It is a vigil of frustration that will never end in life.

Little ould puffed-up Puff, the only dog in the world who had ever kissed the Blarney Stone, and one of the smallest dogs in Ireland, awoke after a while and waddled down to the drawing room. He watched that bleating calf of a Cushy from his satin pillow high up there in his elegance with the disdain of the Mandarins.

Now and then he condescended to nibble at a scone that Paddy had placed beside him, considerately touched with a bit o' bees' honey.

The sun had gone down behind the dark sentinel of old Blarney's keep. The rain, whipped by the winds of Ireland, splashed the outside night and everything in it. In the rays of a Waterford glass chandelier piercing into the churning courtyard, Puff contemplated a crayture of confused instincts. Acushlamachree, the erstwhile pulse of his heart, her tongue hot and as long as her tail, and her flews dripping with juices of torment.

That giantess of a collie female Cork girrl wearing a rain-soaked coat of Angora wool was walking on her hind legs as the trained dogs of Darlys & Co. of England do, trying to gain the windows of the New Castle for a sign of Puff. Darly's world-famous dog act provides shop windows for poodles and sassy such, some pushing baby carriages past miniature papier-mâché mercantile establishments within easy reach of their vision: Sadie's Hat Shop; I. Cohen Bros., purveyors of bones; I. M. Sorri, a dispenser of dubious kennel goods of some sort that make the dogs turn up their noses and little girls like Adrian laugh fit to be tied and say "Golly sakes! We're dashed," when their mummies take them to London; the Snake Pit Saloon, the Craven A Tobacconist, Pluto's Hotel and the Police Station, an engaged W. C. and no lampposts, but convenient parking meters.

The heated she-wolf left her blood and her laboring hair and her hide on those jaggy frowning walls, O! And when the rain washed them off, she put them back again.

He watched her jump and jump and jump until he became completely bored by the whole unladylike exhibition. Dashed if he would sit there and regard such vulgar goings-on any longer. He might be a Chinese Mandarin by accident of birth, but, confound it, he was a British gentleman of sorts, by adoption, after all. He sniffed contemptuously at his unfinished scone and honey and waddled upstairs to his continent couch of velvet. There was nothing else he could do.

Moral: The blarney is a perilous thing.

We must hurry with the O'Boys to the Bing Crosby cinema in Cork. It is almost curtain time, but we cannot leave Tex and Miss Japgess stranded in the moonlight atop old Blarney Castle.

They were there so late because nothing that Tex could do prevailed to make his modest companion kiss the Stone in all-revealing daylight.

"Go ahead," Tex urged, "kiss it, ma'am, for God's sake!"

"It's for His sake, I'm not," she said firmly.

To buss the Stone some brave man, or men, would be required to hold her legs. Miss Japgess was adamant on this point, at least while the sun shone, and it was hours later after every other pilgrim had departed that she finally agreed to compromise and permitted Tex to take her honor, her life and her limbs in his hands.

The details of Tex's arduous experience and the revelations that met his bulging eyes even in the moon and starlit darkness that night had best be left untold. However, when Miss Japgess finally lay sprawled upon her big canvas, with Tex prayerfully gripping her ankles and looking anxiously as she raised her lips to the shrine, his sliding feet accidentally pushed aside one of the rocks that anchored her skirts. A prankish gust of wind billowed the folds disclosingly.

"Good God! World without end!" ejaculated Tex. "I wouldn't of believed it possible!"

The shock was so great that he all but permitted Miss Japgess to fall to her destruction.

Miss Japgess emerged from her contact as a person comes out of a trance. Possibly the glow of her face was caused by the flood of blood that gushed to her head as she kissed the Stone. But a great change was apparent in her behavior which now was almost warm. Tex looked in astonishment as she got to her feet and pirouetted on a single toe. She breathed deeply and executed several steps of a gallopade. Tex rushed forward to offer assistance. Miss Japgess brushed him away.

"It's just a little dance," she said.

"A . . . a dance! Whew, ma'am. Thought for a second it was th' blind staggers."

Miss Japgess was humming softly. Tex scratched his head.

"Well, ma'am," he said finally, "guess I'll be gittin' my mouth full of oratory now." He took his coat off, placed it on a merlon, and studied the dangerous vacancy under the Blarney Stone with some concern.

"Go ahead, Tex," said Miss Japgess gaily, "I'll hold your legs."

Tex was too dumbfounded to comment. But he had private thoughts. "If I didn't know better, I'd swear she'd et loco weed!"

A transformed, transported and suddenly uninhibited Purity Leaguer held a wary Tex with the ease of a splinter. She was actually joking about it.

"First time I ever even so much as *touched a man,*" she confided laughingly.

"But go easy," Tex begged, "you're cuttin' off circulation!"

Tex's lips wooed the powers of the Blarney Stone. His head was far back and through the cavity under it. After one kiss, he risked a look toward the ground below. In the moonlight the yawning space was like an abyss of witches climbing a treillage of hell. The limbs of the trees and clutching ivy reaching for his head, made him uneasy with eerie sensations. A man lying flat on his back at night under such conditions experiences dread and shuddering reactions. The wise kisser of the Blarney Stone keeps his eyes closed at all times. Tex's were popping out of his head when Miss Japgess gave him a playful push.

"Kiss it again," she giggled. "Kiss it lots and lots!"

She joggled Tex's precarious body again. He slid inches further out over nothing. He howled in panic.

"Calf-rope! Ma'am! For God's sake, calf-rope!"

Miss Japgess did not comprehend the term of the range. Obligingly, she shoved Tex's body several feet further. His torso was dangling from the knees straight down the castle wall. He waved his arms frantically and bellowed like a bull under the brand.

"Calf-rope, you big heifer! You . . . you dairy! I hollered *calf-rope!* That means a unfortunate critter gives up!"

Miss Japgess pulled the frightened man to safety. He scrambled to his feet, the veins of his face popping dangerously.

"Why, I thought you asked for *more* rope. I thought you wanted to be lowered further."

Tex controlled his apoplexy and replaced his coat.

He calmed down quickly, for he had kissed the Blarney Stone, although the full total of results was yet to be counted. Miss Japgess was buzzing all over the parapet with her shoe box and canvas.

"We're going to have a picnic in the moonlight," she announced breathlessly.

"Don't keer if we do. I'm about played out."

The spread covered the yardage, enough food for a troop of hungry Girl Scouts. Miss Japgess pressed Tex's unresisting hands full of deviled eggs and second joints of fried chicken.

"Just wait until you taste my chocolate layer cake," she enthused. "Made it by guess and by God all the way over here in Ireland without an American measuring cup. But a pint's a pound the year 'round. Isn't it, Tex?"

With the mention of "pint," Tex quickly tapped his pants' hip pockets. Luck was with him. "Whew!" he exclaimed thankfully, through a mouthful of picnic, "they didn't fall out!"

"Oh, Tex, if they only had!"

Tex's mouth was crammed with the most delicious food he had ever tasted. He reached for more.

"Best goldurned fried chicken I've eaten since th' pigs et my little brother!"

Miss Japgess studied him longingly.

"Tex," she said slowly, "have you . . . as you would say . . . ever thought of getting . . . well, er hitched?"

Tex choked on a chicken back.

"No, ma'am," he sputtered, "not . . . just prezackly. Why?"

"Oh, nothing, I guess," sighed Miss Japgess, "but why don't you stop saying 'ma'am'? Just call me Apjie."

Lo, the spell of the Blarney Stone at last was working its magic on Tex.

"Apjie Japgess is shore a mouthful, ma'am," he said softly. "Mind if I call you Appie?"

"Not at all, Tex."

"You know, Appie, there ain't a goldanged thing wrong with you. Yore bark's worse'n yore bite. You ain't said 'how dare you' once since you kissed that piece of rubble. All you need's a little softenin' up."

"And if you'd only stop drinking that . . . that white mule."

Tex arose and walked over to a parapet. Miss Japgess heard a crash of glass against the precipice below and a splash in the Martin River where enchanted fishes slept.

"Goodness! What's that?"

"I've swore off," Tex said. "This time, Appie, it's fur good!"

He sat down close by Miss Japgess' side and allowed his hand accidentally to brush against the warmth of her throbbing wrist. It caused her great confusion. She reached nervously into the depths of the shoe box.

"Any husband lucky enough to git a gal like you, Appie, would always know where she was, anyway. He wouldn't never have to shake th' sheets to find *her*. That's *one* shore thing, as shore as bacon goes with liver."

"Stop talking about liver, Tex. It's so . . . so unromantic."

"Guess you're right, Appie."

"Here, Tex," she said in trembling, dulcet tones, "try this nutted cream cheese sandwich. Eat a half a dozen or so, Tex. All you need is just a little fattening up."

The glow of a romantic moon bathed golden silhouettes of two midnight picnickers on the heights of Old Blarney Castle, where medieval knight and fair lady linked their arms and sighed in days of yore. A nightingale, whose family founder had won the gift of song from a faithful stone, lifted a serenade to love.

Chapter Seventeen

"Top o' the Morning"

Ho! And what fine jokes they made and what fun our O'Boys had on their trip. They had left the country and the smell of turf fires coming through the doors of the cottages and damp dog hair drying. They were in the city now.

This was the city of which Daniel Corkery wrote:

". . . As humdrum a collection of odds-and-ends as ever went by the name of a city—are flung higgledy-piggledy together into a narrow double-streamed, many-bridged river valley."

It is built on land reclaimed from the marshes and the bogs by the pagan Danes.

There is no lack of great sights in Cork! St. Patrick's Church, St. Mary's Holy Trinity, Christ the King, Father Matthew's Memorial Church, St. Mary's Dominican Church, SS. Peter & Paul's, the Augustinian, the Franciscan.

O'D.'s little eyes were snapping at the panorama like the bark of a feist, and his neck craned over the spire-pierced panorama.

"Ho!" laughed O'K. " 'Tis from Macroom that O'D. comes, I see!"

O'D. came out of his reverie grinning sheepishly and enjoying the joke as much as anyone.

"Yirra," he said, "ye poked a hole in me thoughts as big as a badger's head! But it's not from Macroom that I come. I know where *I* am, O'K. 'Tis *you* who think that this is America!"

"Pooh!" chuckled O'K.

It was the kind of codding that cheered the spirits. The very mention of *Macroom* made people laugh, anyway. Although that little town is only twenty-four miles from Cork, it is said that most of its residents have never ventured beyond the city limits since the landing of the Norse sea rovers in Ireland in 795 A.D. That is, save one doughty group who decided sixty years ago to emigrate to the New World. With their possessions on their backs and their womenfolk hooded with hundred-year-old Spanish shawls, the courageous men finally arrived in Cork, thinking it was the end of their journey, the great city of New York.

Small wonder because Cork, with a population of 75,000, is the second largest city in the Republic of Ireland, and in comparison with the tiny Elizabethan village of Macroom presents a bedlam of sights and sounds usually associated with the greatest metropolis in the world. Someday Cork will be even larger, the natives believe, and the city fathers are grooming for first place with many modern plans. The prophetic doggerel that heartens its citizens for the growth to come, and is quoted by civic patriots, goes like this:

> Limerick was,
> Dublin is,
> But Cork will be
> The greater of the three.

"It does look big after Blairney, though," suggested O'U.

"In some ways, yes," promptly replied O'G., "and in some ways no. All put together there's nothing in Cork City as big as th' Blairney Stone."

" 'Tis so, 'tis so!" echoed those of his approving companions within earshot. They threw their shoulders back a bit further now. Soon they would be seeing the Blarney Stone growing even greater in the role of a movie hero. Only O'D. seemed to be depressed.

"Come now, man," said O'K. soothingly. " 'Twas only coddin' ye I was about Macroom."

"Why not, friend, that I do know," agreed O'D. " 'Tis just that coming to Cork always makes me sad and blue. Taking for example yon sky-piercin' abomination on th' horizon."

O'D. pointed a trembling finger toward the spire of beautiful St. Finbarr's Cathedral, rising 204 feet from its great central tower and dominating the skyline of the city.

"There," he exclaimed, "that monstrosity and national disgrace, th' biggest church in Ireland and th' house o' th' very divil himself."

O'D., who forever concerned himself with the weightier matters of the Catholic Church, usually attended to by the hierarchy of Rome, wavered his words with passion.

O'K. frowned understandingly.

"Aye, O'D., 'tis true, and a sad and lamentable spectacle it is! But St. Finbarr's has not always been a Protestant cathedral!"

"What!" exclaimed O'D., crossing himself as though lightning had struck.

"Once it was properly a Catholic edifice," explained O'K., "but four hundred years ago th' Protestants stole it from th' very saint himself."

"Th' thieves!" exploded O'D. "But didn't they drop dead?"

"They're all dead now, I guess," said O'K.

"And as they *should* be," retorted O'D. emphatically.

" 'Tis bad luck to touch th' fabric o' th' church. Look what happened at Blairney! Th' hounds o' death barked for that Colthurst!"

Our excursionists passed many groups of nuns and friars of many orders, and many priests.

"Every year in Cork," O'D. observed proudly, "we see more and more."

"Why not," said O'T., "more and more; soon everyone in Ireland will be a nun or a priest."

"Who will be feeding them now?" asked O'C.

"Yirra! Ye disecratin' ould cod," snapped O'D. "Have ye lost th' sense o' yer sowl? Ye're just like a jug handle, always off! *Ireland* will feed them, that's who!"

"But," reasoned O'T. stubbornly, "when everyone in Ireland wears th' cloth, there'll be no more sowls to save."

"Oh, well," said O'D. philosophically, "they can always find needed work to be doin' on th' Protestants!"

Now, with no more interruptions save those necessitated by several stops at pubs encountered innocently enough on Green Street, Shanndon Street, Pope's Quay, and some likely establishments patronized on Oliver Plunkett Street and South Mall, in self-defense and only to catch their collective breath after they had lost their way as many times, the pilgrims contrived to lose their sense of direction just once more, and took their bearings at a last and final emporium, having a last look back toward Cork's old Strawberry Hill.

It was a holiday in any sense of the word, stimulating every emotion, recklessness and abandon. They were spending their money like bug-eyed farm boys at Puck's Fair. Lavish were their shopping plans. At one pub O'D. excused himself and came back a few minutes later from the market, grinning like Santa Claus. Under his arm he carried a large sack of smelly merchandise.

" 'Tis for Herself," he said gently. "Herself would trade her sowl for a yard o' thim, and stairve in hell altogither."

Mrs. O'D.'s gourmandish and spiritual preference was for the hellish *drisheens,* for which Cork City is peculiarly famous. The *drisheen* is a pudding curiosity consisting of dried sheep's blood and herbs mixed together and stuffed in lengthy sheep's guts. The Cork Irishman relishes this vile sausage as the gods their nectars on Olympus.

"They'll do," said O'K., "but th' Cork *crubeen* is th' true heaven on *this* airth. Th' boiled jelly in a pig's hoof is a fair trade for th' joys o' th' blissid hereafter. *Crubeens* and trotters in a trade for hell would be a bad bargain for th' divil himself."

The very thought of the celestial succulence of pigs' feet boiled with their cloven hooves, and sheep feet prepared in the same manner, with the exception that the water used for the latter is carefully preserved, cooled, scented with a mystifying perfume, and sold as "Trotter Hair Oil," sent O'K. dashing out for a shopping excursion of his own.

He rejoined his comrades proudly bent under a weight and variety of amazing purchases. One item, carried in a huge crocus sack over his back, left a trail of water dripping from his coattails after him.

"Yirra!" shouted O'L., who had not forgiven the argument about Blarney Lake, "behold this strange manner o' man! Wearin' his poppin' bladder where his protrudin' posterior should be!"

O'K. dropped five pounds of *crubeens,* five pounds of trotters, one pint of Trotter Hair Oil, and one hundred pounds of ice crashing to the floor, and sprang at the taunting O'L. The O'Boys, laughing convulsively over the best joke of the day, permitted them three blows each before stepping in to stop the fight.

" 'Tis ice!" blustered O'K. " 'Tis for th' Americans. Th' furrst in me pub. As for yer own posterior and as to its location, O'L., ye have not th' shame o' a chicken in th' barnyard! 'Tis not even covered by a whisker o' a feather under yer nose!"

"Come, me lads," urged O'D. placatingly, "th' cinema!"

Rubbing at the inflammation of a cheek bone, and unimpressed by the roars that had greeted his bark, O'K. grumblingly recovered his cargo of foodstuffs, replaced his ice on his shoulders, and trudged after his fellows.

Little the worse for wear, they arrived before the portals of the cinema revived, fortified and cheered.

They shuffled down the quiet, plush magnificence of the

Savoy's aisles and finally took their seats with the deep inner happiness they had brought with them down the winding Commons Road. They nudged each other knowingly in the ribs, by way of showing they were old hands at the play.

O'K. placed his historic purchase of ice on the slanting floor before him and gripped it with fierce possessiveness between his knees. As the ice melted, forming a little stream that trickled beneath the seats of patrons ahead, many were the haughty and accusing stares suspicious neighbors indignantly and unjustly cast in each others' direction. The unusual odors of *crubeens, drisheens* and trotters in the hot auditorium were the cause of much sniffing, indicting neck-craning and embarrassed squirming. Palpably, each neighbor was guilty by implication, at least, without benefit of trial.

One especially horrified woman wearing shoes with low insteps and whose stockings were constantly wet by a remarkable and bountiful stream that seemingly had no ending, abruptly left her place with a loud exclamation of outrage and went home, blushing violently, to wash her feet.

All of this commotion the O'Boys, descendants of kings, weathered complacently and regally.

The lights went down, the music came up and there appeared the greatest actor in this world on the screen before them. The O'Boys leaned forward in their seats gripping the arms with damp fingers. There was the star of stars in technicolor that made even the colors of their village seem dark by comparison, and if they could believe their eyes, this performer, of a glittering magnitude to be found only in one place this side of the Pearly Gates, was smiling at them, bowing like an old friend, and bidding them a warm and friendly welcome. It was the Blarney Stone.

The souls of the O'Boys soared with the elation of pride and kinship. The cockles o' their hearts glowed like a warm turf fire, and a supeen o' Paddy's on a damp Irish night.

They were fiercely proud of their village, and they had ample reason. There was much to boast of.

Blarney Village could point to a notable distinction, a handsome paneled bridge built over a visionary, nonexistent canal which was never cut, through which and under which, respectively, water never flowed. The man who put the bridge before the water, so to speak. It was constructed by one of the Mahony family who today operate the tweed mills.

Blarney is further distinguished by the first bath installed in Ireland, that famed one in the New Castle. It is a museum piece, and still in use, a china monstrosity standing on four great iron feet, and surrounded by an amazing elaboration of pipes and taps.

Residents of less distinguished Irish communities say with some envy that the Blarnearian thinks "Blarney is the only place in the world." Certainly, as we know, it has officially been called the "center of the universe."

The McCarties, always patrons of the arts as well as arms, supported and encouraged the last Bardic school in Ireland. (In 1142 Cormac McCarty, King of Munster, who headed the Irish Reformation, built at Cashel in County Tipperary a tiny chapel so exquisite and beautiful of workmanship and design that few others in all of Europe may even be compared. His little chapel is like a jeweled chip of heaven shining there.)

The McCarty school was located in Blarney, and flourished there in the 18th century until the royal supporters were despoiled of empire and starvation forced the poets to seek other lines of endeavor. The English, who had always frowned upon the Bards because they kept alive the heroic opposition of the Irish people to the Sassenachs, hailed the decline and fall of these dangerous enemies who since the time of St. Patrick had wielded weapons more powerful than their best iron arms.

Although now the village, with its little square which comes to life only once each year with the tourist season, is a ghost of its so-called former glory, what is lost in harsh and ugly commercial importance is compensated by charm, and today finds it mellowed and softened with a patina of memories older than any machine, memories exclusively its own and shared by no other in all of Ireland. . . . Its thatched cottages and tiny whitewashed stone houses—the "castles" of its proud peasants —dot the rich undulating country all around, and not a man there would swap his own hearth even for the great New Castle of the "ould man on the hill."

The O'Boys beamed their happiness in reflected glory. It was a sensation short-lived and rudely shattered as they stared while the production unfolded. It tightened like cords around their true and honest hearts.

First, they squinted with a slow, hurt realization of disillusionment. The colored, musical screen blurred momentarily before their eyes as it flickered its monstrous betrayal, things of Hollywood, upon startled reactions. Embarrassed feet shuffled upon the floor and the coughing as of a pulmonary sanitarium filled the auditorium. This was succeeded with a unisonant and horrified "Begob!"

Their minds were yellow and green with bruises that are old as suddenly as they are new. Their complexions were the color of an Irish pound note. Their hearts pumped the dye that makes the blood turn to bile.

"Look!" exclaimed O'S.

"Sweet son o' God!"

Chapter Eighteen

"Father Prout"

Far more than to Queen Elizabeth, King Cormac McCarty, Oliver Cromwell, Ireton, Lord Broghill, Fairfax, King William III, or even the poet Millikin who wrote the "Groves of Blarney," so puckishly appropriated by "Father Prout," does the Stone of Ireland owe its fame to that gay Roman Catholic priest, Francis Sylvester Mahony, of Cork, Paris, London, Rome and Switzerland.

At a period when few of his scribbling countrymen except for Thomas Moore were greatly distinguishing themselves, Mahony was a spirit whose genius in its prime burst like a Roman candle over a nightfall of Irish letters. The resultant fireworks were created by a combination explosion of body, soul and Muse, to the joy of the world and the consternation of the Bishop of Rome. They were not altogether of the type approved by the most liberal interpretations of prescribed canonical behavior and temperance.

Still, it was a God-given time, when the literary sun was shining over British Isles rife with genius. English authors were lavishing a spate of diamonds on the pages of their master-pieces. The sun of letters beamed the rays of Carlyle, Thackeray, Coleridge, Ainsworth, Scott, Jerrold, Browning and Dickens. Mahony pulled his own sun out of the East, the Blarney Stone of Phoenicia, and did some fine prosy decorating of the literary horizon himself. Contending with the best of his contemporaries, who seared their enduring fame on the script of the ages,

Mahony never lacked in comparative fahrenheit of feeling, and his own sun cast shadows and light where it willed.

He was the most refreshing literary scamp in Irish history, an adornment of the world of literature, and such a refreshment to the printed word that the type faces of his day beamed refrains of gratitude. The plainest block danced the minuet as gracefully as the cursive when Mahony's prose provoked the printer's fonts to rhapsody. He also fired the metal, when the notion suited him, with temperatures of his own peculiar foundry of satire, whimsy and caprice, that frequently made it scorch the touch, but always so lovely it was, and is, to read. His writing was the classic of the languages and the glory of Erin. Sometimes Mahony bit the type with his teeth to make it fit. He was the soul of Ireland's wit and humor. In private life, he was the spirit and the essence of camaraderie. It was his conviviality that cost him a cardinal's hat.

It was he who awakened the Blarney Stone from slumber, and it was the Blarney Stone that loosed his tongue to dream.

He was the Blarney Stone's most vigorous champion and its best friend. It was his holy crusade alone that revived its fame about a hundred years ago, after it had lain largely dormant for centuries, and spread the story of its tongue-tonic powers to the masses of the world. The masses certainly never read "Father Prout," but the religion of his teachings got around by word of blarney mouth, and self-appointed apostles were not lacking to further its glory where men had ears to hear and were ambitious for the glory of verbs.

His *Plea for Pilgrimages* did not go unanswered. It was following the publication of this mischievous thesis that the Colthursts noted the increase in Blarney Castle traffic that brought about the shilling turnstile. So, directly to Mahony is traced that source of dollars for those ancestors of the "Jeffers." His works were excellent advertisements and brought in a lot of hay, enabling them to live in the manner to which he had imputed their mode in his polyglot version of Millikin's verses, describing it as similar to the existence of heifers, usually well fed in Ireland.

Before Father Prout's astonishing emergence, the Blarney Stone was the private panacea for the song-happy birds of the Blarney demesne and the fortunate few humans possessing special privilege, knowledge and higher education. For centuries, therefore, the gift of blarney was a monopoly of these providentially elect.

Father Prout tells Sir Walter Scott that the Blarney Stone is "of a basaltic kind, rather unusual in the district." But the boast of its eastern fame was challenged when a learned scholar wrote to Father Prout denying the "soft impeachment" that he had kissed the stone at all. He had been mentioned as a "proud and incontestible instance of the virtue and efficacy of the talisman."

This man claimed it would not stand "chemical analysis."

Mahony has him threaten to expose the stone.

"If you neglect me . . . I'll prove that the block at Blarney is an 'aerolithe' and that your statement as to its Phoenician origin is unsupported by historical evidence."

This unfortunate publicity, however, did not deter the true believers, who started visiting the "heritage" in droves.

Had the protective Mahony attended the showing of *Top O' The Morning* with the O'Boys that day at Cork's Savoy, his gifted wrath would have flayed the movie treatment of his shrine. The resentment of the O'Boys over the portrayal was lost in the futility of their incoherence, the limitation of an audience and the power of the pen. Mahony was confined by no such restrictions, but unfortunately his corpse had been in its grave for about eighty-five years when Hollywood starred his beloved palladium.

In the picture the unbelieving eyes of the O'Boys beheld a Blarney Village composed of "ye olde Englishe tea shoppe" type houses and cobbled streets that do not exist there at all. Large fluffy donkeys trot about briskly, drawing smart gigs (of a type never seen on earth). It bristles with "Colleens"—dressed like Breton peasants—saying "Begorrah," a word never used in Ireland without contractions—except by visiting Americans. There are innumerable shots of a swan lake, gleaming like treacle (molasses) surrounded by cardboard rocks and lovers, as a background for Bing Crosby to sing "Irish Eyes."

Heavy and irreverent hands were being laid upon the shrine. It was unthinkable. How the O'Boys needed Mahony now!

"Begor!" shouted O'K. angrily. "And look! They're stealin' th' Blairney Stone, too!"

The heat in his knees burned into his precious block of ice. Mahony would have had the words to burn the cheeks of Hollywood.

Although Mahony in jest once wrote that the keys to Cork City were presented to distinguished visitors in boxes carved out of the Blarney Stone, he would sooner have buried his beloved Father Prout than so much as scratch a match upon its sacred surface.

His gifted wrath would have flayed Hollywood for having it stolen.

Mahony loosed his satire on a fatuous Mayor of Cork, "the most respectable civic worthy that has worn the cocked hat and chain since the days of John Walters (who was beheaded for boldly proclaiming Perkin Warbeck, the pretender—in the reign of Henry II in the market place of that beautiful city of "Rebel Cork"—as Richard IV, King of England and Lord of Ireland), by commending him for his campaign against mad dogs.

"His favourite pursuit during the canicule of 1825, was the extermination of mad dogs; and so vigorously did he urge the carnage during the summer of his mayoralty, that some thought he wished to eclipse the exploit of St. Patrick in destroying the breed altogether, as the saint did that of the toads. A Cork poet, the laureate of the mansion-house, has celebrated Knapp's prowess in a didactic composition entitled *Dog-Killing, A Poem*;

in which the Mayor is likened to Apollo in the Grecian camp before Troy in the opening of the Iliad."

Had Mahony known that St. Patrick was also the patron saint of Puerto Rico for his achievement in driving the ants out of that island, one may be sure he would have praised the unfortunate Knapp as the "Insect Slayer."

St. Patrick won his chance in Puerto Rico by lot. During a terrible scourge of ants in the year 1536, the natives, in desperate need of a saint to whom they could appeal for relief, impartially put the names of *all* the Catholic saints in a single hat. St. Patrick's name came out in the first draw.

Never having heard of him, it was decided to try again. St. Patrick's card was replaced in the hat, but it would not stay there. It appeared again in the second draw even after the most thorough shuffling.

Deeming this incontestible evidence of his power, the natives prayed to him for help and, sure enough, that night the heavens opened up to deliver a rainstorm that washed every last ant to kingdom come.

The sixteen O'Boys were like a hill of mad ants themselves that day in the Savoy cinema. Their shouts of outrage were highly disturbing to the other patrons. They took the theater over entirely as a private forum for their indignation.

"And to think," sputtered O'D., "th' ould man on th' hill invited th' American producer and wretched photographers, and all th' bloody cinema minions twice to lunch in a row."

"Twice in a *row,* ye mean," corrected O'K. "Not like a *row* in a field. Like a *row* in a brawl."

"Begob! Brawlin' in th' castle now?"

" 'Twas good as one, ye might say. Th' cinema ye view now with such nauseous disgust, could have been worse had the brawl not occurred just as it did."

"What!"

"Th' mendacious buggers wanted a dire tragedy in it," explained O'K. "Th' oreegenal idea was to have th' Blairney Stone stole fer good and all time. But th' ould man on th' hill made th' presumptuous Americans change it around."

"Steal th' Blairney Stone!" exclaimed O'H., who had been asleep. "Putting ideas like that in people's minds! 'Twould be th' very ruination of Ireland!"

"Still, we got it back," suggested O'T.

" 'Tis th' difference between a belch and a burrp!" retorted O'D. "Th' insinuation o' th' thing is there!"

"Aye, bad enough like 'tis," grunted O'O. bad-humoredly. "Even if th' castle did get th' Blairney Stone back. Th' turrible idea o' th' thievery was put in th' minds of people, anyway."

"Just imagine an Ireland without th' Blairney Stone! 'Twould be like taking th' green from th' very fields! And—and—"

"Or th' shamrock from the sward?" suggested O'C. helpfully.

"Aye, 'tis so," replied O'D. with gratitude welling through his high emotion. "Or sellin' th' lovely Lakes o' Killarney."

"Don't think *that's* possible, now," interrupted the realistic tub-conscious O'K. "Guess all th' bathtubs even in America couldn't hold th' Lakes o' Killarney. But th' Blairney Stone, now, could be speereted away in an ass cart."

" 'Tis for years that th' beggars have been tryin' to take it away. 'Tis no peace they give th' ould man any more. And 'twas th' same with his father before him."

" 'Tis th' temptation o' th' very divil they put in his way," said O'H. "But he would niver in this wurrld give in."

"All Ireland would come to his hangin'," roared O'D.

" 'Twould be a fryin' he'd be gettin'," corrected O'K.

"Aye!" the O'Boys agreed so loudly that they drowned out all of the hissing of their neighbors.

"He'd be boiled like a *crubeen!*"

"Dead or alive, th' Stone will stay. Ireland will see to that!"

There is a sublime, popular and widespread feeling among the Irish that the great land-holding descendants of the Sassenachs occupy their estates by sufferance, and the generosity of the people, which given, could also be taken away.

"But would ye tell me," demanded O'O. suddenly, "what would th' foreigners be wantin' th' Blairney Stone for in th' furrst place?"

"Why—why—why—" sputtered O'D., being taken somewhat by surprise, "why—now—er—"

"Why?" asked O'K. abruptly. "Ye askin' a question like that! Why to *kiss* it, ye ideeot, that's why!"

O'D. sighed thankfully.

"To be shure," he said. " 'Twas just what I was about to say. What else do ye think now, O'O., they'd be doin' with it?"

"Aye, to kiss it," agreed O'O., "and 'twas a sad day they came here, an ungrateful day! And here politely we listened to them tellin' us Bing Crosby was second only to God, and Hollywood greater than heaven! Th' maneness o' th' thing; coddin' us, too!"

"Could it now," suggested an outraged O'T. suspiciously, searching for some slim motive for the treatment of his village, "be some type o' diabolical subtile Protestant propaganda?"

"Foo and tosh!" exclaimed the landlord. "It says nothin' against th' true Church and they have Catholics in America, too."

"Begob, not like Ireland."

" 'Tis true . . . God save them . . ." replied O'K., "but still and all, not many countries are like Ireland; th' church is th' very sowl of Ireland."

He changed the subject with a dark and popular thought.

"But British money, now, that might have had somethin' to do with it!"

"Ah! 'Tis so! 'Tis so! Bribes!" agreed O'T. violently. "Somethin' havin' to do now with pirtition?"

"Possibly," solemnly answered O'K.

It was the result of a plot, whatever it was. That was patent and all agreed.

Loudly, the disgruntled O'Boys decided they had seen enough of the pusillanimous celluloid, and they all stormed out of the theater together.

The applause of the remaining patrons that rang in their ears was not for Bing Crosby.

Chapter Nineteen

"Wayward Child of Genius"

The roguish Hibernian, Francis Sylvester Mahony, was actually a leprechaun in disguise. His bald head haloed by white fuzz, his mischievous specs far down the bridge of his nose overlooked by twinkling gray eyes, and the mind of a conniptious but fun-loving sprite belonged in the roots of trees where puckish faeries dwell. But, as it was, Mahony did very well on higher ground, where as "the wayward child of genius," he carved monuments of letters rather than cobbled the shoes of enchanted dwarfs. He caused enough deviltry in human form. What would have happened had he been a pooka is enough to make Ireland pale. His most masterfully sculptured prose was about the Blarney Stone. His masterpiece of poetry was "The Bells of Shandon."

The son of poor middle-class Cork parents, he was exposed after vainly prefixing his own honest name with an unjustified O, apostrophe, to indicate a relationship to a castle-dwelling, socially exalted family of O'Mahonies. No O'Mahonies of the name, before or since, have achieved a modicum of the fame of their patronymic imitator. The most important of these, soon after the fraud, might well have been pleased to drop their O's and with O's of awe formed by their mouth, claim kinship with him.

His critics asked: "Do you wish for epigrams? There is a shower of them. Have you a taste of ballads, varying from the lively to the tender, from the note of the trumpet to the note of the lute? Have you an ear for translation which gives the semblance of another language's face? Do you delight in the classical allusion, the quaint though profound learning of other days?"

All of these "and more" are to be found in the works of this "wayward child."

Mahony's personality expressed in his works is the best example of why the world laughs *with* and not *at* the Irish race.

Dickens was his admirer and edited some of his work for *Fraser's Magazine* in London. The great and the near-great took him to their hearts, the writer, the artist, the Bohemian, the publican, the roisterer, the housemaid and her lady, alike. His contemporaries described him as "a combination of Voltaire and Rabelais." He was intemperate, gaily rebellious, and a more gifted priest never wore the cloth of Rome.

Sadly, the Church admonished him and pondered the reckless behavior of her brilliant and precocious son, but Mahony, who preferred the wee-hour revels of the artist and the writer to the company of the priests of the Society of Jesus, was incorrigible with a lightness that baffled discipline.

Under the spiritual and educational guidance of the Jesuits in their colleges of Amiens and Paris since the age of twelve, his brilliance from the outset had astounded his teachers. Mahony's easy and natural gifts, demonstrated especially in the mastery of languages, with phenomenal facility tested the erudition of his teachers. It was his remarkable fluency in the oral and written classic Greek, ancient Hebrew, Latin, French and Italian that first made his "Father Prout" possible of creation.

With his allegation that Millikin's "Groves" was a translation of the Greek original, it was his ability to produce his "proof" that introduced this character to the scene of letters in his most refreshing performance.

As the creator of "Father Prout," the parish priest of Watergross Hill, near Blarney Castle, Mahony infused with brilliant and fictional fire a dull old country churchman, imparting to his simple mind the imagination, the wisdom, and the searching and scholarly attributes and cynicism of Diogenes, the satirical power of Moore, the slashing poise of Voltaire and the rollicking humor of Rabelais.

Moore, with whom he had often been compared for his "light, airy, playful, yet elegant satire," said Mahony "ran through each mode of the lyre and was master of all." All of this genius Mahony bestowed upon "Father Prout."

After "Father Prout" with his purloined "Groves of Blarney" became more famous than the author of the original, Mahony, who was enjoying a period of probation for some charming ecclesiastic misdemeanor in Rome, relaxed in a nocturnal resort and contemplated the great popularity of his impishly plagiarized creation, over a bottle of wine.

"Any road," he said, "leads to Rome, but would it not have been odd had I got myself there through the Groves of Blarney?"

Certainly, Mahony's improvements gave life to the verses of Millikin never enjoyed by the original. His last verse in which he says the "Jeffers lived like heifers" is a rare example of his felicitous perception.

With "Father Prout" as a vehicle for his own wit and charm, Mahony consorted with Erato and Clio in the green groves of Blarney and made of the magic Stone in the heights of the Castle his literary throne.

At errant moments, he did not spare even himself of that satirical indulgence so dear to his heart. It was Mahony about whom Father Prout wrote of his own affection for Bacchus when he described in verse his happy weakness for wine and fair maid:

> For buxom Maggy, careful soul,
> Had two stone bottles found,
> To hold the liquor that Prout loved,
> And kept it safe and sound.

And:

>Now we sail
>With the gale
>Through the groves of Blarney, O!
>Where old Prout
>Is drinking stout
>And whiskey with Kate Kearney, O!

Another of Father Prout's versions of Millikin's poetry of Blarney further points up his appreciation of the scenery of the demesne:

>'Tis there's the kitchen hangs many a flitch in,
>With the maids a stitching upon the stair;
>The bread and biske', the beer and whiskey,
>Would make you frisky if you were there.
>'Tis there you'd see Peg Murphy's daughter
>A washing praties forenent the door,
>With Roger Cleary, and Father Healy,
>All blood relations to my Lord Donoughmore.

Obvious imputations are to be gathered in the relationship of His Lordship to Peg, Roger and the good Father Healy.

Millikin's delightful absurdity, however, appeared to have caused him some apparent genuine pangs of conscience for the tomfoolery which the verses excited. Just before he died, he wrote this apology:

>O! Blarney, in my rude unseemly rhymes,
>Albeit abused, lo! to thy bowers I come—
>I come a pilgrim to your shades again,
>And woo thy solemn scenes with votive pipe.
>Shut not your glades, nymphs of the hollow rock,
>'Gainst one who, conscious of the ill he did,
>Comes back repentant! Lead me to your dens,

Ye fays and sylvan beings—lead me still
Through all your wildly tangled grots and groves,
With nature and her genuine beauties full;
And on another stop, a stop thine own,
I'll sound thy praise, if praise of mine can please;
A truant long to nature, and to thee!

Mahony drifted, or rather floated, away from the Church on
the wings of his own songs, although fierce and sincere at times
were his efforts to conform to its tenets and to restrain his irrepressible fondness for the life of the Bohemian.

He entered suit for libel, alleging $10,000 damages against
a magazine of the day for describing him as a "suspended
priest," and won a beseeching and abject apology.

In one last effort, he begged the priests of the Jesuit College
of Clongowes Wood in Ireland, where he returned in bad health
from Paris, for a last chance to redeem himself. The good fathers
accorded him every consideration, first appointing him Prefect
of Studies and later Master of Rhetoric.

Shortly thereafter, while chaperoning a group of boys on a
night of wild revelry in which he joined so enthusiastically that
he became heavy with wine and brandy, he met disaster. One of
the drunken students, a red-headed youth being transported in
a rented dung cart, was playfully thrown into a tub of scalding
water on arrival at the school and severely burned. "Prout" departed for Switzerland. He never returned to Cork, except in
death. They brought his body home from Paris where he died
in 1866, at the age of sixty-two, and buried him with tender-
ness in the Shandon Churchyard.

There sleeps "Father Prout" on the banks of the River Lee,
where the beautiful Bells of Shandon toll out over his grave in
perennial eulogy to the author who rang their chimes across the
seas:

With deep affection and recollection
I often think of those Shandon Bells,
Whose sound so wild would
In the days of childhood
Fling round my cradle their magic spells.
On this I ponder, where'er I wander,
And thus grow fonder, sweet Cork, of thee;
With thy Bells of Shandon
That sound so grand on
The pleasant waters of the River Lee.

One of Mahony's fondest plans contemplated the construction in Blarney of a super-Blarney University dedicated to the "national acuteness" of Ireland. It was to be the world's only educational institution for the cultivation of fun and geniality, the development of wit and charm, its graduates *cum laude* attaining rare degrees. Michael O'Rourke, B.G. (Bachelor of Gaiety); Francis O'Driscoll, B.W. (Bachelor of Wit); Terrence O'Connor, B.R. (Bachelor of Revelry); and knowing the penchant of its would-be creator, the degree B.B., or Bachelor of Bacchus. The highest of all, however, was to be another B.B., Bachelor of Blarney, reserved for Father Prout himself.

Quite naturally, Mahony envisioned the Blarney Stone as the cornerstone of his exceptional seat of learning.

Never at any time did Mahony subscribe to the obscure theory so often advanced in Ireland that St. Patrick was the creator of the Blarney Stone, by miracle. Throughout his life the author adhered to his favorite postulation of its Eastern origin.

St. Patrick's first miracle, according to the ancient book of Lismore, written by the Irish monks, was the miraculous transformation into a stone of a draught of poison introduced into the womb of his mother, Concess. This occurred before St. Patrick was born.

Here is how the old monks of Lismore reported the incident:

Now as to Patrick, of the Britons Ail-claude ("Rock of Clyde," i.e., Dumbarton) was his father; Potitus, the Deacon, was his grandfather; Concess was the name of his mother, daughter of Ochmas of France, a sister of Martin was she. And in Nemptor was he born; and when a false oath is taken under the flagstone on which he was born, it sheds water as if it were bewailing the false declaration; but if the oath be true, the stone abides in its own nature.

This is Patrick's first miracle and in his mother's womb he wrought it. A son of the King of Britain came to the place where the woman dwelt, and she washed (his feet) for him, and he received entertainment from her. Wherefore his wife through jealousy gave a drink of poison to Concess, who drank it. And Patrick seized the poison in his grasp, and made thereof a *stone* in his hand, and thus was he born. God's name and Patrick's were magnified thereby.

Gradually, this *stone* of the womb, not that of the weeping flagstone, also became magnified in size and fame until it wound up on top of McCarty's castle, according to the legend. No one will know the truth about the St. Patrick theory until the meeting of Doom. At that time, say the monks of Lismore, "the men of Ireland will go to meet Patrick at Down and wend along with him to Mount Zion. . . . And then will Patrick sit on his throne and judge the men of Ireland. For Patrick is the apostle of Ireland, and he is the father of teaching and faith for Irishmen, and he will judge over them on Doomsday. And after the sentence of Doom, those who have fulfilled his command and his teaching, in fastings, in prayer, in alms, in compassion, in gentleness, in forgiveness, and in the other divine commands, will go along with him into the heavenly kingdom."

Mahony's scholarly and almost mathematical "proof" of the Blarney Stone's Phoenician origin in Father Prout's discourse with the Presbyterian Sir Walter Scott, is a classic of contrivance and sheer audacity that greatly increased his fame as a humorist.

Prout: This palladium of our country was brought hither originally by the Phoenician colony that peopled Ireland, and is the best proof of our eastern parentage. The inhabitants of Tyre and Carthage, who for many years had the Blarney Stone in their custody, made great use of the privilege, as the proverbs *fides Punica, Tyriosque bilingues,* testify. Hence, the origin of this wondrous talisman is of the remotest antiquity.

Strabo, Diodorus, and Pliny mention the arrival of the Tyrians in Ireland about the year 883 before Christ, according to the chronology of Sir Isaac Newton, and the twenty-first year after the sack of Troy.

Now, to show that in all their migrations they carefully watched over this treasure of eloquence and source of diplomacy, I need only enter into a few etymological details. Carthage, where they settled for many centuries but which turns out to have been only a stage and resting-place in the progress of their western wanderings, bears in its very name the trace of having had in its possession and custody the Blarney Stone. This city is called in the Scripture *Tarsus,* or *Tarshish,* which in Hebrew means a *valuable stone, a stone of price,* rendered in your authorized version, where it.occurs in the 28th and 39th Chapters of Exodus, by the specific term *beryl,* a sort of jewel. In his commentaries on this word, an eminent rabbi, Jacob Rodrigues Moreira, the Spanish Jew, says that Carthage is evidently the Tarsus of the Bible, and he reads the word thus (Yiddish), accounting for the termination *ish* by which *Carthage* becomes *Carshish,* in a very plausible way: "Now," says he, "our peoplish have de very great knack of ending dere vords in *ish;* for if you go on the 'Change, you will hear the great man Nicholish Rotchild calling the English coin monish." (See *Lectures Delivered in the Western Synagogue,* by J. R. M.) ...

But, further, does it not stand to reason that there must be some other latent way of accounting for the *purchase of as much ground as an ox-hide would cover,* besides the generally received and most unsatisfactory explanation? The fact is, the Tyrians bought as much land as their Blarney Stone would require to fix itself solidly—

Taurino quantum potuit circumdare tergo: and having got that much, by the talismanic stone they humbugged and deluded the simple natives, and finally became the masters of Africa.

Scott: I confess you have thrown a new and unexpected light on a most obscure passage in ancient history; but how the stone got at last to the county of Cork, appears to me a difficult transition. It must give you great trouble.

Prout: My dear sir, don't mention it! It went to Minorca with a chosen body of Carthaginian adventurers, who stole it away as their best safeguard on the expedition. They first settled at Port Mahon—a spot so called from the Clan of O'Mahony's, a powerful and prolific race still flourishing in this country; just as the Nile had been previously so named from the tribe of the O'Neils, its aboriginal inhabitants. (Is he trying to make a dirty crack at the O'Neils or claim Egypt for the Irish?) All these matters, and many *more curious points,* will be one day revealed to the world by my friend Henry O'Brien, in his work on the Round Towers of Ireland. Sir, we built the pyramids before we left Egypt; and all those obelisks, sphinxes, and Memnonian stones were but emblems of the great relic before you.

George Knapp, who had looked up to Prout, with dumb amazement, from the commencement, here pulled out his spectacles, to examine more closely the old block, while Scott shook his head doubtingly. The learned doctor continued:

Prout: I can convince the most obstinate sceptic, Sir Walter, of the most intimate connexion that subsisted between us and those islands which the Romans called *insulae Baleares,* without knowing the signification of the words which they thus applied. That they were so called from the *Blarney* stone, will appear at once to any person accustomed to trace Celtic derivations: the Ulster king of arms, Sir William Betham, has shown it by the following scale.

Here Prout traced with his cane on the muddy floor of the castle the words "Ba Le AR es iNsulAE = Blarnae!"

Scott: Prodigious! My reverend friend, you have set the point at rest for ever—*rem acu tetigisti!* Have the goodness to proceed.

Prout: Setting sail from Minorca, the expedition, after encountering a desperate storm, cleared the Pillars of Hercules and, landing in the Cove of Cork, deposited their treasure in the greenest spot and the shadiest groves of this beautiful vicinity.

Scott: How do you account for their being left by the Carthaginians in quiet possession of this invaluable deposit?

Prout: They had sufficient tact (derived from their connexion with the stone) to give out, that in the storm it had been thrown overboard to relieve the ship, in latitude 36° 14", longitude 24°. A search was ordered by the Senate of Carthage, and the Mediterranean was dragged without effect; but the mariners of that sea, according to Virgil, retained a reverence for every submarine appearance of a stone: *Saxa vocant Itali mediis quae in fluctibus aras!*

And Aristotle distinctly says, in his treatise *De Mirandis,* quoted by the erudite Justus Lipsius, that a law was enacted against any further intercourse with Ireland. His words are: *In mari, extra Herculis columnas, insulam desertam inventam fuisse sylva nemorosam, in quam crebro Carthaginienses commearint, et sedes etiam fixerint: sed veriti ne nimis cresceret, et Carthago laberetur, edicto cavisse ne quis poena capitis eo deinceps navigaret.*

The fact is, Sir Walter, Ireland was always considered

a lucky spot, and constantly excited the jealousy of Greeks, Romans, and people of every country. The Athenians thought that the ghosts of departed heroes were transferred to our fortunate island, which they call in the war song of Harmodius and Aristogiton, the land of O's and Macs:

And the "Groves of Blarney" have been commemorated by the Greek poets many centuries before the Christian era.

Scott: There is certainly somewhat of Grecian simplicity in the old song itself; and if Pindar had been an Irishman, I think he would have celebrated this favourite haunt in a style not very different from Millikin's classic rhapsody.

Prout: Millikin, the reputed author of that song, was but a simple translator from the Greek original. Indeed, I have discovered, when abroad, in the library of Cardinal Mazarin, an old Greek manuscript which, after diligent examination, I am convinced must be the oldest and *princeps editio* of the song. I begged to be allowed to copy it, in order that I might compare it with the ancient Latin or Vulgate translation which is preserved in the Brera at Milan; and from a strict and minute comparison with that, and with the Norman-French copy which is appended to Doomsday-book, and the Celtic-Irish fragment preserved by Crofton Croker (rejecting as spurious the Arabic, Armenian, and Chaldaic stanzas on the same subject, to be found in the collection of the Royal Asiatic Society), I have come to the conclusion that the Greeks were the undoubted original contrivers of that splendid ode; though whether we ascribe it to Tyrtaeus or Callimachus will depend on future evidence; and perhaps, Sir Walter, *you* would give me your opinion, as I have copies of all the versions I allude to at my dwelling on the hill.

Scott: I cannot boast, learned father, of much *vous* in Hellenistic matters; but should find myself quite at home in the Gaelic and Norman-French, to inspect which I shall with pleasure accompany you: so here I kiss the stone!

No wonder, then, the proud Blarnearians were affronted by the "stage Irish" treatment on the offensive celluloid.

The great heart of the master, greatest bard of Blarney, is stilled in the churchyard of St. Anne's, but after the showing of the movie that day in Cork, Mahony's rebellious spirit lived again as the other O'Boys carried on for him in the vigilance of their hearts and cold dudgeon on their faces. Their homeward journey found the joys of Ireland's loveliest countryside lost to their lowering eyes.

More than half of O'K.'s ice had melted from the raging furnace of his anger.

Chapter Twenty

"The Pebble"

Slow as some miner saps th' aspiring tower,
When working secret with destructive aims,
Unseen, unheard, thus moves the stealing hour,
But works the fall of empire, pomp and name.
                                    —*Ogilvie*

The O'Boys met that night in O'K.'s Snug Pub on the leafy lane of Blarney. The truculent agenda made the suds of stout mugs fly across the bar. The anti-American sentiment was growing.

They found Kane seated in his usual place, drinking gin-and-mix, and Maggy, her cheeks rosier than ever, extending such possessive attention that some of their number winked prophetically.

"If th' Yankee does not marry Maggy, now," said O'D., "afther all himself's brazen deceitful love-making that's transspired under our very noses, th' poor girrl will not be able to hold up her head as high as th' snoot o' a root. Poor, innocent and outraged Maggy'll have th' hangdog look o' Cushy now that ould Puff's turned lion."

"Just what *has* gone on?" asked O'O. "Has he popped th' question? If Maggy's hearrd him speak a worrd, herself's th' only one and I am given to understand that was 'wh . . . wha . . . what.' 'Tis a new and secret language if th' meanin' calls for banns."

"Such subjects do not have to be *popped* by th' mouth," explained O'D. testily. "Not a sound is necessary. Th' all-important pairsonal and sacred subject can be broached by th' *manners* o' men. Eyes can pop such a question as well as mouth."

"Then 'tis th' table that's spoken for," said O'O. "Th' Yankee's eyes have niver left it. If that's th' sorrt o' marriage it 'tis goin' to be, th' priest should now declare it null and void, before it 'tis too late."

"Too late for what?" laughed that evil-minded divilish O'M., th' rougue. "Th' likes o' him would leave th' cover on th' table 'til th' legs got tired o' holdin' it up."

"Still 'tis me own guess himself'll break th' poor Colleen's scandalized hearrt," said O'D. stubbornly. " 'Tis th' American way!"

O'D. emphasized his opinion with a heavy fist crashing the bar. Maggy and Kathleen jumped, but Kane's eyes remained downcast.

Even jumpier than Maggy were the O'Boys. The rumor of the American syndicate's all-out efforts to obtain a lease on the Blarney Stone, despite precautions and safeguards worthy of international secret service and cloak-and-dagger intrigue, had leaked out. The code word for the Blarney Stone, "The Pebble," used by the conspirators in discussing their prize objective, now was common property. The presence of dread and hated spies, infiltrated into Blarney Village in the guise of innocent tourists, was more than mere gossip. Every Yankee in street and pub was a suspect.

Ludicrous reports of all sorts were rife in the village. A group of giant American Air Force bombers, whose mouth-watering crews had flown them to Dublin from their English bases at the invitation of the American Embassy to enjoy a meal from Ireland's plenteous board, excited scary reports of all sorts. The Irish press was horrified, angered and questioning about the propriety and the purpose of their visit. Some went so far as to assert a charge that the planes were atom bomb carriers, on a mission of dire secrecy and intrigue. But not so the indignant Blarneareans.

The flight, in their opinion, coming on the heels of spies, was no coincidence but was palpably part and parcel of the conspiracy to take the Blarney Stone to the United States. Why the atomic bomb was deemed necessary to capture it was not quite clear, but the extent to which America would go to obtain possession of Ireland's heritage was obviously implied in connection with the power and importance of that country's prime weapon.

At first, the U.S. aviators were amused by the fluster of the press, and then became pained and hurt when it dawned that the protest over their "sinister" presence was in deadly earnest.

"Honest to God," they said in dismay, "we only came over here to put on the feed bag."

They had no intention of bombing Ireland at all! They flew back with dyspepsia.

The poor Yankees were merely conforming to a well-established and popular English custom.

Every hungry Englishman who can escape for a time his own austere board at home goes to Ireland for at least one square meal per year. Ireland's pigs are fat, her horses sleek, her larders are bursting, the udders of her cows are dripping cream. Those who can afford the luxury fly over from London every week end. Even more fortunate Britishers have taken up permanent residence on St. Patrick's moist and well-fed isle, becoming expatriates for their stomachs' sake.

The Blarney Annual of Fact and Fancy, edited by that distinguished Irish scholar, Dr. Reilly, and great scientist, too, not far from Father Prout's immortal parish almost in the shadow of the castle, published this significant report in a recent issue, and reprinted by kind permission:

An Englishman and his son were on a visit to the Tower of London. During the inspection, the son asks:

"Where are the Beef-Eaters?"

"Oh, they're all on holiday in Ireland now," replied the father.

But no logical explanation for the bomber flight could long prevail.

"Bejabers!" exclaimed O'K., "America would declare war itself to get th' Pebble!"

"Callin' th' Blairney Stone a *pebble's* like callin' th' Kerry Mountains molehills," grumbled O'D. " 'Twill be a millstone yet around their necks." He was casting dark looks in Kane's direction. "Wonder, now," he asked suddenly, "if himself's in on o' th' mendacious plot? Th' ould 'Diplomat' should slice his tongue out o' his lovesick head!"

"If himself has one to slice," laughed O'K., "and remimber, now, too, th' ould 'Diplomat' can only smell th' English."

"My pairsonal impression all this time has been th' Yankee was in love with a sartain picture, not th' table and Maggy. There's not been a budge out o' th' man," commented the confused O'G., who took a dim view of the entire romance.

"Ye blind and yammerin' conjugation!" exploded O'D. " 'Tis only to make th' pure girrl jealous and desperit with such dishonorable means."

"But to prove a table . . . er . . . er, I mean himself guilty is anither thing," said the muddled O'G.

"*All* of them are guilty," snapped O'D. with finality.

O'G. was thoroughly squelched and not a dissenting voice was heard.

And Irish-American relations that night in the Season of the Pooka were improved not one whit by the appearance in the village of an old 1949 issue of the American edition of *Fortnight,* an edition devoted largely to an appalling delineation of Erin's poverty, its ignorance, common infanticide of bastards, squalid slums, its powerful, narrow and backward priesthood, slovenly and filthy children and its shabby educational system. It depicted the land of colleen and the shamrock as gripped with general despondency, yet still enduring somehow under a swollen, misguided leadership that evaluates human life as second to the knowledge of the Gaelic language, that is forced on the tongue. The generally unflattering article all but took a census of the lice in the heads of Irish school children, yet it was illustrated with expensive color photographs of the gorgeous castles of peers, neat cottages of the peasantry and happy, well-dressed Irish girls kissing the Blarney Stone. There were busy photographs of a prosperous-looking Dublin; tugboats on the River Liffey chugging out the stout of Guinness toward the throats of thirsty men; the golden Irish Book of Kells, illuminated by ancient monks and as delicate as the wings of faeries and as enduring as eternity, such evanescence and strength it also has, and the most exquisite volume in the history of art and letters. It has been called the most beautiful book in the world.

Then there were shown Abbey Players, Ireland's great Horse Show at Phoenix Park and pictures of the Hunt and the finest thoroughbreds on earth, and others reflecting Ireland's culture. But the damning text also was there.

It left a feeling of melancholy for, at last, free Ireland, as in Scott's words from *Lady of the Lake*:

> Lord of a barren heritage,
> Which his brave sires, from age to age,
> By their good swords had held with toil.

The loud outburst that had startled and hushed the barmaids came from a group of the O'Boys who were cursing the offensive pages and pounding their fists on O'K.'s bar in a display of anger that made the walls shake.

"Now how far can th' Americans go?" cried O'D. apoplectically. His skewer head was swollen with angry blood. "There is no raison on airth for it, it gives a bad impression abroad, and 'tis th' divil's own libel, too!"

O'C. was turning the pages slowly.

"Sure," he said, "but th' pictures are pretty."

"Th' pictures, now!" exploded O'D. "Ye can't tell a book by its cover. Read it, if ye can read, man. Th' stinkin' American tongue!"

"Aye," said O'C., "but 'twas written, it says, by an Irishman. O'Houlihan!"

"O'Houlihan, yes. A Cork man!"

Poor O'D.'s head shrank back to its accustomed size, and his face paled.

"Oh," he whispered, "it must be a scurrilous trick, I'll go bail it 'tis a trick." He wiped his face in a despairing gesture, but brightened momentarily with a face-saving thought. "Still," he said, " 'tis American. It was printed there, and dirty stuff and rank and horrendous it 'tis."

"Why not," agreed O'C., " 'tis all o' that, but th' pictures are pretty."

Somewhat foolishly, O'D. repeated over and over the author's name. "O'Houlihan, O'Houlihan, O'Houlihan," he muttered. "A lefthander, now, I'll bet a bob!"

O'C. thumbed on through the pages.

"Come, man," he said, "there ye go again gettin' feverish over fewtrils."

O'D.'s consternation was not at all surprising for, indeed, it is quite a rarity to read an article by an Irishman criticizing Ireland. This pastime usually has been reserved for foreigners. The monopoly first was noted some centuries ago by the Rev. Geoffrey Keating in his *History of Ireland*. How well he excoriated this alien practice of demeaning Ireland with literary assaults would have warmed O'D.'s heart:

For there is no historian of all those who have written on Ireland from that epoch that has not continuously sought to cast reproach and blame both on the old foreign settlers and on the native Irish.

Whereof the testimony given Cambrensis, Spenser, Stainhurst, Hammer, Camden, Barckly, Moryson, Campion, and every other new foreigner who has written on Ireland from that time, may bear witness; inasmuch as it is almost according to the fashion of the beetle, when it lifts its head in the summertime, to go about fluttering, and not to stoop towards any delicate flower that may be in the field, or any blossom in the garden, though they be all roses or lilies, but it keeps bursting about until it meets with the dung of horse or cow, and proceeds to roll itself therein.

But Spenser, who like Shakespeare disliked the Irish (Shakespeare's mother was an Irishwoman), did have the grace once to admit that their bardic poetry was "of sweet wit and good intention." Thackeray had no good word. In his *Irish Sketch Book* in 1843 he called Ireland a "land of the aliens."

The *Encyclopaedia Britannica* does not agree with Spenser. It points to "serious defects in Irish literary products, lack of any sense of proportion, which naturally goes hand in hand with the love of the grotesque. We are constantly struck by the lack of sustained effort which prevented the *filid* from producing great epics of verse."

As to the style of more modern Irish writers, the editors point to "the inflated style to which the Irishman is so prone." It is "seen at its worst in the 16th century *Battle of Ventry* and we are treated to a nauseous heaping of epithet upon epithet, e.g., we sometimes find as many as twenty-seven adjectives accompanying a substantive running in alliterative forms of three," says the august *Encyclopaedia Britannica*.

Can this possibly be what is meant, these combat scenes from *The Battle of Ventry?*

> ... and the fierce heroes attacked each other in their firm-sided, rough-skinned, broad-footed, strong-tailed ... that were stout below, and let flash the great grey blunt eyes with their shaggy eyebrows, and they gnashed the grey-branched, strong-boned, chewing, wide-jawed, board-like teeth, and they turned up the broad-caved, thin-branched, crooked noses and those two warriors attacked each other, and closed the black and strong, never-sprained, firm-clenching, indissoluble hands across their backs, and gave each other mighty-unequal twists. Or:
> ... they fought a combat sharp, bloody, masterly, evenly matched, valiant, courageous, powerful, proud, murderous, dashing, red-sided, sudden-wounding, wonderful, unheard-of, howling, quick, groanful, red-handed, brave, quick-wounding, eager, close, mad, furious, wound-giving, red-speared, courageous was the battle of the two.
> And then the two battle-soldiers bared their blue-jointed, iron-smooth, gold-ornamented swords and attacked each other vehemently, fiercely, closely, madly and with great blows, with slow feet, actively, strongly, and powerfully, hardily, fiercely and vehemently, and the kings fought a wonderful combat.

When this was shown to a Blarney resident not so long ago, he studied the text with a wrinkled brow. Finally he produced a pencil and paper, engaging himself busily.

"Yirra!" he exclaimed triumphantly. "There they go short-changing the Irish again! There are only 68 adjectives and adverbs in these passages, not 27! Some of the *Encyclopaedia Britannica's* editors quite obviously cannot count. But begob, what could a sowl expect of a book with a name like that?"

Even the foreigner, St. Patrick, was not guiltless.

In his *Epistle to Coroticus,* declaring himself "a sinner and unlearned," he said that "for the love of God I dwell a pilgrim and an exile among a *barbarous* people."

The Irish monks in their *Book of Lismore* go the origin of the Patron Saint's exile and his unhappiness:

> The learned declare that he was of the Jews by origin, since it is manifest from the miracles which God wrought for him, that he was of the Children of Israel, for of them were the Jews besides. For when the vengeance was inflicted by Titus and Vespasian, the Jews scattered throughout the world, and Patrick's original kindred came to Britain, and there a heritage was gotten by them, for in a certain book of his epistles Patrick himself declared that *Nos dispersi sumus per multas regiones terrarum propter peccata nostra, eo quod Domini praecepta et mandata eius non custodivimus.* Wherefore from that dispersion his original kindred came to Britain.

This probably refers to the passage of St. Patrick's *Confessio* in which he said, ". . . and the Lord brought us the anger of His fury and scattered us among many nations, even to the uttermost parts of the earth, where now my littleness is seen, amongst a foreign people."

It was an Irish king named McCarty, of the family of Blarney Castle fame, who precipitated the invasion of Ireland by criticizing the conditions in his country to Henry II. His reports of Ireland's evil ways . . . and riches! . . . were whispered into the monarch's ear after he had fled to England to beg support after raping the wife of Roderick O'Connor and forfeiting his estates into the bargain.

Henry listened diligently, for he needed Ireland, to command her ports and sail the traffic of his conquered seas at will, the Irish Sea, and his far-flung ports of conquest on the Loire of Biscay and the Garonne of the Pyrenees. Ireland was a seaquest, a rounding out of network of harbors in a voyage of sea-pire, from the Forth to the Shannon and the Seine.

Now the crafty Henry II and his agent Salisbury, with greed of empire long before this visit, had looked to Rome for apostolic sanction for the invasion of Ireland, with religious excuses, because no other legitimate reason was at hand. The Irish were neighbors who lived closely on their own island, never giving offense to other races. The necessity of a pretense for a black purpose was answered by the sympathetic Englishman, Pope Adrian IV, who essayed for the convenience of the king of his homeland the role of master of all the known world, and sped him on his way to garner with the sword the hostile souls of Ireland and to put down by any means he might deem necessary the "rampant vice of improperly converted Catholics."

And herein there is a word to be said in behalf of the English: when they invaded Ireland as Catholics they enjoyed a sense of almost divine right to murder Irishmen, for they were empowered to accomplish their mission as conquerors by none other than the former Nicholas Breakspear, once a barefoot beggar boy who, like his father Robert, solicited alms near the English Abbey of St. Albans.

Now in the year 1155, after a stunning and fairly miraculous ascent, occupant of the chair of St. Peter, he was the first and only Englishman to become pope. History describes him as "haughty and aspiring," his reign "rilled with bitterness and anxiety and foes encompassing him on all sides."

Adrian declared at the time, "The Lord has kept me continually between the hammer and the anvil."

Historians of the day pointed to Adrian's "dreary isolation" and the "solitariness of his supreme position . . . which he felt, as an Englishman among Italians."

Indeed, it appears that the English pope at times was despondent and sorely homesick. Now came King Henry II of England to visit him and pay homage and to send deputations

of Norman Bishops of the old Abbey of St. Albans, where once
he begged bread outside its walls. The Bishop of the Abbey
barred young Nicholas as a novitiate, describing him as altogether "dull and indolent." Long since, his father had deserted
him to become a lay brother and later a monk. But now the
Bishops brought rich gifts, of which Adrian refused all except
three miters and a pair of sandals. The greatest gifts were the
cheering visits of his countrymen, one of whom, John Salisbury,
came from the court of Henry II telling of the deplorable condition of church and state in Hibernia, of its population of rake-
hells, of its barbarity, lawlessness, depravity, of its sins and its
shames in the eyes of the Holy See, and indeed that all of the
flesh of Ireland had corrupted the way of the Lord. Fifty years
before Salisbury's visit, critics in England and Rome had written
in horror of conditions there. One said later that in the year
1105, "all Ireland was a trembling sod." The pope's sovereignty
over the island was in a state of disorder, and morality allegedly
was nonexistent.

The lonesome English pope lent a sympathetic ear to the reports of his old countryman and friend, Salisbury, and before
this agent of Henry II left Rome the Holy Father had issued his
notorious *Bull Laudabiliter* donating all of Ireland to the British
monarch.

Although controversy has raged around the authenticity of
Adrian's famous or infamous *Bull,* depending on the point of
view, its genuineness has never been disproved, even the official
Catholic Encyclopaedia accepting it as fact removed from doubt.

Authorizing Henry II to invade Hibernia with necessary force
and annex that island to his crown, the monetary consideration
was the collection of Peter's pence, a tax of one penny for the
papal see from every household in Ireland.

As to spiritual considerations, Adrian's *Bull Laudabiliter*
pointed out to his countryman, King Henry:

Your highness' desire of extending the glory of your name on earth, and of obtaining the reward of eternal happiness in heaven, is laudable and beneficial; in as much as your intent is, as a Catholic Prince, to enlarge the limits of the church; to declare the truth of the Christian faith to untaught and rude nations, and to eradicate vice from the field of the Lord.

Salisbury in his *Metalozicus* explains Adrian's legal right to give Ireland to an English king:

At my request he granted to the illustrious King of the English, Ireland, to be held by hereditary right, as his letter testifies to this day. For all the islands by ancient right are said to belong to the Roman Church by virtue of the donation of Constantine, who founded and endowed it.

The principle of Adrian's outright gift of Ireland to the English was confirmed four years later, in 1159, by Pope Alexander III, and again twelve years after Adrian's death in 1171, when at last Henry II actually invaded Ireland and ran into violent difficulties with resisting Celtic kings. The Holy See promptly affirmed the rights of Henry II as the sovereign lord of the startled and coveted country. The clergy of Ireland also confirmed the kingdom to him and he was crowned king at Waterford in the presence of 400 of his knights and 5,000 men in arms he had brought with him. This ended the 2,500-year-old reign of the ancient Irish (Milesians) which began just nine years before Daniel was thrown into the lions' den.

Eighty-eight years after publication of the *Bull Laudabiliter,* the Irish Parliament enacted a law acknowledging Adrian's donation and decreeing excommunication for any Irishman resisting it:

As our Holy Father Adrian, pope of Rome, was possessed of all sovereignty of Ireland in his demesne as of fee in the right of his Church of Rome and with the intent that vice should be subdued had alienated said land to England, by which grant the said subjects of Ireland owe their allegiance to the King of England as their sovereign lord, all archbishops and bishops shall excommunicate all disobedient Irish subjects, and if they neglect to do so shall forfeit 100 pounds.

The Irish Parliament, at Trim, also made it law that no Irishman should grow hair on his upper lip. This legislation was not inspired because the moustache was a carrier of germs, which in those days were unknown, anyway. The Irish legislators were concerned only with the fact that moustaches made Irishmen resemble the English.

Some church apologists for Adrian's *Bull* have asserted that the pope believed that the "leaven of Norman culture might prove as beneficial in Ireland as it had in other countries," but whether the English came as Catholics or as Protestants, the Irish found their culture repugnant, their presence repulsive, their rule bloody. Fingering their decades of rosary beads and saying *Hail Marys,* they first arrived as Catholic enemies to garner rowdy souls and remained as Protestant enemies when they repudiated the Vatican which had in the first place given them the Holy Spoils of Hibernia, bent on sending the same rowdy souls that first they had come to save, now to hell.

It was not so long ago, as time goes in Ireland, that another man proposed a solution to the Irish problem. He was Jonathan Swift, who wrote during that part of the 18th century when Ireland possibly suffered more than in any of the other seven centuries of English overlordship.

If it is true that today, as the Cork Irish writer says, the living standard of the republic is so low that bread, tea and potatoes constitute the basic diet of the poor and that an oc-

casional egg and a sausage are luxuries, Swift doubted that anyone could even find human feces on the dirty cobbles of Dublin
during his lifetime, because the people had nothing to eat at all.
He proposed to channel whatever food there might be available
in the island to the stomachs of pink and rosy little Irish babies
so that they might be specially fattened for roasting or stewing
purposes and shipped over to spill their gravy on English boards.
Swift made it clear that the English had already devoured their
parents. Apparently, the grandparents were too tough to eat and
were too old to cause much trouble, anyway.

The scholarly Dean of St. Patrick's clearly proposed a solution of simplicity—cannibalism.

The menus of England would advertise roast young suckling
Irish infant with pippin in mouth, a tender and succulent *pièce
de résistance* on already human-greasy dining tables across the
Channel. Now wasn't this a dainty dish to set before the king!
It would have eliminated all of the troubles in no time at all.
Just as a tree falls in the forest and makes no noise when there
is no one around to hear it fall, so too can no troubles exist
when there is no one around to cause them.

O'C. was still looking at the pretty pictures in *Fortnight* magazine when a conspicuous American tourist stomped toward the
bar.

O'D. stopped muttering and temporarily suspended his glass
of stout just under his throbbing nose in mid-air to regard the
newcomer with some malignance.

He was just at the point of making further serious charges
against all of the forty-eight states in general, and prepared he
was with new and vital evidence.

A flying saucer had just landed in the Mountains of Kerry,
causing great excitement. Some witnesses said it shone like silver,
making a dull, booming noise; others that it resembled a black
mist and moved quite silently. A few compared it to a double-
decker bus without wings. The shape and character of the latter

could have but one meaning to the suspicious O'D. The "bus" of a secret weapon had been flown in to fly the Blarney Stone out. As everyone well knows, all flying saucers originate in America.

Even the bank strike in Ireland that dried up the circulation of currency gave rise to the incredible statement that Blarney Stone conspirators, with trunkloads of cash at their disposal, had created the drought in order to further tempt the ould man on the hill. The Blarney Castle steward drove about the roads of Cork with a tractorload of trees in lieu of a purse, and bartering farmers, for a day's shopping, drove herds of cows to the city. Patrick Street was roamed by lowing cattle, hissing geese, grunting pigs, gobbling turkeys, quacking ducks, cackling hens and baaing sheep. Noisier currency no one could imagine.

But O'D. was forced to defer his splendid elucidation of this damning condition for a later date because of the appearance of the alien.

"Bet a bob he wants to telephone New York across th' ocean," O'D. grunted sourly. "Tellin' how fast they can ring up, how fast they do things over there. How well *we* do it. Such does not go over, over here."

"Aye," agreed O'K., "in a moment himself'll be sayin' to Irishmen who've niver been on a train that he flew over here on an aeroplane twenty thousand feet in th' air goin' three hundred miles an hour!"

"Faith, and pray, what was there to shtop him up there?" demanded O'D.

The Yankee had not missed the remark.

"Not even Paddy's pigs have wings to block the way, up there," he said.

The new arrival had unmistakable United States briskness in his feet and privilege in his manner. Even the fashionable London suit of clothes he had picked up in Bond Street could not disguise his origin. An American abroad will look like an

American in turban, fez or feather, or arrayed like a sultan in a seraglio. Nay, even the way he rides a camel past the Sphinx is different. Distinguishable is the American by his origin, be he vestured as a Bedouin, be he gawking on the Ganges, sailing in a dahabeah on the Nile, jouncing in a rickshaw, lumbering in a howdah, fainaiguing in a fiacre or Fiat, or flouncing in a filibeg, he is stamped, he is registered, he is copyrighted by his maker, U.S.A. There is no mistaking this phenomenon of identity. Even in the way he kisses the Blarney Stone. His buss, when the blood rushes to his head as he leans back dizzily on the parapet of the castle, most likely will be accompanied by a curdling "Oh, boy!" He is a man apart.

"Begob," shouted O'O. trenchantly, "a John Bull Yankee!"

"Hist," whispered O'D. to O'K., "himself looks th' sorrt who'd be afther gettin' th' stone! Th' sartain thievin' look about th' eyes altogither."

"Whisht! Wait! That we'll see when himself's good and dhrunk. 'Tis possible that God-sent ice will loose th' Yankee's tongue."

Chapter Twenty-One

Yankee Doodle Don't

It is almost impossible for Irishmen to dislike Americans. America is Ireland's second home. Few are the Irish who do not have relatives in the United States who have maintained and preserved the best of their ancient traditions of royalty in the New World. The Irish there dominate as Princes of the Church. They are kings of the labor unions, the police, sanitation, fire departments and barrooms, and more important—as the political rulers of the nation's voting machines, the Irish are kings of the government. They have always been kings so they are quite at home in this role, and very successful at the job they are too. And coming from a land of castles and kings, the Irish in America quite in keeping possess more "castles" in one state alone than dot the green hills in the moody distances of their native land.

His conspicuous success abroad possibly has been partly responsible for the oft-repeated assertions of one school of Englishmen residing in Ireland that "an Irishman never amounts to anything until he leaves Ireland."

"John Bull American!"

From the Irish point of view nothing could have been more damning than this gratuitous lumping in O'K.'s pub of Uncle Sam and John Bull in one and the same breath, producing a centaurlike creature, as it were, a gray-whiskered monstrosity wearing a red, white and blue top hat and possessing the body of a superannuated male animal with a big Union Jack waving

on the folds of a beef-and-kidney stomach. The very insolence
the author of this genius gave his words made it quite clear to
everyone that in no wise had he intended to imply that the
monstrosity in mind was akin either to the noble king of the
beasts or to the proud, feathered monarch of the skies. No, it
was not the griffin that O'D., the garrulous tweed carder, con-
jured up with his words. O'D., who possessed a great body
topped by an inordinately small head sparsely crowned with
carotene furze, stood grinning patiently at the object of his
sarcasm. The American stopped and studied the glowing tippler
in amusement.

"My, my," he said. "Oh, brother, what a character!"

Our friend from across the Western Ocean was treading on
dangerous ground. He was not the first to meet and joust—and
lose—with the only being in the world, except a wife, who always has the last word. Quite naturally, this rare creature is an
Irishman, but also a special brand of Irishman he is too, with
whom even Irishmen hesitate to tangle.

For of all the eloquent Irishmen of Ireland the residents of
Cork are most renowned for their gifted tongues. Living in the
shadow of a wonderful little slab that makes pygmies out of
monoliths, well they might be, too, and no one from the "outside" who has ever encountered the experience of a verbal set-to
with a Corkagian has come off anything but second-best. His
adversary has ever retreated in confusion, has stuttered in in-
coherency, has floundered in his incapacity to retort. He has
failed in repartee, has bogged down with weak response and his
notions have found no voice to utter. He becomes as an ould
woman talking to her cat.

The origin of this Corkagian talent obviously derives from
that main source that seems to say, "Come, all ye of timid
tongue, come to the groves of Blarney, kiss me—ye who would
have the golden eloquence of the gods!"

The American walked brightly over to the bar and ordered bourbon.

O'K. eyed him suspiciously and the natives shuffled their feet.

"Bourbon? Yer in Ireland now," he said, "and that whisky takes th' blackmail dollars o' which there's a lamentable international shrinkage altogither."

"As if I didn't know," laughed the Yankee.

"Paddy's?" suggested O'K. " 'Tis foine indeed, and made right here in Cork, and foine it 'tis as a Cork chimney."

"Chimney? I don't get it."

"In Cork we do things well. Ye must know how a Cork man builds a chimney?"

"Can't say as I do."

"Well, ye must know how smoke can back up in a cottage from a turf fire?"

"We use oil."

"Anyway," continued the patient O'K., "when a Cork chimney builder's asked if th' chimney he would build would draw smoke, he says, 'Well, if I don't make it so it 'twill draw smoke, it 'twill draw talk.' "

The Yankee bit his lip and made no comment.

"So try some good Cork Paddy's?" invited O'K.

"Nope, guess not."

"Maybe ye'd try Jameson's, then. Almost as good, snob-British as Dublin is, keepin' those royal spit and polish traditions alive. Jameson's comes from a Dublin distillery, ye know, but it won't kill an American, I guess."

"No," the American said maliciously, "whenever I do drink Irish whisky, I order Bushmill's."

"That's Protestant whisky! Belfast ditch water!" blurted O'K. angrily. "Faith, and I wouldn't have a drop in me pub!"

O'D. made a face.

"Bejabers!" he exclaimed. "Protestant shellac!"

"Och whisht! Now, man," said O'K., winking, "don't get

ye'self stairted off on religion again. And mind yer manners. This gentleman's a guest o' Ireland for only a fortnight, maybe."

"Don't mention *fortnight* to me!" snapped O'D. " 'Tis an obnixious and pee-yewseelanimous worrd in Eire! Slurrin' a good half o' Ireland's unfortunate colleens!"

"He intimated but a *few*," said a severe O'K.

"Nothin' *few* is implied," retorted O'D. "Sayin' they'd rather go to hell than have their neighbors know."

"But now maybe," said the American, ignoring the generally bad-humored atmosphere, "I might take a swig of that Johnnie Walker there on the shelf. I might belt that shebullie, maybe— that good old Irish-Catholic Scotch of yours that I see you're stocking."

"Foo!" sputtered O'K. "Yer th' cliver one, but ye didn't catch me on *that!* It *'tis* Scotch, I'll admit, but 'twas made in Scotland. That makes th' difference."

"I don't see how."

"Scotland is Celtic," said O'D., "and so are th' Irish. Only Scotland is still under th' British heel."

The American scratched his head.

"Oh," he said weakly.

" 'Tis that which makes th' difference," said O'K. " 'Twas made in Scotland, altogither."

Somewhat proud of himself, O'K. tapped his fingers on the bar.

"I do not run me pub like a church. We drink here. Would ye be havin' some Scotland whisky, then?"

"Naw, it tastes like Sneaky Pete to me, and after all, bourbon's my drink."

" 'Tis a foine big thurrst, then, that ye'll be workin' up in Ireland," said O'K. sarcastically.

The American laughed in good humor, but O'D. bristled.

"Ha!" he asked suddenly. "And where would ye be goin' this threatenin' night, Yankee Doodle?"

The American looked over at O'D., frowning and grinning at the same time, but said nothing.

"We've had dry weather for a month," O'D. went on, "but looks like they're goin' to give us somethin' else. Ye might be gettin' yer foine duds wet."

"Doesn't matter."

"If ye go far now, say as far as th' 'pebble,' they would be soaked, if ye ask me. Where was it now ye said ye planned to go?"

"Didn't say, but if you must know I'm going to look for a leprechaun, one with a green hat small enough to fit your head."

O'D. rubbed at his scalp ludicrously and took a menacing step, but O'K. restrained him with a word. The innkeeper was laughing in spite of himself, like all the rest. O'D. was stammering foolishly. "But, O'K., be . . . begob now . . ."

"Th' man intended no harm, O'D. Just coddin' he was. But say, guv'ner," he said craftily, turning to his amused patron, "I see ye believe th' 'Little People' *are* to be found in Blairney."

"Sure, just as sure as Catholics grow in Ireland."

O'D. choked on a throatful of stout and sputtered through sudsy lips.

"See! See! I as much as told ye! Listen to th' man! Divil I heard th' like!"

"Hold th' tongue in yer head a minute now, O'D. We see th' Yank's an expairt on th' subject o' faeries."

"But not on Catholics," protested O'D., "comparin' thim with *weeds!*"

"Tosh, O'D., ye've become too sensitive on sairtin subjects. He gave no deeleeberate offense."

"Offense?" demanded the American. "Holy Moses!"

"Cursin' too," grumbled O'D.

O'K. and the other O'Boys laughed tolerantly.

"Ye *are* a bit unraisonable," said O'K. "Moses was no saint, O'D."

"Maybe not, but let no man call me unraisonable! The proof is in th' ballot Ireland cast for the furrst President of Eire, and a blissed Presbyterian at that!"

" 'Twasn't yer vote and 'twas th' Cabinet's unfortunate but ginerous way o' fightin' narrow Protestant bigotry, and nobody was runnin' aginst Douglas Hyde, anyway! But, as I was sayin', as man or boy, by night or by day, niver did I lay me two eyes on a leprechaun, and niver did I go out o' me way o' meetin' one, for 'tis not afeard o' one I'd be.

"But there was queer old Leahy, th' farm hand now, and he th' only one in Blairney who claims iver he did see th' crayture. 'Twas at th' Castle's swine sty he saw it, but a queer old divil Leahy is, too.

"Leprechaun-looking himself, he is, and we wondered if it was not his very own twin he saw that night he sat up with th' ould man's sick pig. And a foine and beautiful prize boar he was, and th' grunts o' death rattlin' his tusks.

"Ould Leahy nursed that dyin' boar 'til he exhausted himself to a noddin' state. Towards mornin' he heard a turrible groan.

" 'Yirra!' Leahy cried. 'Th' ould man's boar is gone!'

"He made to get up with a jump, he did, but what he saw made him jump th' more. There sittin' astride th' dyin' boar's shoulders was a little green man no bigger than a shoe. He was rubbin' th' swine's nose and yellin' like a banshee.

"In a second th' boar gave a great and mighty powerful grunt, and sprang to quick live life faster than iver ye see that swine run for a ripe sow. They galloped off togither. Th' little man left one o' his faery shoes, and shure and begor I know who has it. There's not a worrd o' a lie in it."

"Whist, O'K., ye make a goose run over me grave," said O'D., shivering.

"Yer impolite interruption is somewhat in order, for speakin' o' graves now," said O'K., with a sly glance at the American, "a lot o' people go to their graves prematurely because o' goose-flesh. Those geese, I mean, who meddle with such things as *pebbles*."

"And a lot more'll be movin', too, if th' *pebble's* not let alone!" O'D. shouted with heated point.

The American took a step backward as O'D. eyed him.

"Th' *pebble*," O'D. repeated. "Th' PEBBLE. Iver hear o' that worrd? Th' *pebble*?"

The O'Boys squinted their eyes in interest over O'D.'s clever trap, but it failed to snap. The Yankee bit his lips but did not faint, as O'D. had hoped. O'K. moved in again.

"Th' guv'ner doesn't answer ye, O'D. 'Tis possible, ye know, himself's niver hearrd o' th' pebble."

"You were talking about a leprechaun," suggested the Yankee nervously.

"So I was," said O'K., somewhat disappointedly. "There we left him a-sittin' on th' boar's back. But still th' *pebble* can be more dangerous than ridin' th' backs o' lions o' boars. When 'tis approached th' right way, th' ould Stone will do no harm, but th' goose that tries to fly away with it ends up in a stew. A goose stew, guv'ner."

The American was frowning thoughtfully.

"Aye," continued O'K. cunningly, "th' ould block likes his home where it 'tis. Th' Blairney Stone's traveled enough already. Some geese who've tried to peck off a little parrt o' it did not sharpen their beaks—they lost their very wings. Lucky, too, is such a goose that dies and does not linger on in turrible and everlastin' mortal and heinous punishment on this earrth. I' spite o' th' heinousness o' th' crime, sin and offense against God and man he's still much better off stone dead!"

"Dead? But, how . . . how . . . ?"

"Yes, dead. There was th' thievin' Yankee sailor lad who tried to steal a single splinter o' th' Blairney Stone. Th' unfortunate crayture fell from th' castle walls in a horrible mess o' human flesh, but 'twas to heaven he went, anyway."

"Heaven?"

"Aye, ould Twomey, th' gardener, saw him fall and hearrd th' turrible splash like a poppin' bladder. He dropped his spade and hobbled over to his side. When he tried to raise that mangled body, th' sailor's neck lolled like a hat feather over his shoulder.

" 'Och, now,' cried out ould Twomey, 'he a dead one for sure and all, neck and body clean atwain.'

"Ould Twomey bowed his reverent head and made th' sign o' th' true cross.

"Then it 'twas th' turrible sickened and horrified tourists and workers came a-runnin'. Ould Twomey was standin' there with a gintle smile on his face.

" 'Standin' there grinnin',' someone rasped like a file. 'Why don't ye do somethin'?'

" ' 'Tis done,' ould Twomey said, as calm as an angel.

" 'Then call a priest if he's dead! No one knows when th' soul leaves th' body!'

" 'No matter when this lad's soul leaves *his* body, 'twill wind up all right when it gets to where 'tis goin',' said ould Twomey. 'If it 'tis furrst to hell it goes, he'll be talkin' his way out o' there, and if it 'tis at heaven he applies, there's no chance St. Peter'll be havin' th' minute he opens his mouth! He kissed th' Blairney Stone before he fell, th' lucky thief!'

"Ould Twomey walked serenely back to his spade and went to diggin' again on his flowers as though nothin' had happened altogither."

The Yankee was flexing his fingers nervously.

"But that leprechaun, what happened to him and the pig?"

"Ah, yes, th' leprechaun." O'K. rubbed his chin whiskers reflectively.

Such cliver strategy that O'K. deployed. Such a foine gineral he was! The admiration of the O'Boys glowed as red as Irish whiskers.

"Maybe yer real purpose, now," he said carefully, "is to

capture a leprechaun and take th' poor crayture prisoner back to America in a matchbox."

"Nope. We have mostly book matches in God's country. You can bet your sweet bottom dollar we'd never think of mashing a leprechaun."

O'K. was crestfallen, but he came again.

" 'Tis said there's tribes o' leprechauns in th' Derrymasaggart Mountains and in Macguillycuddy's Reeks.

"Th' Derrymasaggart Mountains make th' leprechauns happy, too, they say. Since th' craytures like to feel small, why not? Those mountains are two thousand feet high."

"What a wonderful time they'd have in Denver. Why, their egos would soar. Our Denver mountains are a mile high. They'd feel like ants."

"How high do leprechauns grow in Denver, guv'ner?"

The Yankee snapped his teeth together.

"You . . . you . . . say . . ."

"Niver mind, guv'ner. We have some healthy ones in Ireland. Very healthy they are, on th' shores of Lake Leand. Th' waters are foine for th' faeries' bladders."

"Didn't think faeries had to go."

"Heh, heh, such Yankee coddin'. But faith, guv'ner, that's what makes th' dew o' Erin."

"In your hat! It's green!"

"Heh, heh," laughed the victorious O'K. "In th' leprechauns' hats! They are green, too. And it takes a lot o' hats at a dewdrop per hat to sprinkle th' dew over all o' Ireland."

The American felt a trifle foolish.

"What a way to water mushrooms!" he managed.

" 'Tis what makes green cheese," laughed O'K. "It 'tis what makes th' grass grow."

"And what makes the moon go 'round, too, I suppose you'll say next," snapped the American in somewhat poor grace.

"Th' moon is th' sun o' th' leprechaun, guv'ner, and green, too, so 'tis to th' man in th' moon ye'll have to go to find out."

"I'll bet that character's an Irishman, too!"

"Now, just how do ye mean that?" cried O'D. abruptly.

"Cheese it!" grinned the Yankee. "Come on, what happened to that leprechaun on the pig's neck?"

"Oh, him?" said O'K. "Himself's fingers were nimble as a girl's on th' dyin' boar's nose, and he was singin' to th' animal like a reed whines in a bog. Th' boar stopped his groanin', and with great and marvelous relief he turned over on his side in a deep sleep, snorin' in peace, and awoke completely recovered. And a most wonderful engagement he had indeed with th' brood sow.

"Now, guv'ner, bein' as yer an expairt on such things, would ye put a bit o' stock in ould Leahy's tale?"

"Why sure," said the Yankee promptly, and with some relief, "matter of fact, I've seen a leprechaun myself."

"Ah, now, listen! But just one?"

"Yes, just one."

"Most Americans now," said O'K. slyly, "claim they see more than one, being what ye might say, Americans."

"Big eyes we have," laughed the Yankee.

"Why not," agreed O'K., because an Irishman never says "yes" or "no," but "why not?" or "fair enough." "But one American woman who came here ran into me pub with her two eyes big as umbrellers opened for a rain. 'Twas *seven* she said she saw."

"Seven leprechauns?"

"And at th' same time, too, mind ye, and that day I niver will be forgettin'. Down she gobbled four straight gins before she could get her words to rollin' out. Belonged to a secret American Protestant sect, th' Mairthadist, she admitted, and shamelessly said she taught school on Sunday."

"Ha, ha," laughed the American, "now that *is* funny!"

"Indeed, and it 'tis," grinned O'K., "but th' funny part is she didn't see *any* leprechauns at all."

"D.T.'s, I guess."

"Now there's where yer downright wrong, man. She saw th' Little People, all right, crawlin' on their hands and knees straight up th' steps o' Blairney Castle, seven o' thim with short little arms and short little legs, like babies they were, one followin' th' other right up th' high stone staircases, slippin' and trippin' and fallin', squirmin' all over th' ould stones, all currsin' to beat th' very divil in German.

" 'My God!' yelled th' American Lady, fairly fallin' out o' her many foine American lace petticoats. She must have been bad ascared for her hair had turned purple before she panted into me pub, her skirts, outer and under, ripped and tore."

"Bejabers, now, and which road would it be she had taken?" asked O'O. "Th' Bog Road?"

"Th' bog herself took altogither! She made her own new road, leppin' as she did over hedgerows and through the brambles like a purple-headed deer. Th' poor swine, sad craytures, will lose thimselves on that strange, dangerous and unfamiliar road.

"Ah, a fright she was. Faith, and if 'twasn't for th' shtring that be holdin' herself togither, th' feathers o' cherubs, she'd be needin' to hide her nekkid skin, that bad her dress was bursht and ripped. When she remembered her remarkable flight she screamed again, 'Oh, my God! Ugh! I might have been bitten by snakes!'

" 'Modom,' I told her, 'ye're in Ireland!' "

"You told me that once, too," reminded the American.

"Aye, and that I did for sure, but faith and for different reasons. Can ye imagine a schoolteacher niver hearin' about St. Patrick! I tried to tell her, but she had swooned away as into eternity itself. After all that gin, too!"

"Maybe that did it. But you said the leprechauns were cursing in German? I thought leprechauns spoke Gaelic."

"Not these, guv'ner, these were German midgets. Th' cirrcus was in Cork that day."

"Heh, heh," laughed O'D. "Heh, heh, now."

"Now I'll be damned," said the American somewhat foolishly.

"What about *your* leprechaun?" O'K. insisted.

"Funny thing, the one I saw couldn't speak Gaelic either. Polite chap, too. Introduced himself as Chauncey, as I recall, and wore a monocle that was always falling off. 'Pick it up,' he said one day to me. 'Pick it up yourself,' I said. 'You're closer to the ground than I am.' "

"Och whisht!" exploded O'D. again. "A British leprechaun!"

O'K. had been caught in his own trap, but he motioned for silence and though somewhat ruffled, tried again.

"Ye should have caught th' little crayture," O'K. said. "If ye hold a leprechaun and look him straight in th' eye, he'll give ye a crock o' gould."

"But I did catch Chauncey," the American said. "Only he had kissed the Blarney Stone. Sure talked himself out of a tight place. But I might catch him again. I need some more of those blackmail dollars."

The O'Boys now were shuffling uncomfortably, but O'K. would not retreat. O'D. started to blaze again, but O'K. again lifted a restraining finger.

"Wait," he said.

"Wait?" grumbled O'D. "Weight broke down th' turf cart!"

The O'Boys laughed nervously, and O'K. doggedly pursued his man.

" 'Twill be a wet night, I fear, for you to look for Chauncey."

"If it rains the faeries will get wet, too."

"Yourself's dry wit could not be otherwise, seein' as what ye've ordered, but they say faeries shed water. Rain sticks on mortals and their British clothes. Now I have me Guinness ruined with ice for Americans such as you, so why not stay here dry—on th' outside, anyway—under me roof, and drink spoiled stout. Chauncey won't be drownin'.'"

"No, mine host," replied the American stubbornly, "only bourbon could keep me here within this night, and you don't have that."

"Ah, true," admitted O'K., "nor yer humpbacked cigarettes, either, and none in th' length and breadth o' Ireland. 'Tis th' shortage of ye own dollars, man! But we've Irish brew aplenty and cold it 'tis with ice trucked on me own froze shoulders out from Cork."

The Yankee shook his head.

"Well, since ye won't drink me Guinness now," O'K. said resignedly, "all that glorious, imported, unnecessary ice will go to hell . . . I mean, er . . . purgatory."

The American grinned unsympathetically.

"Now to what better place could it go?" he asked. "There's good use for ice in purgatory! It must be warm there anyway, since I understand it's close to hell."

"Foo!" rejoined the host. "Irish sinners would never touch th' stuff!"

"Well, well, now whadda you know!" exclaimed the American triumphantly. "Then you mean to say that only the Irish go to hell . . . I mean . . . er . . . purgatory!"

"Foo and tosh!" exploded O'K. "Not that we'll get stairted off on th' dangerous subject o' religion, but it's not that th' Irish do not *go* to purgatory, and Irishmen not likin' ice has little to do with th' question. It's simply that once in purgatory th' Irish don't *stay* there long enough to work up a good, healthy thurrst. When they go to heaven, they leave th' ice behind for you Americans such as has a lease on th' place!"

"Wow!" exclaimed the Yankee. He opened his mouth, trying to say something else, but the bedlam of O'Boy cheering and the slapping of O'Boy backs was such that any worthy rejoinder he might doubtfully have thought of, would have been lost.

Frankly, he considered himself vanquished by the superior firing powder of a nimble-witted Gaelic tongue, and he fled through the door with a feeble American "Aw nuts!" He had dazedly intended saying something like "The devil wouldn't have you," but when the cool air and the first drops of drought-breaking rain refreshed his forehead, he was glad that he had not. Somehow, he was instinctively conscious that the deadly innkeeper would have boomeranged this back down his throat.

A gentle shower was falling on the immunity of Irish faeries' wings, and on his own absorbent Bond Street clothes, but his collar had long since wilted from another kind of moisture in the pub. He raised his face up against the downpour to try to clear his ringing head.

"Whew! Lace-curtain Irish, hell! Those pugnacious Micks are cannibals! Man alive! Why, they'd eat a man alive! What one hell of a job I'm up against. What a giddy and delirious gamble it is."

Fearfully, he looked back at the little inn on the leafy lane of Blarney Village. The sounds as of a broiling cauldron came through the doors into the night air, and the rain became hot on the Yankee's cheeks.

"Lucky to get away without a Mickey Finn," he thought.

With a heavy heart, he walked toward the private road leading to the New Castle on the hill. He walked fast, for already he was late for his twentieth exasperating conference with Sir George Oliver Colthurst. He was a mentally entwisted crayture.

"It's positively eerie," the Yankee muttered. "The Pebble! They even know about the *crack* in the Blarney Stone! But, God, it's worth a man's life to trifle with it, and even if I do get a *splinter* of it, I'm afraid it will take take the atom bomb to blast it out of Ireland.

"But I feel sorry for them," he said. "Irish wit is the wit of frightened sowls, the wit of heartbreak, dust that will not be settled by a gentle rain. You only laugh when you're scared!"

The cablegram from Macy's New York department store crinkled urgently in his pocket: TEMPUS FUGIT; QUO VADIS?

"Why in hell didn't somebody eat Paddy's pig? Was it too tough?"

The promoter bent his neck against the rain and pushed ahead through the darkness. O'D.'s weather forecast had been far too accurate. The slanting downpour was soaking his foine duds, and saw-tooth Irish lightning sliced at a feinting green-cheese moon. The scrappy orb was boxing with thunderclouds. Frightened corncrakes made the noises of crickets. Fieldfares rose like feathered helicopters over their nests singing reassurances to their young. The flashes splashed the private road with spooky light. The trees and the hedges took weird forms and the old yew trees in the haunted Rock Close, swept by the brawling wind, fought a thousand giants of darkness with as many fists. The Ice Witch of the neolithic cave was cackling in her hellish kitchen. Damned if he did not smell smoke! The promoter shuddered.

The monsters of Blarney taunted him. The dead lives of ten thousand witches' cats hissed in the night. The promoter had yet a mile to go on the lonely way. A bolt of the storm crashed its fire against the turrets of the old castle and split into hordes of luminous green and yellow demons who danced on its surface. They chattered livid tongues. It was a Tower of Babel. A ghostly tower stormed by a blazing language of pyro-imps. They dazzled in the frying footlights, converged upon the Blarney Stone and drenched it with light.

"Damned if they aren't thumbing their noses at me," he muttered.

Three times the lightning struck old Blarney and curled the castle with a protective fist. The heaven's leaping fingers gripped and clenched. The promoter's face was a ragged haggard silhouette.

"What was it that Irishman said? 'Th' weather is more fun

than anything else. If you don't say it's a nice day, then, faith, you don't like somebody.' "

"Cripes!" he said. "I've worked myself into a fine state! Been one hell of a strain. That coy stone. How hard I've tried to get it!"

He had answered every question, he thought.

"What if the Constellation falls?"

He had countered to ship it by sea.

"What if the ship sinks?"

"Hell, the Blarney Stone has been shipwrecked before! It could even talk to Triton. And if it can't speak Greek, why, a million dollars would raise the *Titanic*."

"Aren't you exaggerating slightly?"

"Well, maybe; but a million dollars would certainly raise a ton of sandstone."

"Please speak in terms of pounds."

The storm cursed him in Gaelic. It was a crackling oath that shattered the Martin Valley and made the river blush. The forks of lightning jabbed accusing prongs at the wayfarer from the castle walls.

"It's giving me the works," he said.

Barbed-wire lightning crashed over the castle again and old Blarney haughtily shrugged it off to entangle the stars. Sudden admiration for her strength and glory surged in the promoter's heart.

"Look!" he whispered in awe. "It's like the Holy Grail!"

She was ablaze with liquid radiance, raked naked by the lightning of her ivy gown, but she was presently covered with an emerald sheen of joy, robed in a neoncandescence of nudity.

Heaven itself was shining her light upon the Blarney Stone, a light as soft as a mother's eyes on her firstborn, the love light that coos into the cradle where the infant sleeps.

"My Lord!" exclaimed the promoter. "What Coney Island would do with her! 'Hot dogs, cigars, cigarettes, popcorn, chewing gum, candy.' Think of it! They'd make a weenie joint of Blarney Castle!"

The thought was stunning.

"They would kiss it with English mustard on their lips!"

The old kingmaker would rage her resentment. It would brook no such. The stone of the ages was in her keeping! It crowned the fortress of the Irish monarchs, and it was now bejeweled with the tricky lightning of the storm. All over the surface it cavorted in giddy pranks, raising the dickens and Tom Walker.

The verse of Father Prout came to his mind, and made him shiver with its prophecy. The poetry of Francis Sylvester Mahony might have been written there. Such a queer thought—the Blarney Stone, a desk for genius.

> But still the Magic Stone
> (Blessings on it!)
> Is not flown.

There was lonesome melancholy here in the cycles of the past, and it crowded a futility of regrets.

There loomed the Blarney Stone, the master of speech, before him, its facets polished like a diamond ring, rising aloof in its superlative patina, in a well-earned glory, O!

The promoter wrote his own words, and emblazoned them in a graven force upon the sacred surface:

"Bladhmann-go-brath!" (Blarney foriver!) It was not "Eire-ann-go-brath!" (Ireland foriver!)

He toyed with his thinking.

There was no raised shamrock there. There was no Latin inscription. It was a hefty Irish power inscribed. The Blarney Stone was getting its Irish up. It screamed back at him its sentiments in trenchant Gaelic.

"Bladhmann-go-brath!"

The Gaelic challenged in angry calligraphy akin to the scratching of a fighting cock.

"Blarney foriver!"

"What a pity," said the promoter, "to take it away. That heritage. Blarney foriver, 'til the doom of judgment. I feel like a vulture. Blarney is really all that Ireland has."

It was a sad thought, and the American was committed to the project, but he eased his conscience with a convenient inspiration.

"It's only for a little while," he said. "You'd think I was stealing it for good and always."

He had no choice to indulge his sentiment and let his heart drip so much for Eire.

Hopefully, he searched for efficacy of Sister Brigit's vision on the face of the prize:

> Oliver Cromwell, he did pummel
> And broke a breach in her battlement.

"Maybe one of his cannon balls *did* hit the stone," he mused, as he strained his eyes. "A half a loaf is better than none."

The lightning was fickle now. He could not be sure.

"Here I am actually *begging* Sir George to take a million dollars as rent for a little piece of rock! Hah! That emerald, that stone and color for happiness."

The hubbubing of the aerial freshet whipped him on his way and imps rode his Bond Street shoulders. The New Castle's hall lights gleamed ahead over the hill where the descendant of Sassenachs was waiting for the interview with a Yank.

"I wonder if he's giving *me* the blarney?" the promoter asked the hitchhiking demons of the old demesne.

The fingers of the sky were gripping at the night. The New Castle was their target now. A bolt hurtled against a brownstone turret from Scotland, and a Benjamin Franklin lightning rod buried it in the ground. The castle was doused with ink, and the promoter was showered with gravel chips. He flinched against a wall. His ankles rubbed against a huddled growling Angora of a female giant. The startled promoter yelled as the lightning revealed her and pulled his hair. The giant was sensuous Cushy, ever faithful in her vigil, even in an Irish storm. The Yankee sidled away from the snarling bitch and raced for the great iron portals of the castle.

Frantically, he pulled at the gong.

Bong! bong! bong! it rang through the hollow halls, the hollow bong of his own frustration. The Yankee briskness was drained through his toes.

Little Adrian pushed open the metal doors. Sister Brigit stood at the head of the entrance stairs holding a jumping candle. She was like a wraith in her white flannel.

All of the dogs in creation were barking.

"Ssh!" warned Adrian. "Listen! The castle is full of ghosts tonight. The dogs are barking at Oliver Cromwell."

Chapter Twenty-Two

The Seven Dwarfs

Up in the great "New Castle" fronting the ruins of Old Blarney, lives a modern little princess in an enchanted medieval wonderland. Her great-uncle is the king, a king who rules in somewhat shopworn feudal splendor; but he cannot properly be called one of Ireland's "hungry gentry," even if some of his carpets are threadbare in places here and there. He is the "ould man on the hill," an ailing suzerain of a still powerful demesne whose gloomy walls and last years are brightened by the royal child of his heart, one who lives the pages of a faery tale. She is to the castle born, the "godchild" of the Blarney Stone, and the ward of good spirits, friendly ghosts and the colony of leprechauns who live near the witch's cave and make little shoes in the old Druids' Circle in the Rock Close nearby. We already know her as Adrian.

At a pantomime of *The Bad Witch* in Cork, to which she and two young playmates once had gone in company of the doubtful parents of a seven-year-old boy who had nightmares, they had the most wonderful time. The reluctant parents, who feared the effects of the play on their susceptible offspring and that the witch might frighten him out of his wits, had nothing to fear, after all. Seated in a high box over the stage, the sensitive child, when the witch first appeared, recoiled a bit, but when she became *really* witchlike, far from dissolving into tears, he hurled a full, unopened bottle of lemonade straight at her head. Luckily, it missed her and merely exploded on the stage in a perfect shower of broken glass and soda water. It caused more commotion than anything that had happened in Cork's theatrical history until the O'Boys viewed *Top O' The Morning* at the Savoy.

There was one hell of a row, greatly enjoyed by Adrian and her companions. The manager stormed into the box, and the boy's parents narrowly escaped arrest, the witch all the time eyeing them with *real* malevolence.

Adrian has wide, eager eyes, such as make the world young again. There is an ecstasy of excitement in them. Her fancy-hungry mind is a weavery to behold. It creates vivid pictures of enchantment for all to see.

She lives on ground that has been especially charmed, the only little girl in a generation of adults living in Blarney Castle, the favorite of the woodsmen, the groom, the servants and the old folk of the estate and the little village on the Martin River flowing down below, from whom she knows the most intimate secrets of the "little people." She knows the secret hiding places of the crotchety old leprechauns and her sharp ears every day catch the ringing noise of the tiny cobblers' hammers making faery shoes as the old curmudgeons toil to increase their crocks o' gould.

As for toys, Adrian is the possessor of the biggest "doll house" in the world, a real *carrick-a-fouky,* which means faery rock castle. It is old Blarney Castle itself. There in its great rooms inhabited by her enormous collection of "dolls" she plays in favorite high-ceilinged chambers of stone with walls eighteen feet thick, where once the grand ladies and gentlemen of the royal McCarties lived and loved and drank intoxicating usque-bagh from leather goblets, because there were no glasses, and licked gravy of the "wilde deere" and dripping boars' heads from their fingers in the big dining hall strewn with rushes and littered with marrowbones gnawed by the multitude of eternal Irish dogs. From the windows where once were aimed the arrows of the longbow, this little girl amuses herself by tossing pebbles to disturb the sleeping trout in the amber Martin River below.

The forms and the shapes of her "doll house" were parts of her vocabulary as early as she could say blarney. "Bawn," "enceinte," "peel," "oubliette," "merlons," "donjons," "keeps," "corbels," "machicolations," are as common to her speech as "mummy" and "nunk." These are the words that describe the castellation of old Blarney. A *peel* is a tower devoid of a bailey. A *bailey* is a courtyard. *Enceinte* means a protecting wall. A *bawn* is an outflanking fortification. A *donjon* is a dungeon. An *oubliette* is "a dungeon with an opening only at the top." A *merlon* is one of the "solid intervals between embrasures of a battlemented parapet." A *corbel* is "a projection from the face of a wall, supporting a weight." A *machicolation* is a machicolation, and *Nunk* means uncle and *Mummy* means mother.

The castle is a dangerous toy, but Adrian is like a hummingbird within its walls. The poet John Hogan, a hundred years ago, found it terrifying:

> Directly downwards let us drop our sight,
> How creeps the blood, while o'er the deadly height!
> As fancy pictures to the thrilling sense,
> Our various stations if we fell from hence,
> The pier beneath that tops the ruin'd wall,
> Would just receive us in our awful fall.
> Next on the ledges and the rock below,
> Our mangled bodies would successive go,—
> Thence to the bottom, 'mongst the brakes be hurled,
> And there lie gasping for another world!
>
> Let drop a stone—tremendous! Thus it falls!
> What hosts of jackdaw quit the ruin'd walls;
> See how they hover round in boding gloom,
> As if the harpies waited for our doom!
> Nor as we step must caution be forgot,
> Or we may; 'twixt these battlements be shot.

THE BLARNEY STONE

A grown-up youth, some little time ago
Tripp'd and fell inward, on the floor below;
His frantic fellow flew—but found him kill'd—
And oh! what horrors that survivor fill'd.

A fortunate man named Cahill fell off the castle in 1900. He was a native of Cork and a sailor, and semidrunk at the time. In trying to kiss the stone from "wrong side," his legs held by two tipsy friends, he slipped and they dropped him. His fall was broken by the yew trees and he got off with a broken ankle.

James Burke from Charleville, in 1932, accompanied by two friends and slightly oiled, climbed the castle and attempted to do a handstand on top of the battlements. He was seen by Jim Harrington, the keeper, and urged to desist, but as soon as Jim left, he tried again and fell. He broke his neck.

One day at Blarney, as more than a thousand tourists climbed to the top of the castle to undergo the actually neck-breaking experience of kissing the Blarney Stone (it is a definite hazard to life and limb), a drunken sailor, playing an accordion on one of the high turrets and dancing along the walls, lost his footing and plunged over a battlement eighty-three feet to the ground. Many women fainted and others turned their heads away, but soon everyone on high heard the music of an accordion issuing from the topmost branches of an ancient yew tree where the sailor had landed and found a comfortable perch to continue his serenade to the leprechauns. The world pilgrims to Blarney cheered the escapade and later made up a purse of several hundred shillings for the fortunate tar. Later, however, another sailor, who had learned of this easy way to make a fortune, fortified himself with malt and endeavored to duplicate the feat of his friend. It is remembered that his music was very pleasing to the ears, but he missed the yew tree. Gardeners removed his mangled body in a wagon and delivered it to the commander of a destroyer at Cobh.

Although the majority resisted this easy way to pass through the pearly gates, the alarming casualty list mounted annually. Finally, iron bars were placed beside the Blarney Stone so that now all a kisser has to do is merely to *flirt* with eternity. As he lies upon his back holding onto the iron bars with his ankles gripped by strong men, he kisses the Stone with one eye looking toward heaven and another toward hell below. Until finally he is dragged up to safety, it is a certainty that he never knew for sure which way he would go.

Adrian's wings have always saved her from a fall.

Her playmates, in an often incongruous parade, include Cromwell, arm-in-arm with Ireton and Fairfax; Queen Elizabeth, James II, Coleridge, Carlyle, Bing Crosby, Winston Churchill, St. Patrick and Brian Boru.

Adrian's intelligence all of her life has been constantly exposed to that of adults, the great and the near-great, who throng its social walls. She knows that anyone who travels to Tibet must cross through the territory of the Wali of Swat. Her father, a career officer in the English Army, knew the Wali of Swat, and speaks a little Urdu, too. The precocious and unspoiled Adrian is probably the only little girl in Ireland who knows how to say "thank you" in Urdu.

She also is a relative of the late George Bernard Shaw, who had a bright mind, too.

She rattles the skeletons of Cromwell and Anjou with beguiling unconcern. That day when the bees stung her English governess, a hiveful got under old Oliver's armor. He ran out of the New Castle and jumped into Blarney Lake trying to drown his tormentors. She was afraid for a moment while he floundered and splashed that he would drown himself. Now he was back again, making the dogs bark.

Adrian loves the characters of *The Wind in the Willows*; Toad is nice and Mole is a cozy sort of animal, she thinks. She has affection for Uncle Remus, too, and sincerely feels that Br'er

Possum resembles certain humans she knows; but members of the historic warring cast are her favorites. Edward II of England, Bruce at Bannockburn, Cormac McCarty. So brave the McCarties were. Said the Sassenach Reverend Urban Vigors to the Sassenach Reverend Henry Jones in 1641:

> Thursday the 8th of Mar., my Lord Pres. and Col. Lanester and their forces marched from Castle Lyons to the *Cittey* of Corke, and they got into the *Cittey* in good tyme, for the Lord of Mouskerey (McCarty) had waysted his countrey and was very strong. The strongest castle his Lordship hath, wherein he usually liveth is with in three miles of the citty; the name of it is Castle Blarney.
>
> The Irish in those partys say it is one of the strongest castles in Ireland. I have byn often in it and I find it to be a place of great strength.
>
> The late Lord Sir Chas. McCartee built two or three walls about the said castle and walled the garden with very strong walls and turrets with battlements and contrived many plans of defence, I could heartily wish our English Army were the owner of it.
>
> To acquaint you sir with the overthrow we gave the Lord of Muskery near Corke with 500 musketeers, and a hundred fifty horse and how his Lordship's tent was taken there by our soldiers and his armour for his owne body, would be true though stale newes; for I am sure you have seen part of the passages in print.
>
> The Lord of Muskery escaped with life very narrowly at that tyme. I heard that he fell out very sore with his Lady for persuading him to joyne with the countrey in their rebellious actions and desperate attempts.

Adrian has absorbed every scrap of history connected with the Stone that has made her family's estate so famous. Among these ghosts she has her special pets and even enemies. Lord Broghill, the old Druids, the *Filid,* and Brian Boru, all of whom have a definite link to the Blarney Stone, are to her what the pirates of comic strips, Long John, Robin Hood, Little Orphan Annie, Little Red Riding Hood, Pinocchio and Peter Rabbit and Mickey Mouse and Humphrey are to American children.

At will, Adrian conjures Dermot McCarty, King of Leinster and owner of Blarney Castle, who was put to flight for rape, and brings him to life all over again out of 1170 A.D. into the present, when the dramatis personae gather again before the walls of the old citadel where the attack occurred.

Shady and unchivalrous conduct of certain personalities in those times of inveterate prejudice, conduct of wars and politics, empire building, get a going over as old rivals and enemies meet for the first time since. These clashes and the raking of old coals when English and Irish enemies come face to face at Blarney produce raging debates between representatives of the various stages of history in which the Blarney Stone has performed. From the great dramas of the Phoenicians and the Milesians and the Old Testament the Blarney Stone steps out of the wings of mythology and takes its bows before the footlights in the times of the Crusades and the wars of Bruce of Scotland, and taunts Queen Elizabeth with its "splendid effrontery."

The only ghost that she really fears is that Indian Chief Tipoo Sahib, whom her great-great-grandfather slew with a sword in the Indian Mutiny to get the diamonds and emeralds in his turban. When he comes snooping around Blarney, looking for his jewels, it is positively flesh-crawling the way he peers and leers through the windows. He is harmless, however, because only his head comes back to haunt the ground. Adrian's great-great-grandfather saw to that by cutting his head off. So he has no pockets to put the baubles in, even if they were still around to be found. He might gobble them up in his mouth, but there were so many he would be obliged to swallow them, and having no stomach, he is out of luck on this score too. It's just the way he leers and peers in the galleries of pitch pine that makes him such a nuisance.

She lives in a wonderland different only from Alice's in that its inhabitants, aside from pookas and leprechauns and enchanted cows and an occasional ghost of a ring ouzel, are the lively ghosts of real persons who every once in a while get lonesome for their old Blarney home and come back for a visit singly or in great hordes for a convention, often with exciting and even dangerous complications. Events are popping in ghostdom now. It is to run the greatest risk imaginable to mix some of this company in the massive halls and drawing rooms in Blarney Castle. Anything can and does happen. When Cromwell and Cormac McCarty arrive at the same time, the ringing of their mail and armor in an ensuing personal battle makes such bedlam that it is enough to awaken the dead. It matters not at all that only Adrian and the dozen-odd dogs in the castle hear it. It is the most natural place in the world for these ghosts to come, to the hallowed ground where they lived and fought and died and where with longbows and boiling oil, sword and pike, they helped make and change the history of the world.

Even though some of them are grumbling old men who are not pleased with anything they find, Adrian treats them with the form of politeness due her elders. However, they are often most trying. Some of the arguments they have are outrageous. They do not agree on anything. They talk about their tactics and their sieges and their battles. One of them starts a terrible controversy over the impregnability of stone against wild fire and cannon. One sure thing that is finally agreed upon is that castles of the future will have to be made of iron.

"In that case," Adrian asks, "would you have an *iron* Blarney Stone?"

"Pshaw, but a trifle," snapped an old warder with rude impatience.

"You should have kissed the Blarney Stone yourself," Adrian

reprimanded him sharply. "Possibly that would make you more polite. After I finish these peaches and cream I'm going to take you to the top of the castle and push your mouth against it with my own hands."

Sometimes Adrian's playmates follow her right out of the Old Castle into the New Castle and sit down, uninvited, to dine.

All of these visitors have simply terrible table manners, too. They even try to eat with their fingers because they never saw a knife or a fork in the Old Castle. No one sees them but Adrian.

Old Dunivan, her favorite dog save one, Puff the Peke, growls over in the corner every time they come in. He knows. And sometimes the other dogs bay at the moon as though death were near when "they" clutter up the castle.

Since the arrival of the American with his wretched million dollars, the Irish ghosts have become completely unmanageable. Led by Cormac McCarty, they picket the castle every night in clanking phalanxes of angry dead. The dogs go wild. No one except Adrian can sleep. She is as fresh as a daisy, but she has her hands full.

Queen Elizabeth is delighted that the stone may go.

"Cast the wretched thing into the sea!" she cries. "It made a fool of me! Out of my Empire with it!"

"Ssh, Your Majesty, I'm sorry, but Ireland is not a part of the Empire any more."

"Send that English ghost back home!" the Irish pickets shout.

The ghosts use the ancient game table in the billiard room from which to orate their grievances under an enormous oil painting of "The Rape of the Lapithi by the Centaurs." This was done by Sebastian Ricci, and Adrian's great-great-great-grandfather refused $2,500 and a horse that won the Ledger for it. The great soapbox is now occupied by Oliver Cromwell. He is storming up and down the green felt stage, lecturing and fussing and covered with the positively disgusting shredding shrouds of his Tyburn grave.

"I'm not so sure any of my cannon balls *ever* hit the Blarney Stone. I wasn't even there."

"Ask Lord Broghill," suggested Adrian.

"He won't leave England. He's had enough of the blarney."

"God knows I have, too," shouted Queen Elizabeth, as she espied Cormac McCarty outside. "Jugglyng traytor, denounced in publicke!" she cried.

Her Majesty's loud and shattering ire made "The Five Senses," by Nogari, tremble on the wall, and shook "Pyrrhus and Andromache," by Lazzerini, until their teeth chattered.

That Irish King McCarty who did something perfectly terrible to the wife of Roderick O'Connor 799 years ago is in a clanging fracas in the courtyard with none other than Roderick himself. Like all Irishmen, he has a long memory, too.

There is never a dull moment at Blarney Castle.

Even the Seven Dwarfs of Snow White in their flesh and bone, have come to visit Adrian in Cork, real little dwarfs, tiny freaks rented for the play from a London Circus, enough like the faery cobblers of Blarney to be their septuplets. Adrian was mad about them, as one can imagine, and so were her two young friends, Valerie and Deborah, who went with her to the show and applauded and laughed and cried, and became so excited that they twisted their dimity pinafores into knots.

They talked in rapture of the Seven Dwarfs all the way back to Blarney where the kindly old king had invited them all to tea.

Never had Cork, in their opinion, received such important visitors as the seven talented dwarfs. Why, they were as beautiful as talking dolls and the little girls had wanted to hug and squeeze them all. Back at the castle and bemused by faeryland, they scarcely touched their delicious but mundane chocolate cakes and cookies and biscuits, just freshly baked by Mary the cook. They were transported to a realm that called for pies made with singing blackbirds, curds and whey, magic golden

apples and the kind of food, whatever it was, that Little Red
Riding Hood carried under her arm to her grandmother through
the woods. Faery rings and mushrooms filled their thoughts.

The king had not yet come down from his countinghouse, and
the butler had taken his silver tray from the drawing room to get
something in his pantry. They were left all alone and pensive
and far away, sad that the wonderful spell was breaking. But
suddenly one of them had a great inspiration.

"I know!" she cried ecstatically. "Let's kiss the Blarney
Stone!"

Now that was magic, even though one could not eat it, of
course, like an enchanted golden apple, but it enchanted one
more than Mary's chocolate cakes! And it was not a hundred
yards away. They believed they all had thought of it at the same
time and with spontaneous and delighted oh's and ah's and little-
girl squeaks and cries and squeals of pleasure, they raced out of
the drawing room, through the castle's great strong door and
across one of the most beautiful gardens in Europe. Past shining
cattle chewing four-leaf-clover cuds in the *bawnafinny,* or pretty
Gaelic pasture, orchis-pied, and sprinkled and starred with
primroses, peonies and lupine, mischievous little flowers that
flutter their eyelids on the bossies' ticklish damp noses as they
crop the shamrocks, and make them sneeze.

Never, the children thought, did Snow White see such a faeryland. Their happy laughter made the cows look up, and the
tourists high atop old Blarney's battlements saw them and waved
their handkerchiefs. The emerald shade beneath the trees was
patterned with shell-blue fragments of blackbird egg, white of
the pigeon, and the palest blue of the robin, cast from the nests
by the mother birds, now worried about their young and screaming at them as the three little girls fill the branches with their
shouts. What a pity that American Sunday School teacher did
not retreat from the seven leprechauns through this lovely
avenue of escape rather than flounder in the briars.

Old Katy Ford sees the girls coming and pulls the rusty iron bolt on the old castle gate. They rush through together and head for the great winding staircase of the keep. They are breathless now, up the steep spirals, nearly to the top, past the famous "Earl's Chamber," where once lived "Laider the Strong," who slept on the rush-covered floors and kept his prize hunting falcons perched beside him, and are nearing the high kitchen placed in the topmost floor for safety and the stomach's sake, and with ovens fourteen feet long and six feet deep, big enough to roast a whole ox at one time, when all of their breath leaves them. They stop in consternation and push their backs against the cold walls in a busy hush, transfixed by the identical spectacle that had driven the American schoolteacher out of her mind! They can hardly believe their eyes.

There, in person, are the Seven Dwarfs of Snow White, dwarfs in the flesh and bone, sliding, slipping, hopping, struggling, and horrors! cursing their unhappy way down those treacherously slanting steps worn to danger by footsteps which echoed back into the centuries.

But in what a different mood is this miserable group of dwarfs than when seen on the flat stage of Cork's Opera House! They are screaming and berating each other like a cageful of little demons.

Adrian, Valerie and Deborah gasp their astonishment. They are *not* dreaming. The Seven Dwarfs of Snow White are real! They stare at them in reverent ecstasy. The Blarney Stone is forgotten.

Dopey, the smallest dwarf, is being half-carried by the harassed Prince Charming himself!

"Damn!" shouts the trembling and bad-humored Dopey. "Be careful!"

"Quit your bloody squirming, then," snaps Prince Charming. " 'Oose 'orrible, 'ideous and hidiotic hideah was it, anyway, for Hinglish midgets to be climbin' a blarsted Hirish carstle!"

Prince Charming possesses a mouthful of English squirrel teeth and seems to talk through them with his nose.

"Why, they are Cockneys!" exclaims Adrian, as indeed they are, professional London midgets on a tour. They are not Germans, at all, as the unfortunate American Sunday School teacher had so mistakenly reported to O'K., but that is understandable, since the poor thing was so wrought up that she might well have thought the terrible language they spoke was the tongue of hell itself.

The midgets are screaming out advice and calling each other by such unfaery names as 'Awkins, 'Arris, 'Illsmith, 'Eath, 'Ayden and 'Alliday. Prince Charming, it seems, is named 'Arry Grimes.

Dopey's little face is squeezed like a bath sponge and the perspiration of fear is draining down his neck, as he contemplates the terrible spiraled distances below. Grumpy, Sleepy, Doc, Happy, Sneezy, and Bashful, all in a great dudgeon, are crouched precariously on the steps, angrily calling each other names the overjoyed and well-bred little girls had never heard before.

Dopey is giving Prince Charming no end of trouble. The climb, up or down, the steps of Blarney offers a challenge even to a sure-footed unfettered mountain climber. Poor Prince Charming, already exhausted by a three-hour ordeal of pushing the dwarfs up the endless heights, is not equal to the demand of carrying them down, and with a sudden terrible scream he lets go of his howling burden as he struggles to keep a foothold to prevent himself from falling. Dopey plunges forward. His little bottom bounces three steps upon the hard stone before he snatches a little hand at safety and finally holds on to the ledge of a time-smoothed boulder.

"Good gracious!" cry the little girls, closing their eyes. They have never been so thrilled in their lives!

Slightly stunned and terribly outraged, Dopey gets to his feet, and on shaking knees rails away at his tormentor.

"Bloomin' giant!" he screams in a high-pitched voice that sounds like a curmudgeon of an old leprechaun being tortured for his crock o' gould. "Blimey, cawn't you 'old a man!"

"Blimey, yourself," retorts Prince Charming angrily, " 'ell hitself cawn't 'old a 'orrible wrigglin' arse that won't stye still!"

The other six dwarfs now having been given an example of the fate that awaits their own descent of the steps, in Prince Charming's unreliable keeping, burst out with a torrent of resentful abuse at their big custodian.

Prince Charming is sorely tried and bedeviled. He is perspiring from his labors and his suit is covered with the gray dust of old Blarney. All day long he has literally had his hands full of squirming midgets, each with a great distemper.

With each excruciating step he had negotiated in the upward journey with his charges, he had emitted a protest. He was forced to push them with his shoulders, nudge them onward with his elbows and even with his head.

"One step," he grumbled, "one step's 'igher than their own 'eads."

When the little pilgrims finally arrived at the summit, not one kissed the Blarney Stone when they realized what they had gotten themselves into. When they espied the great size of the opening and the sheer drop to the ground, alarming even to a man of normal size but magnified to mountain height in their little eyes, they emitted a concerted doll-like shriek, shrank away in terror and fled for the exit.

And now that Prince Charming has let go of Dopey, all of their frustration is leveled against him.

"Monster!" they shout, "you 'eld 'im by the neck like a bloomin' kitten!"

Prince Charming has reached his limit. With a roaring unprintable oath he slaps the sandstone dust from his palms.

"You hall," he shouts, "can go streyt to 'ell!"

And with that, in the most unchivalrous act ever recorded in the conduct of a Prince Charming, he deserts his charges and plunges recklessly down the steps alone.

" 'Arry, 'Arry," the midgets call after him, "come back 'ere! Come back! You big freak! We'll never get down!"

" 'Ell and be damned to you," retorts 'Arry.

" 'Ow, 'ow, 'ow," cry the midgets now in great alarm, "are we goin' to get down this mountain?"

"Hin this hinstance hi'm 'ighly hindifferent, you bloody mites!" 'Arry yells back. "Hi'm washin' my 'ands of the hintire mess. *Fall* down!"

That is how the Seven Dwarfs of Snow White were so cruelly left stranded in such a dilemma as Blarney Castle had never experienced within its old walls for five hundred and five years of varying fortunes and sieges.

For that is how long Blarney Castle has stood on its "maine rock" overlooking the precipice of the Martin River, since first its builder inscribed a Latin verse on a remarkable stone and placed it in an honored position in the topmost battlements:

Cormac McCarty, bould as bricks,
Built me in 1446.

Only five hundred and five years? No, it is unlikely that ever before in history had a group of midgets been trapped in a medieval castle of Europe.

The hearts of Adrian, Valerie and Deborah go out to them in their terrible quandary.

"Oh, please," they cry, "do let us help you!" They plunge forward to the rescue.

The midgets, their faces suddenly screwing up like mashed tennis balls, stare in horror at the energetic little girls descending upon them.

"Get back, get back, you Hirish hinfants," roars Bashful. "Bring some Hirish *men!*"

"Don't be afraid," shout the girls encouragingly, ignoring Bashful's silly orders. "We'll save you!"

Adrian fairly pounces upon the struggling Dopey who, kicking, protesting and scratching, finally is deposited safely below by the seat of his pants. One by one, in flight after flight, the girls run up and down the castle steps clutching the balky dwarfs with all their strength. Never once do they give ground, holding fast to their noble purpose, oblivious to scratching and heaping imprecations.

"Hofficious little brats!" howls Sleepy. "Leggo me. Wow! Leggo! Mind your own business!" Adrian had first grasped him firmly by an ear the size of a thimble.

Valerie has Doc in her arms and holds so tightly around his neck that his face turns purple and he emits the agonized sounds of a man who is choking to death.

Six of the seven dwarfs are stretched out upon their backs, panting to recover, when Deborah, whose thumb is sticking in his eye, finally brings down the miserable Happy, who is doing anything except living up to his name. She dumps him beside the others, but all of them soon get to their feet and start screaming again and jumping up and down.

The girls were terribly disillusioned. They were not at all as they were on the stage. And such language! If their governesses could only have heard them! Good lands! They did not know how poor Snow White could put up with it.

Blarney loomed over their agitated little bodies like Gibraltar. Truly, now, as Prince Charming had said, it *was* "a 'ell of a place for midgets."

Soon they stopped blaming the girls, and began fighting among themselves like a lot of Shetland ponies.

Now neither Adrian, Valerie or Deborah cared one whit how long it would take their little legs to carry them on the six-mile hike back to Cork, or whether the play went on that night or not. The girls had carried them far enough already. Actually too far. Possibly they should have left them up there in the castle to starve, as bad faeries do in story books.

The great exertions of the girls had made them ravenous. Without so much as a backward look at the ungrateful Seven Dwarfs of Snow White, the brave little heroines raced back across the *bawnafinny* to devour all of Mary's cream bun goodies.

Chapter Twenty-Three

The Swan Song

In the vaulted galleries of the New Castle that life-sized oil of King Charles XII of Sweden, done by a student of Cuyp, is flirting in majestic restraint with a Mrs. Vesey, another valuable oil by Hamilton, wearing a pink dress and a profusion of dark curls. Mrs. Vesey is a Colthurst ancestress who has been blushing under the stares of the king in coquettish competition with a sedate Miss Oliver, by Hogarth, for about two hundred years. The portrait of the king was a personal gift to the Jefferyes after Sir James had saved his life in that battle with the Danes. The king is wearing a dark uniform, lined with buff, and the buff gauntlets that were described by Voltaire. By his side lie his crown and ermine mantle. The king's attention to the two handsome ladies has not gone unnoticed for some time by a critical and somewhat stalwart Lady Lanesborough, in pastels. Lady Lanesborough has been restrained from violent action, one may be sure, only by fear of the sword hilt King Charles grips rather skittishly with his left hand.

During these past centuries, every visitor who has ever entered the various libraries of the Jefferyes and the Colthursts in the castles of Ardrum, Ballybourney and Blarney has been forced to sidle past His Majesty's threatening mien to enter the room where important interviews have been traditionally held. It is a forbidding experience. Mrs. Vesey, Miss Oliver and the withering Lady Lanesborough have made the gauntlet of those monarchal, stabbing eyes somewhat less arduous. This Swedish king,

so feared by the Turks that he was called by such Turkish names
as "The Head of Iron," has a tendency to overwhelm the timor-
ous and even subdue the brave who venture within range of his
gaze. It is remarkable that Lady Lanesborough has bristled so
long before it. Many other ladies have faded in his presence.
Some Gainsborough School portraits and pencil sketches by
unknown artists of less redoubtable and unknown females of
undetermined value hanging there were removed to the faraway
billiard room and the boudoir in less than fifty years.

The American promoter found the king actually terrifying.
When on this rainy Irish day he came to Blarney Castle for his
last interview with the ould man on the hill he was, as a matter
of fact, beginning to find everything in Ireland terrifying. He
cringed past His Majesty as though he, this Swede too, might
be Irish. The sword of the Swede was as the sword of Damocles
over his head, and well might it be. The Yankee was as skittish
as the hand on the hilt. Things added up almost to a point of
hysteria.

The sword of Damocles had a special meaning for him in a
reversed and confused sort of way.

He himself should have been Dionysius and the ould man on
the hill his guest at the royal banquet. That sword suspended by
a single hair was suspended over the wrong person, in his
opinion. It was the American whose neck now was at stake.

In connection with that flattery of the fates of kings of which
Damocles was accused, it is noteworthy to point out that this
was one of the earliest instances of classical blarney mentioned
in the reigns of the kings of Syracuse. It further points up the
more or less modern moral that the blarney *can* be a perilous
thing.

The American was glad to have the company of the butler.
He showed him to a great brown leather chair under the
bookcases overlooking the lake. The rain had stopped at last.
The wide lawns stretching to the *bawnafinny* were a feast of

colors. There were hints of the yellow, crimson, orange and flame in the trees that would soon be rioting in the blue mists of the autumn evenings to come. This season would bring the Virginia creeper and the Harvest Festival, and the smell of leaf smoke in the groves, leaf smoke, smoky blue dew.

"God!" murmured the promoter. "I've been here all summer long!"

He was nervous and depressed with premonitions. He felt like a swan song.

He riffled the pages of an old book by the Rt. Hon. Silver Oliver, owner of Castle Oliver and a Colthurst ancestor, strongly advocating an English income tax, giving pompous advice to the government on how to beat Napoleon and criticizing the "insipidity" of the expression of Scipio in "Venus and Achilles," which he put down to continence and labeled chastity as a passive virtue unsuited to the genius of painting.

He fingered through a postscript to "An Essay on Man" by Alexander Pope, written in 1795, consisting of nine vellum pages written in small copperplate handwriting by the same Rt. Hon. Silver Oliver.

The first part of this is headed "Proofs of a God." The next: "My attempt to give some idea of the Instinct impressed by God on Man." Then comes "Reason." After this a separate essay called, "Oliver's Scheme to give Government ample support for the War, till France shall agree to a Peace that will protect Europe from her Mad ideas of Universal Domination, Robbery, and Pillage without the additional burden of a Farthing on the Poor, on Manufacturers, or on Trade." And he adds: "This I sent to Earl Campden soon after Lord Malmsbury's return from Paris."

It is mainly an indictment of the policy of the British government and a perfect diatribe against the French. It ends with the following drastic suggestion: "Therefore let the War be continued in God's name, till we make Great Britain, Ireland and

Europe safe. This cannot be done without great, and unheard of exertions in these countries. . . . I have some trifling Property, and will with pleasure, agree to what I shall now propose:— Let everyone, (during the War only) who is possessed of a hundred pounds a year, in Lands, Houses, Tythes, Fines on renewals, by Interest of money, Employments Jointures, or Annuities, be obliged to contribute one fourth of his clear income to the Expence of the War, first deducting out of it Agency, Crown, Quit and Composition of Rents, and Interests of money he pays: also Demesnes kept by Noblemen, and Gentlemen for the support of their houses."

The American found this very like tax proposals being recommended in his own country, as though he were not already depressed enough. It served to make him lonesome and homesick for people and things he could understand and who could understand him.

He soon threw this aside and idly fingered a set of chessmen. They had belonged to Tipoo Sahib, from whom that Jefferyes had also stolen the Colthurst diamonds, when he sliced off his neck with a sword—those diamonds that now decorated the neck of Lady Alderly in palace ballrooms of London. The chessmen are in carved red-and-white ivory, and ornamented with gold. They look as old and worn as the tormented promoter.

"There's nothing 'lace-curtain' Irish about this," he thought, and then recalled that, after all, it was really English, not the Irish ha'p'ny copper coin with a brood sow and suckling pigs on one side and a harp on the other.

He has had a very trying season altogether, and today had a particularly upsetting and almost nightmarish experience in Cork on the way to the interview with the owner of the Blarney Stone in the New Castle. It had put him in a strange mood, which was finished off by the scrutiny of the Swedish king. Now he felt finished off himself.

As he walked toward his car near the Western Road Bridge,

one hell of a great swan lit down on the wet road in front of him. (Thinking it, the road, was a river?) The startled American, who had never seen a swan anywhere except in Central Park Lake, was astonished. He had good reason to be. The angry and surprised bird bristled its feathers, stuck out its neck, and charged to attack! The Yankee sprang back with a wild shout of terror. Rather, he recoiled like a spring of startled flesh and bone, but it was his brain that he was worried about. The swan hissed a few times and spread its wings, making off down the road center like a Constellation. A bevy of cyclists scattered before it. Now fascinated, the Yankee followed after the swan, which, just getting air-borne, hit a black horse. The horse, unable to believe its eyes, jerked sideways, tangled in its harness and ran away with the wagon of pigs to which it was hitched. Cages of squealing pigs fell to the street, bicycles were entangled with the racing wheels. A great Irish wolfhound the size of a calf leaped barking with excitement into the melee of everything there is to make a melee of: swan feathers, wire, pigs, squeals, barks, hisses, a runaway wagon and a horse gone insane over the whole thing. A crowd of corner boys came to the rescue, set pigs, horse, wagon, dog and hapless cyclists to rights, and tactfully shooed the outraged swan away.

The Yankee thought he must be losing his mind. He stood flat-footed and watched the most curious procession ever noted in Cork since the O'Boys paraded into the Savoy with their smelly trotters, *drisheens, crubeens,* and O'K.'s dripping ice. First, an enormous swan paddling along on vast blue feet with all the dignity of a Lord Mayor, behind it the crowd of "shooing" corner boys followed by a wary Irish wolfhound, a cursing Irish farmer chasing an escaped pig, and behind all of this on Western Road a long line of hooting busses and other traffic, including a funeral. When at last the swan got to the River Lee it glided off without a backward glance, while on the banks there was wild cheering and a covey of hats in the air.

The American left the scene hurriedly, beads of perspiration as from a jugger of Paddy's breaking out all over his forehead. "It's from what I've been through," he said. "I'll never mention this. It couldn't have happened, even in Ireland! What in the name of peace is the matter with me! That damned Irish swan! I'll bet *he* never kissed the Blarney Stone."

Bells were ringing in his eyes as he departed. They were the visual bells of an impossible photopia of bedlam and colors of hairs and hides and other things. Bells also were ringing in his ears. Those were the light Bells of Shandon from St. Anne's churchyard, cast in Gloucester, and the words of Francis Sylvester Mahony cast in the heart of Cork, sounding off with those chimes, O!

There's a bell in Moscow, while on tower and Kiosk O!
In St. Sophia the Turkman gets,
And loud in air calls men to prayer,
From the tapering summits
Of tall minarets.
Such empty phantom, I freely grant them;
For there's an anthem more dear to me—
'Tis the Bells of Shandon
That sound so grand on
The pleasant waters of the River Lee.

"I'll bet a dime," said the foreigner, "that dowdy is derived from O'Dowd, and that looney has nothing to do with the moon. It must come from O'Looney."

So that is the mood in which we find the promoter now as he awaits in the New Castle library the arrival of the ould man on the hill. An estate tractor drawing logs through a distant faery glade moans like a demon in his ears.

Paddy, as smooth as a crystal chandelier in his butler's uniform, appears with a large silver tray, with a pitcher of cistern water, an array of glasses, and Turkish cigarettes. In the center of the burden reposes a large cut-glass decanter of amber whisky.

"It 'tis good to know you'll not be retairnin' out there to America empty-handed, sir," Paddy said.

The Yankee jumped out of his chair.

"Paddy! Paddy, wait!" he shouted. "You've heard something! You mean to say he's going to let me take the Blarney Stone?"

Paddy cleared his throat uncomfortably.

"Th' Blairney Stone niver did I mention, sir. It 'twas to Christmas trees that I was referrin'."

"Christmas trees! Are you gone mad?"

"It was Sister Brigit, that religious and devout sowl, sir, who was tellin' me about th' Christmas trees. Th' ould man . . . plaise ye, Sir George . . . is very proud of his Blairney trees. Sister Brigit says he will sell ye ten thousand Christmas trees so it won't be that ye'll have to go back out there to America empty-handed, after all."

"Good God! Now, Paddy, what in hell *would* I do with ten thousand Christmas trees?"

"Plaise do not be quotin' me, sir. Th' ould . . . Sir George . . . will be tellin' ye, sir. But I hope that ye'll niver be lavin' Ireland, with o' without th' Christmas trees. Ye're a grand and foine man, sir. Ireland is proud to have ye here as our guest."

"Well," said the American helplessly, "if I've got to buy ten thousand Christmas trees to get the Blarney Stone, I'll buy 'em. Hell! I'd buy every tree in the country to get the Blarney Stone. It would be worth the price."

"It did not have, somehow, to do with th' Blairney Stone," said the discomfited Paddy. "Th' Christmas trees are just to keep yer hands from bein' empty, sir, Sister Brigit said."

Sister Brigit was very kind, the visitor knew.

She was *so* very kind and good that she would even cry for birds that had never been killed by an Irish gun. For man, bird or rabbit she would cry. And did.

"O, th' woodcock," exclaimed Sister Brigit. "Such a delicate little birt it 'tis. The hunter uses small shot, size twelve, to kill it, shot like dust, it 'tis. A speck o' it will kill a poor, delicate woodcock. It would fall to th' ground from th' hot breath o' yer mouth on its poor little wings. But a cliver divil it 'tis when it gets between you and behind a tree."

Sister Brigit sighed for the fate of the woodcock. And other craytures of nature, too.

"St. Francis of Assisi would cry with blushin' shame o' red birds' feathers o'er th' slaughter that goes on in blissid Ireland," she said. "Those who eat sparrows will eat hot stones in turrible purgatory's board. Some there are who put a little mess o' somethin' on th' ground, and standin' off a little piece, wait for th' sparrows to fly down to eat their feast o' death. Their shot takes twenty off their feet at th' same time." Sister Brigit smacked her lips.

"But you'd eat them with bacon, I see."

"O!" said Sister Brigit. "O!" And she blushed like the feathers of a cardinal. But she preached on the gospel of the gentle St. Francis.

"Here in Eire," she said, "th' sin o' th' ages o' hell is greyhound coursing, a turrible sport it 'tis, crueler than war on babies. A wretched unfortunate tame hare, likely th' pet o' a little child, freed and hounded to torture by man and beast—caught and loosed to run again, given hope, and over and over again released, th' tremblin' crayture, pantin' its burstin' lungs, lookin' over th' hills o' freedom it will niver see. Only God, finally sick to His stummick, maircifully lets it die exhausted in a hero's hands. Hound and man would niver kill it. There!

"And some o' th' great brave ones pull th' claws o' cats and throw them to th' greyhounds' pens to give th' hounds th' killer instinct and blood lust. Th' poor cats with bloody paws fight with surprise instid o' claws. They can't hurt those valuable greyhounds."

Sister Brigit's chin was a warm Niagara, but she did not stanch the flood with drying eye or Irish linen. Headlong, she cursed and assailed the wicked things of her native land. A great crime of modern Ireland she considered the heartless shipping of old horses for the abattoirs of Belgium, England and France.

"Sportsmen," she said, "who niver in this worrld would allow a race horse on a ship except in fair weather, and a smooth crossing, sell their poor wretched old farm horses that have about been worked to death to men who whip their weary living skeletons into stinking, crowded, kicking neighing holds, shave off all their hair, because there's a profit in horsehair as well as horse meat—send them riding into storms for four days, unfed and unwatered from Cork to the continent, old horses, old hunters that have worked for twenty years, faithful old craytures that have earned th' pasture, sent to hell in hell without breakfast.

"Th' oldest ones, so on their last legs they are like to die, are given injections of stimulants—just enough, because stimulants cost money. Th' stimulants are measured very carefully.

"They are tumbled into those stinking holes, galled rump to galled bald rump, bleeding from careless shaving blades, jaw to jaw, hoof to hoof, sagging shaky knees making th' noise o' coconuts bumpin' in Africa, packed in a hot steel can thrown on the waves of storms, seasickness in their empty stomachs, their old eyes full o' wonder and fear.

"So, they sail to the ovens of Europe, parboiled and tenderized on th' way. It makes things easier for th' cooks that way. Their old precooked carcasses trembling for the oven of death. When they were young and could earn money for their masters, there was an apple in their mouths, or a piece of sugar, but now their time is over and they cannot haul or dray. Their worth is under their hides because man has forgot. God will hear the neighs of those faithful old horses in heaven some day.

The harps of the angels will be thrown off key and heaven will stop singing to listen while faithful old horses cry their wonderment.

"Now there's th' rabbit again," she said, "asleep in its little bed, under a blanket o' snow. He has to breathe and th' breath a-comin' out o' th' crayture's cozy bed makes two little pinhole chimneys o' white smoke that gives his home away. There ye can catch him with yer own two hands and th' sharp eyes in yer head. So ye break his neck, take him home and skin him. And fast ye must cook him, too, for if ye hang him up for too long in th' cold weather th' poor rabbit's flesh will be frostbit."

The American's eyes were gorged with bewilderment.

"Sister Brigit!" he exclaimed, "if you were not a saint, I'd think you were a cannibal!"

"Och whisht," said Sister Brigit, "I do not like to see th' rabbits either killed or cooked. And it 'tis th' same with greed," she whispered. "If it 'tis greed that makes ye want so much th' Blairney Stone, ye may be turned into th' tail o' a cow!"

Kind Sister Brigit without further word or ado, arose and walked away from a startled American.

"Jeepers!"

It was from other sources that the Yankee had to learn the mysterious meaning of Sister Brigit's allusion to a bovine terminal appendage.

It 'twas that greedy divil o' a Macroom O'Looney who became th' prolongation o' a moo-cow's rear end not so long after the Milesian Irish kings arrived in Ireland in all their emerald glory from Spain.

O'Looney was caught in the act of stealing milk from an erstwhile heifer, that milk intended for the poor children of his village. The children were fairly starving as morning after morning the puzzled village milkmaid stripped the heifer's dry teats and brought home an empty pail.

A witch came to this O'Looney man. She was the witch o' conscience.

"Listen here," said the witch, "you're taking the milk from the mouths of babes! A man who loves milk so much would sell his sowl for milk. Would ye trade yer sowl for all th' milk ye can drink?"

"Would I?" asked O'Looney. "Lead me to it!"

The witch took O'Looney's sowl and made him the tail of a cow, leaving his greedy face as it 'twas.

"Drink to your stomach's content," said the witch, holding O'Looney's sowl in the palm of her hands. O'Looney was the happiest man in Ireland. His mouth was in switching distance of the creamiest cow udders in all of Ireland. He sucked and he sucked. When the cow went dry, he nearly starved, but when she became fresh again with calf, he butted the calf to death in the *bawnafinny* with the whip of the tail he was, and got fat again. He became so heavy that the poor cow could hardly drag her tail around. O'Looney was the master of the cow. He forced her to graze night and day. He was a cruel master and so greedy for her milk that thinner and thinner she became. When bulls came around to visit the cow, O'Looney thought they were after her milk and whipped them away with the tail he was. So the cow had no more calves and she finally died under O'Looney's punishing regimen.

Even today near Blarney Castle one can hear O'Looney screaming for milk as the tail he is drags a skeleton of a cow around a haunted *bawnafinny*.

"Wouldn't you *ruin* the Blarney Stone?" Sister Brigit asked the American one day. "If you took it away out there to America with greed in yer hearrt?"

"Hope ye like Paddy's, sir," said Paddy briskly. "Very good Irish whisky, sir, ten years old; made right here in Cork."

The promoter sagged in his brown leather chair.

"God!" he said weakly. "Where *have* I heard that before!"
The experience shook him anew.

"Give me a *big* snort, Paddy."

Paddy passed him a half a tumbler dancing with pearly beads.

"Pity ye have to be waitin' so long, sir. It 'tis lonesome havin' no one to talk to."

The Yankee gulped the raging brew. He found it very smooth.

"I'll talk to the Paddy's, Paddy," he said.

Paddy laughed.

"Do yerself good, but it 'tis only me duty, sir, to warn ye that Paddy's will talk back to ye. That Irish whisky has no manners, sir."

"I'm not surprised," grunted the Yankee. He left his chair and helped himself to another stiff drink. "But just let it open its big fighting Irish trap to me once, if it gives me any mallarky . . . any gobbledegook," he snapped, "and I . . . I'll . . ." He clenched his fists into red hammers. "I . . . I'll . . ."

"Is there something wrong, sir?" asked the astounded butler. "Should I call Sister Brigit?"

"No, no," said the promoter quickly. "I'm all right. I'll be all right."

Paddy backed into the hall.

"Just ring, sir," he said anxiously, "if ye need me. But a great one like yeself would niver be needin' nothin', that mind ye have in yer skull, sir, bein' what it 'tis. It 'tis bigger'n a badger's head, sir."

"God, how big *is* a badger's head?"

"What I was cummin' up to say, sir, it 'tis not so big in itself; it 'tis th' hole that it can make that's big."

"Gad, Paddy," said the promoter, "if the Irish had any sense, they could rule the world—but don't they anyway, without any sense? It's the dexterity of their tongues, I presume."

" 'Tis th' luck o' th' Irish, sir, seein' as ye mean th' blairney."

Paddy grinned and went on his way to the pantry.

"Damn it, I feel awful," said the American.

He hit the cut-glass decanter of Paddy's again with a wallop that made a boiler-maker seem like wine.

He turned again to the library shelves. An 18th century volume in handsome parched old leather caught his eyes. It was Crose's *Antiquaries*. His eyes were slightly glazed, but he read with interest what he saw, for the book described Blarney's Druidical monuments and the *logoon,* or Rocking Stone, in the Rock Close by the Witch's Cave where Adrian had so often taken him for briefings.

The American read the strange text:

> These are huge stones so exactly poised on a point, as to be easily caused to rock, or vibrate, if touched at a certain place. Some of these are artificial, and others natural rocks, cleared of the circumjacent earth. These were probably used by the Druids as instruments of pious fraud, like the statue of St. Rumbold, by the monks of a monastery in Kent; which statue, though only the size and figure of an infant, could not, it was pretended, be lifted by anyone labouring under an unexpiated offence, that is, one who had not by alms and offerings purchased their absolution. The figure stood on a pedestal against the wall, to which it was secured by a secret peg, which might be put in or withdrawn on the other side. If the penitent was niggardly in his offering to the saint, the peg was applied, and the figure became immovable even by the strongest man; and, on the contrary, a liberal benefaction made it easy to be lifted, even by the most delicate girl.
>
> In like manner these stones might be so managed as to vibrate, or not, according to the will of the Druids, who might impede its motion by wedges, or direct the application to be made at the wrong point. Some of these stones had rock basins on them, as perhaps a sacred ablution made a part of the ceremonial.

"Damned frauds!" exclaimed the promoter. He hurled the book to the floor and polished off for himself a great drink of Irish whisky.

The Irish brew, an imperial quart of it, reposed on a piece of Chippendale near a photograph of the ould man on the hill. It was a photograph of youth, a young ould man on the hill, in the decorated uniform of an officer in the British Army. A stripling of a picture it was, of a Norman youth, and a handsome divil of a Norman youth he was, with eyes as quizzical as the nonsense of a wise man's mind, a bachelor's eyes that had turned the hearts of the loveliest ladies of Europe.

The face of the disturbing photograph was reflected in the flint glass of the decanter.

The promoter addressed himself to the decanter.

"Listen, Sir George, you old Druid," he said, "I know all of your answers already, but before you come down to the library, let's have a little rehearsal, eh? I'm here for the last time to talk to you about the Blarney Stone."

He drained some pearly beads from the bottom of his tumbler and sat down again. He wagged a finger at the cut-glass facet where danced the likeness of the ould man on the hill.

"Listen here, Sir George, tell me! What is this all about— these Christmas trees?"

Chapter Twenty-Four

A Million Iron Men

From their encounter with the Seven Dwarfs of Snow White, Adrian, Valerie and Deborah race into the castle's drawing room.

The sounds of a distressing argument come from the library, where it seems that the ould man is conferring with a most unreasonable visitor.

"Hey, are you giving *me* the blarney—like McCarty gave it to Queen Elizabeth?" demands the guest.

The ould man is giving as good as he gets.

Here came the Americans again bearing a million dollars, tempting him with their wretched American money, after he had said no so many times before, and still was saying no.

Still, if it *is* broken, Brigit's vision may be a sign that he could at least permit a *part* of that block, the Shrine of Ireland, to go out there to America as some of his family and friends urged.

If the Blarney Stone is all that Ireland has, then what country has more? A great truth gave the promoter a lofty inspiration.

"Why that . . . that indestructible old son-of-a-gun is Ireland's good-luck horseshoe! It is nailed over every door in the world. The Irish use it as a pass key to get in everywhere! Blarney, blarney, blarney," he said excitedly. "Can't you see, Sir George! That old rogue of hearts! That Blarney Stone, why millions of Americans will kiss it!"

"Do you think that will do the Blarney Stone any good? They might wear it out with their osculation." Sir George laughed.

The Yankee did not appreciate the humor.

"This is an Irish stew! A perfect seasoning of impudence," he exclaimed. "I always thought a million iron men would buy anything! I came to stay a week, it's been months! My reputation as a promoter is at stake. The people back home won't understand what a nutty proposition I'm up against."

"I did not promise you a sanguinary thing," Sir George says with great dignified elegant nasal resonance in basso buffo, O! "I said *maybe* a little piece if it's *really* broken!"

"Now," the visitor storms disgustedly, "I've got to depend on a dream! We've *got* to have a showdown!"

"We'll see tomorrow morning," says Sir George, "whether Sister Brigit's vision is accurate. She says there's a fissure there. Oliver Cromwell might have hit it, you know."

"A vision! A dream!" wails the unhappy man. "Oliver Cromwell! Ireland, a little bit of heaven, hell! Eireann go *brat* is really the way it's spelled in Gaelic. The *brath* spelling is just for phonetics."

"Ireland is not *broth,* anyway," says Sir George. "You know you're invited to tea," he adds charmingly.

"What better place to 'get the blarney' than at Blarney Castle? That lingual circumambience. What a goofy deal *this* is, that a million iron men won't swing. You should name that Blarney Lake 'Lake Jerk' and throw me in it! 'With soft words intended to deceive without offending.' High teas, low teas, cocktails, dinners, champagne. I goggle in consternation. I am not pandered. I am charmed. How could I be otherwise? But I am not mollified."

> But the smooth tongue can more than woman woo,
> Her lord and master takes it kindly, too;
> And if laid over, just too slightly slick,
> More than mere puppies like a little lick!—

So grateful feel its oil, till anger burns,
Then to what rank rancidity it turns;
Loaded with which, the slippery tongue extends
Its service still, to daub the dearest friends;
Nature must ever to herself be true—
So all who lick are quite as sure to spew!

Chafing from delay after delay, the restive promoter is losing his temper. Yesterday, Adrian had worn him to a frazzle running him up and down the wishing steps of the Witch's Cave. He was most reluctant under her prodding.

"It seems to me, knowing what you're after," she said, "you would run up and down these wishing steps all day long."

"Cripes!" he said. "Those coffin tacks. My heart! You'll plant me in the roots of trees with your leprechauns."

She had dragged him up and down the cruel steps of the castle so often to kiss the Blarney Stone in this land of ghosts that he was a wraith of his former self. Exhausted from this harrowing strategy, puzzled and perspiring, on one specially trying day he blurted the gravest of heresies:

"To hell with it, this munificence! This is all baloney!"

Adrian jammed her fingers into her ears, because she personally believed that the Stone was not efficacious for doubters.

Another cable from New York insisting that the stone must be the "original" reposed in his wallet.

"Damn!" screamed the harassed promoter. "If they mean that 'acrobat' stone only an eagle can kiss, I'm sunk. I've crawled every inch of the castle. Can't even find it! They must want to exhibit it at the Bronx Zoo or in the Rocky Mountains!"

He was pulling his hair when Adrian turned airily on her heel and left him to gnash his teeth and stew in his own juice.

The irritation continued to grate from the library into the big bow-ended drawing room with its seven high windows—

Those four looking south, over the tennis courts and croquet lawn, across a yew hedge and a stretch of park, to the lake. The east windows, at the bow-end of the room, overlooking a wide lawn bordered by plantations of flowering shrubs, and on one side by the yew hedge which divides this lawn from the entrance drive.

Into the drawing-room walls that are painted a pale blue. The armchairs and sofas, covered in chintz, in an old-fashioned design of blue, rose and gold. Into the floor of parquet, carpeted with Persian rugs. And the antique furniture in the room, and a particularly fine buhl writing table, also a carved rosewood piano by Broadwood, of London, ordered and designed by Louisa Jane Colthurst, and a French satinwood, upright spinet, that is now used as a china cupboard. And also the various showcases, containing collections of miniatures, Battersea enamel snuffboxes, and many other "objects d'art."

Into the walls hung with pictures, and into this room containing some of the best in the castle, into the large painting of "The Supper at Emmeus," by Nogari, and a very pleasing picture of Sir Nicholas Colthurst, one-time Mayor of Cork, by the Irish artist Martin Shay, hanging over the door. He is very severe now.

And into the ears of the disapproving old Countess of Desmond hanging over the Adam mantle, and of Adrian.

"Listen," she said, holding her hands over her ears, "it's perfectly frightful!"

"What *is* he fussing about?" asked Deborah.

"Oh, he wants us to be millionaires."

"My goodness!" said Deborah. "Puff should go in and bite him!"

"He did—that night of the storm. The wretched American without even a Wellington on, was *dripping* wet and completely *showered* poor Puff."

"He might have worn a mackintosh. Poor Puff!"

"The Blarney Stone is biting him now. I've tried *so* hard to help that wretched American," Adrian sighed. "So has Sister

Brigit. It's *such* a good cause—it's for sweet charity, for poor American and Irish children. Everything would be so dignified. No hot dogs at all."

"Hot dogs! My goodness, Adrian."

"They are sausages," Adrian explained. "The wretched American promised faithfully the Blarney Stone would positively *not* be shown in amusement parks. Only in departmental stores under green lights in a shadow box. There would be soft background music, 'Come Back to Erin,' most likely on a talking machine. The Americans would kiss it at mouth level as they walk by, he says."

"At mouth level? Whose mouth?"

"Why the Americans' mouth, of course," said a somewhat exasperated Adrian. "Why else would they have it at mouth level?"

Valerie was engaged with a big thought.

"The Americans seem so decidedly odd, don't they?"

"They just do things differently out there, I guess," said Adrian. "Sister Brigit says we should love everyone regardless of how peculiar they are. All men are our brothers, she says. We must love even our enemies. As Irish as Sister Brigit says she is, she told the American she didn't hate the Wali of Swat, just because his name is not O'Brien."

Adrian's reporting of Sister Brigit's views on bigotry was correct, but incomplete. Adrian had pedaled off on her bicycle to visit Ranti, Belinda and Redwing in the stables and feed her guinea pig colony before the good nurse had finished her discourse on tolerance. The unhappy American was particularly cross that day and inclined to be snappish as he always was when he received a cable from the United States. Sister Brigit was merely attempting to comfort him in his misery. She chose the Wali of Swat as an extreme example of the differences in people and the barriers and misunderstandings such differences caused, by reason of the fact that Adrian practically knew the

Wali of Swat by being able to say "thank you" in Urdu. The American was morosely preoccupied.

WHEN ITALICS ARE CLOSE ITALICS YOU GOING TO SHIP THE PEBBLE QUESTION IMPATIENCE HERE MOUNTING.

That was what the cable said.

Sister Brigit said: "The Wali of Swat doesn't speak Gaelic, of course."

The American made no reply.

"The Wali of Swat is certainly no O'Brien," she repeated, laughingly.

"I Urdu the first time," the Yankee said crossly. "But with a gashouse name like Swat, he should certainly be named O'Something. We'll just call him O'Swat."

He was so sharp that Sister Brigit dissolved into tears.

"Pshaw! That Irish wit! It's a kitchen match. So brilliant for a moment, but it goes out fast. It ends right there."

"On the point, I would say. And it leaves a glow," sobbed Sister Brigit. "I tried so hard to help you. Your plan would be good for Ireland. I even had a green vision for you."

"My God, Brigit! A *green* vision? What on earth *is* a green vision?"

"You will find out," said Brigit mysteriously. "When St. Brigit answers a prayer, it 'tis th' most frightenin' responsibility in this worrld. I hope what I asked for was not wrong."

"Listen here, now! I thought your vision was that Cromwell's cannon balls cracked the Blarney Stone. These Irish riddles! I can't settle down here permanently to figure them out!"

"Be patient," Sister Brigit replied. "Time flies. One month calls for anither, and February will soon be Marching!"

"Please! Don't keep me here 'til February! But wait! February-Marching! March 17! Why, Sister Brigit, you must mean I'll get the Blarney Stone for St. Patrick's Day in New York!

Marching! Marching!" The promoter could scarcely contain his excitement. Every inch of him was trembling with imagination. "Listen," he whispered, "do you know what that means? It's a showman's dream. We'll have the Blarney Stone lead the parade right up Fifth Avenue! The Irish will go wild! Why it will be like . . . like the Second Coming!"

"Do they plan to steal the *entire* castle?" Deborah asked.

"Oh, no," replied Adrian in horror. "That would *never* do, to put it *all* in a departmental store. The Americans would fall off in droves. The American explained that the wretched shoppers would drop from the turrets like 'dead pigeons.' So they are going to have a castle made of cardboard sprayed with green sand."

"It is so elaborate," Deborah said, "that it makes one fairly breathless, but why do the departmental stores want it, though?"

"The American said it was to attract millions of people who would bring their babies to kiss it and buy more prams and things they will see in the stores."

"Prams?"

"Prams, he told Nunk. But maybe he means other things, too."

Deborah shook her head.

"Prams, indeed. I should think they are not *all* that babies need. I hope the Americans would buy them a cream puff, too!"

"Anyway," said Adrian, wearily, "they'll pay millions of iron men to kiss it."

"Iron men, now?"

"It's really American money. The American calls dollars *iron men*. It's peculiar American speech. Nunk would prefer him to express himself in pounds. He cannot understand dollars, either."

"Things are so complicated," sighed Valerie.

"No, just the Blarney Stone, he thinks. Every American who

kisses it would get a shamrock, a block of peat from th' bog, a shillelagh, a four-leaf clover and a gramophone disk of Bing Crosby singing 'Irish Eyes.' But there will *positively* be *no* sausages."

"My," said Deborah. "The poor Blarney Stone."

"Sausages would seem to be undignified out there in America, and Nunk will positively have *nothing* undignified about it. He has put his foot down on *that*. Nunk can be *very* firm when he wants to be."

"But I can't understand what *sausages* have to do with the Blarney Stone," spoke up puzzled Valerie.

"It's an American custom of some sort," replied Adrian, and thereby dismissed the entire subject.

She began singing snatches of a song that drifted into the library. The sentiments had an understandably apoplectic effect on the disconsolate promoter. The title was "A Perilous Thing is the Blarney."

> "But people get used to a perilous thing,
>   And fancy the sweet words of lovers are true,
>   So let all their blarney be passed through a ring,
>   The charm will prevent all the ill it can do,
>   The blarney, the blarney,
>   O, the peril that lies in the blarney!"

Temper was jumping in the promoter's neck cords.

"Eireann go brat!" he said.

"Just listen!" exclaimed the horrified Deborah. "That *pushy* American! Screaming for money! He will jolly well be turned into a cow's tail," she prophesied. "He only wants the poor dear old Blarney Stone to get more iron men."

One can hear him all the way down to the game larders, the dairy, the footmen's room, and the manservants' bathroom. Into the Estate Office where the agent works, and from which all the business of the Estate is conducted, into the sideboards bearing their arrays of silver, into that heavy buhl cabinet that was made originally for the Prince de Condé, and came from the Tuileries, in Paris. That cabinet, which once spent several months under the sea. The ship in which it was traveling to Ireland from France was wrecked off the coast of Cork. That cabinet that was insured for four thousand pounds, so that no one wished it to be salvaged, but it was. Into every recess of the castle the voice of the promoter resounded, rattling even the massive entrance doors and the stained glass in the domed ceiling.

"It will make you rich! Rich!" he cries.

All of the elaborately carved family crests in the castle are a-twitter. The lace collars and the curled hair are standing up. The records of the potato famine crackle in the tin strongboxes.

"Sir George, how *can* you turn me down? Why, Macy's Department Store will even purify the stone after every kiss with ultraviolet rays. I've thought of everything! They will even make ultraviolet *green* if the Irish want it! Full-page ads, radio, television—announcements even in Gaelic, parades, bands, skywriting, balloons. We'll have to raise 'Hail Columbia' with it, of course, but dignity, dignity! There'll always be dignity everywhere! Even the Irish cop guard of honor will wear green gloves!"

"He gave Sister Brigit an umbrella," Adrian said. " 'I'll pray for you every time I touch it,' she said. 'Then you'll pray for me every day in Ireland,' he said."

"He should have bought an umbrella for himself too, I should think," remarks Deborah practically. "Look what happened to poor Puff."

Now enter the great neighboring Lord and his English Lady—she in a hat of lacy duck-egg blue and baggy-seated tweed suit, he quite proper too in striped trousers and a Bond Street jacket for calling at Blarney at such an hour, in drooping mustaches resembling those of an Alaskan sea otter, reminiscent of the fashion of the late King George V. The Lord talks right out of his stomach. Adrian bustles a polite welcome, but it is unnecessary. They make themselves at home, mixing their own Cusenier and Gordon's gin waiting in the great silver cocktail shaker on the rosewood piano.

"That American bloke," says the Lord, "is driving poor Georgie mad. He has already received warnings to burn him down."

"It would be terrible actually burning him though, wouldn't it?" asks the Lady.

The mighty Lord wipes some yellow bubbles from his sea-otter handlebars, and humphs cavernously from a large cavern, not so empty, but full of grottoes.

"Silly ass! *Not* the American, the *castle*. The American was very unreasonable about that. He said it should be *insured.*"

"It's all so complicated," sighs the Lady. "There must be *some* way of getting rid of him. If the stone is cracked won't he go on away with it?"

"Sssh!" whispers the Lord, "but the stone is not cracked! What looks like a crack from the wrong side is *lichen!* It's just a straight line of green fungus!"

"Oh, goodness me, now what?"

"No one has really had the heart to tell him, I guess. Ho! Just listen to him carrying on."

"Does poor Georgie know the stone is not cracked?"

"Yes, Adrian told him. Georgie said this whole affair is a confounded fungus. Georgie further says he's dashed if he wants anything more to do with any part of it. He says he thought all along permitting the stone to leave Ireland would be very unlucky. But, to quote Adrian, his heart is as soft as a guinea pig's stomach. He can't bear to tell the wretched American. He has been kept here waiting and hoping, for so long. Poor Georgie is afraid the shock will crack him."

"Poor Georgie?"

"Silly ass. No! The American."

"Goodness!" exclaims the fine lady, "then the Blarney Stone isn't going anywhere."

"Bloody well right, for once," responds his lordship.

Ould Puff is growling there in the corner over his puzzling dreams about the size of Cushy. Dunivan is growling too.

"They're growling at Cormac McCarty," Adrian says.

The importunate American is at it again.

"You actually owe it to humanity to let it go," he is arguing. He is becoming positively lyrical with his inspirations. His face is glowing like a pippin. The imperial quart of Paddy's is alarmingly low. "Why, the more scientific and hard-boiled the world has become, the more the values of the Blarney Stone have increased, the more it has woven with its great magic the creative powers of imagination. Why, Sir George, the Blarney Stone is the answer to world peace!"

"Hey! Come again!"

"Yes, world peace, and the Irish problem, too. You owe it to the world and to Ireland. We will enact another law in a law-weary world. The enforced kissing of that gay pebble. I have saved this argument for my very last! We will tour the world of war-makers with the Blarney Stone: Moscow, London . . ."

"Moscow?"

"Yes, even Moscow! The Blarney Stone has an engaging personality. It will not bite the war-makers. It certainly has no fear of them. Look here, in its time it has been kissed by many warriors without contracting the disease of war. It is free of those deadly germs. It has a magic prophylaxis all its own, and even Stalin could not contaminate it!"

He stopped in high excitement to wipe his dripping forehead and to catch his breath.

"Moscow, Dublin . . ."

"This *is* Ireland, remember."

The American raced on.

"Washington, London, Peiping, Tokyo, Washington! What a

pity Hitler failed to visit Blarney—a melancholy example of what happens to dictators who fail to kiss the Blarney Stone.

"After this tour, all future wars then would be fought with the golden tongue and not with exploding isotopes. And who will deny that the smooth purl of blarney lies sweeter on the jangled ear than does the voice of splitting atoms? Did you realize, Sir George, that people still say 'cold as hell' because that was the way the old-country Irish used the English language?

"So in every Capital, let the war-makers, and those capable of making war, come to kiss the true symbol of diplomacy, to worship it and woo it for the peace of mankind. The cultivation of blarney by the men of Mars could save all of creation from destruction; it could even save the United Nations. This fantasy would capture the imagination of the world!

"And the world is worth saving, for there are swans that sleep like great white pompoms at night on the waters of the River Lee and swim in the day with the visiting signets from the Irish Sea, and vie with grace the hours away. And the long golden hair of a girl of happy Cork watching them from St. Patrick's Bridge shimmers in a glory under the moles shot through by the rays of a lovely foggy sun. The deep green pulse of Ireland throbs from the wonder in its breast and the echoes of Killarney are the music of laughing hearts. And the Americans love everything about Blarney."

The promoter is begging the air for breath from his frenzied eulogy.

"That man sounds sick," says Adrian worriedly. "When a man is sick, he can't be well."

"I think you'd better sit down," they hear a worried voice urge the guest. "You don't seem well."

"Why, that sounds like Paddy," Adrian cries. "Listen!"

The American was having one last word. "All of these un-holy holy wars would end," he said. "And what's more, you'll be rich. You won't have to live here in frugal feudal splendor. You'll be RICH! Please, don't you *understand?* Barnum got Jenny Lind out of Scandinavia for peanuts, didn't he? Why can't I get the Pebble out of Ireland for a million iron men?"

A voice clears its throat.

"Ahem, now," it says, "why won't you be satisfied with . . . er . . . er . . . say, to buy ten thousand Christmas trees?"

"Trees! Christmas trees? My God!"

The truth hits the startled Yankee like a Cromwell cannon ball, and the thunder of understanding rocks him.

"Yes," says Sir George, "why can't those confounded American departmental stores, loving everything about Blarney, be satisfied with ten thousand firs from Blarney Castle forests? It would seem to me . . ."

There is a sudden silence and then is heard a dull thud as though made by the flop of a poor, bewildered and confused crayture of a deflated U.S. showman on a Persian rug, O!

"Adrian! Adrian!" Paddy calls out. "Fetch Sister Brigit! Quick now! This wretched American has raised 'Hail Columbia' with himself! Himself'll be disturbin' Sir George in whativer himself's delayin' about upstairs!"

"Oh," exclaims Adrian springing happily to her feet. "I knew Nunk wasn't there all the time! His voice was so strange. Isn't it wonderful and adorable that he hasn't a cold, after all! It's all such a wonderful dream. I hope that wretched American *never* leaves."

Futile cries from a crayture in the library answer the child of enchantment in an American accent.

"Blarney will stop the seed of hell, the atomic bomb, from sprouting and make the honeyed beehives grow. God! What am I saying?

"That bubble of word fest, that Blarney Stone, that mischievous rock, that bubble of butter!"

Gently Paddy puts an Irish linen napkin dipped in warm cistern water over the gasping American's eyes.

"I warned ye, sir," says Paddy, "that Paddy's would be talkin' back to ye. I would have been in long before, but I thought it 'twas th' ould man talkin' to ye with a touch o' laryngitis."

Chapter Twenty-Five

Pooka Pooh

Now, the hooligan pooka disappeared from Blarney Village as suddenly as the dust of the parched square settled with the first drops of green rain that painted the sward of beautiful Cork and restored its national color. Dispositions improved instanter, the natives were freed of absurd distortions, minds cleared, mad exaggerated notions subsided and normalcy again prevailed. All of these manifestations were definite proof that the Season of the Pooka was over, yet still other confusion followed in its wake, mostly from the results of conscience and remorse.

Especially penitent were the O'Boys for their narrow, chauvinistic assault upon the wretched rich American millionaire, literally driven into the storm.

Clear and sober reasoning soon brought home to those who had offended him that 15,000,000 Irishmen lived in America, and who was there among them to say that their victim had not a drop or two of Irish blood himself?

There are more than 47,000 geographically Hibernian namesakes in the United States: towns, cities, villages, hamlets, graveyards, churches, race tracks, pool rooms, billiard parlors, forts (*e.g.,* Fort Kearney, Nebraska), hotels (*e.g.,* the Shamrock, Houston, Texas), mountains (*e.g.,* the Purcell Mountains, of Montana), parks, rivers, creeks, streams, ranches, rocks, lakes, mines, oil fields, counties, islands, beaches, springs and castles. With too many *e.g.*'s to enumerate.

There are Paddy mountains, Tralee mines, Eileen diggings, Wexford motor courts, O'Brien barrooms.

There are twenty-three Dublin towns in the forty-eight United States and only one in all of Ireland. There's a Belfast, alas— in Washington, too. But to make up for this, there are Derry and Muldoon, Colorado; Kildare, Utah; Tipperary, Arkansas; Shamrock, Missouri; St. Patrick, Minnesota; Cork, Kentucky; Kilkenny, North Carolina; Hibernia, New Jersey; Belfast, Maryland; Colleen, Virginia (George Washington was a member of the Friendly Sons of St. Patrick); Limerick, Maine; Doty City, California.

Glengarries, St. Patricos of the Rio Grande, Erin, Kildares, Shannondales, Tralees, Murphysboros, O'Reillies, Antrims, Irelands, dot the map of the U.S.A., but there's not a Blarney to be found in the post office register. Still, the blarney is everywhere, and not a bit homesick in the Land of the Free and the Home of the Brave.

How could the blarney be homesick in such surroundings, with Glenmoras, Kennedys, McCabes, Tyrones and Kerrys to be found as the names of communities from the Atlantic to the Pacific? Blarney is quite at home in Clare, Ohio, Killarney, Ohio, Sligo, Ohio and Londonderry, Ohio, to name a few.

In Florida, Harp, Foley's Landing, Malone, Dowling Park, Kathleen, Carlow, Griffin Lake, Shamrock, Brandon Castle, Milligan, Malone, McCould, McDuffie, Hogan, Fay, McCloskey, O'Brien, Hogue, Scanlon and Hickey are within an hour's motoring distance of McGinty, Alabama.

And hardly a Catholic in a town o' a sainted name. In the U. S. A. there is a Bishop Foley, of the Episcopal Church. A Reverend McManus in the South wears a bow tie. And most Methodists encountered there are as Irish as Wesley was English, O! That Lutheran Gilfoyle of Georgia, O!

One so inclined may multiply this Hibernian geographical

phenomenon in every state of the Union until one so inclined may run out of mathematics. It is no accident. Nostalgic Irish settlers stamped their ould country map names on the soil of America in an attempt to make it altogither a great Irish subdivision and the greatest of all Gaelic real estate developments. Those early Irish settlers were "corkers." They came from County Cork. Everytime a man says "He's a corker," he pays tribute to County Cork and that pendulum of wit, the Blarney Stone, that makes it tick and swim in that fount of the unabridged and flowing tongue. *Quod vide*:

Dublin, Georgia; Dublin, Florida; Dublin, North Carolina; Dublin, Maryland; Dublin, Pennsylvania; Dublin, New York; Dublin, Virginia; Dublin, Alabama; Dublin, Ohio; Dublin, New Hampshire; Dublin, Michigan; Dublin, Mississippi; Dublin, Indiana; Dublin, Kentucky; Dublin, Missouri; Dublin, Arkansas; Dublin, Iowa; Dublin, California; Dublin, Idaho; Dublin, Nebraska; Dublin, Texas; Dublin, Arizona.

Odds were that at least the grandparents of the Yankee promoter were born on the ould sod, or at wurrst his great-grandparents. Why, it 'twas said for what it 'twas wurrth that more Irishmen were listed in the New York telephone directory, alone, than composed the population of the entire Republic of Eire, now dwindled from a one-time peak of 14,000,000 to about 3,000,000 sowls. Why, America was Ireland's second home, and all Irishmen long had held her warm in their affections. Americans were not foul divils.

And good America has been to the Irish, too. In America, Irishmen and their children of the second generation even more so. But good, America has always been to the Irish. Why, look what happened to Cassidy, who rose from brick mason to millionaire in little old New York. Gerald Brennan immortalized him years gone by in a lovely poem, "Shanahan's Ould Shebeen":

This is the tale that Cassidy told
In his halls a-sheen with purple and gold;
Told as he sprawled in an easy chair,
Chewing cigars at a dollar a pair;
Told with a sigh, and perchance a tear,
As the rough soul showed through the cracked veneer;
Told as he gazed on the walls nearby,
Where a Greuze and a Millet were hung on high,
With a rude little print in a frame between—
A picture of *Shanahan's Ould Shebeen.*

"I'm drinkin' me mornin's mornin'—but it
Doesn't taste th' same
Though th' glass is iv finest crystal
And th' liquor slives down like crame,
And me Cockney footman brings it
On a soort of a silver plate—
Sherry an' bitters it is,
Whiskey is out iv date.
In me bran-new brownstone mansion—
Fift' Av'noo over th' way—
The cathaydral around th' corner,
An' the Lord Archbishop to tay.
Sure, I ought to be shtiff wid grandeur,
But me tastes are almighty mean,
And I'd rather a mornin's mornin'
At *Shanahan's Ould Shebeen.*"

Aye, the Irish had gorged the veins of history with beauty
and truth and poetry of the universe, but America, not Ireland,
was the actual sounding board of Irish genius. All the Americans worth a damn, the O'Boys philosophized, have some Irish
blood. But they did *not* agree that there's not an Irishman in
Ireland worth a damn, as some of their English critics say—that
no Irishman amounts to anything until he leaves Ireland. One

of them was humming Goodwin's "Nothing Too Good for the Irish" by way of refuting this all-too-current libel:

> Dutchmen were made for to carry coal
>   And shovel snow,
> Cubans for cigarettes, the Portuguese
>   To sail the seas,
> Scotchmen for bakeries, the
>   French were made for style,
> Russians for mining, Americans
>   For Liberty,
> But the men made for bosses,
>   Were sons of Erin's Isle.
> Then hip, hip, hurrah, Erin go bragh!
>   Nothing's too good for the Irish!

They had proved it at home, they had proved it abroad—God bless America. Yes, America *had* done a lot for Ireland, any way you look at it.

In America, the good Lord answers Irishmen's prayers so fast they can't keep up with them.

Furthermore, America had given to Ireland the statesman DeValera. An Irishman, of Cork, had written a patriotic song about it, specifically thanking God and New York for the favor.

In retrospect, not even *Top O' th' Marnin'* was half as pusillanimous as once it had seemed.

"Maybe it 'tis even th' fault o' th' Irish thimselves that th' Americans want so much to kiss th' Blairney Stone. Oursilves sent th' Irish out there in th' furrst place," O'D. philosophized.

"All o' this tumult and confusion," said O'G., "when even oursilves do not know th' rightful home o' th' poor Blairney slab."

"Begor man," snapped O'D. "Mind yer words. Ye tread on dangerous and traisonable ground!"

Contrition could go just so far and no further!

"That grand American brought a lot o' th' trouble onto himself, though. Divil a one iver I seen like him. Tellin' an Irishman in Ireland not to get his Irish up. 'Twill be into th' diminsions o' his casket himself'll be settlin' before he forgets what his bad manners caused. Such things could bring on a war . . . those Americans who are correct, but not just quite right, those Americans who have a big pocketbook and no brains."

"Even he went so far as to intimate th' British Coronation Stone and th' Blairney Stone are not th' same color."

"Once they were, though," said O'D. "Both so nice and greenish like. But now th' Stone o' Scone is a shameful brown. It blushed itself to that color from being sat upon by th' rear ends o' so many English kings!"

"Still," continued O'D., "aside from iverything else, includin' patriotism, takin' th' ould girrl out there to America and chargin' strangers so much for her kisses—why it 'twould be makin' a . . . a bad girrl out o' her."

"A shillin' here in Blairney *is* different somehow," agreed O'D.

"So indaycent is th' very thought. It would come back ruined and stuck with chewin' gum! It should be against th' law."

"But it 'tisn't gone anywhere, and it niver will!"

The O'Boys had been guilty of appalling things.

A few of the O'Boys, intending to make personal apologies to the visitor and seek his forgiveness, straggled abroad to the green and looked for him in every likely place, the Muskerry Arms and the Castle Inn, but were told that the American had somewhat hurriedly checked out of one of the hotels and had left town forthwith.

"Oh, to be sure! Though it 'twas all th' time I knew th' ould man on th' hill would niver let it go. Too much sense he has to do such a foolish and irriverent thing. Himself's not one to be sayin' th' holy shamrock's a weed."

"Niver St. Patrick himself iver said th' shamrock was holy, as holy as it 'tis. 'Tis only you who're sprinklin' its very roots with holy water."

O'D. shrugged off the charge, because a sense of guilt was heavy on his heart.

No wonder he could not be found! Sputtering something incoherent about Christmas trees, he was speeding in a chauffeured motor car through the moisture of the Irish night to gloomy, rain-drenched Shannon Airport, like Ireland a wet place surrounded by water. The somewhat perturbed Irish chauffeur could not get him there fast enough.

He had his head snapped off the moment he attempted to pass a friendly worrd or two.

"Ireland's so tranquil now, sir," he said. "So peaceful, it 'tis, sir. Why even baggage with British trippers' stickers on it can be left all night on th' street and not a sowl in this free Republic will touch a hand to it altogither!"

"Not even the hotel porters, I guess," the customer responded sourly. "That's why it must have stayed out all night on the curbing. This place is like wild Indians and I've been to Bolivia. Bolivia me!"

This peculiar passenger was enough to disturb any driver, those things he kept asking, O!

"I wonder now whether Sister Brigit's green vision had anything to do with those Christmas trees! Did *she* blarney me, too?"

The Bells of Shannon tolled in sad farewell. That anthem of rebel Cork. The words of a masterpiece came to his ears on the wings of chimes.

> I've heard bells chiming, full many a clime in
> Tolling sublime in cathedral shrine,
> While at a glib rate brass tongues would vibrate,
> But all their music
> Spoke naught like thine;

For memory dwelling, on each proud note swelling,
Of belfry knelling its bold notes free,
Made the Bells of Shandon
Sound far more grand on
The pleasant waters of the River Lee.

They induced a strange soliloquy. Those words by that priest, Francis Sylvester Mahony, who kissed the life of the ages into the Blarney Stone as he might have longed to kiss a girl, a girl like Peg Murphy's daughter washing praeties forenent the door. Cold breasts respond and throb with fire. Mahony breathed life and milk into those breasts. Life is in them now, life to suckle and milk the mouth of the world of nonsense. The breasts of the Blarney Stone. The Blarney Stone, a toothing ring, a sugar tit for the babes of all creation.

The car raced on over grounds of hallowed glory, down the soaking road where Cromwell marched at the head of 12,000 murdering horse and foot; and through heroic Limerick sped the brooding traveler, Limerick besieged and slaughtered by the "Brewer's" son-in-law. The ghosts of Irish babies hanged from their mothers' hair whimpered in the night on the banks of the River Shannon, flowing once with blood, and hordes of massacred Gaelic sowls screamed imprecations from the hedgerows and the desolate bogs, howling out of heaven and howling out of hell, so that neither living man, divil nor angel would ever forget. The reckless rubber screeched back at them the noise of tortles' wilde fire and the rattle of shorte gunnes, and the airport was won.

There, the promoter hurried through formalities in bad grace. A great swan of a bird was warming the blood of her fibers outside Customs to take him home. He raced across the drenching distance to the gangplank of the stratocruiser. An Irish porter ran by his side carrying his small parcels.

"A bit o' moisture, sir, we're havin' in Ireland tonight," he observed friendlily.

"There's that Irish blarney again!" snarled the American. They even blarney the weather, calling this *flood* a 'bit o' moisture.' I hope you and all of Ireland are flooded out!"

"I hope we're all hangin' onto you when we are, sir," retorted the porter promptly.

"Did you ever see them, those swans, coup big?" the American asked somewhat foolishly. "They shake the water off their backs altogither."

Ireland floated away in a ghoulish green mist behind the exhaust of mounting octane wasps and fell away into the sea. Above the urgent air-borne whine of four hearts pulsed against the ribs of wind he heard a greedy ghost of a tail begging for milk.

The stratoswan plunged her wings into the churn, and a skeleton of a cow rattled her bones on the metal feathers. The promoter shivered.

"It's that looney O'Looney," he whispered, "and I'll bet he wants grade A."

The man beside him turned in surprise.

"What? Hey—who?"

"Oh, just a guy I know. He's a cow's tail."

"Now, I've heard of a horse's . . ."

"No, no," interrupted the dejected entrepreneur. "That's what *I* am. You wouldn't understand. This guy O'Looney's a lowing ghost who lugs a cow's skeleton around with him. It's a long story."

It was too long for the other passenger. He quivered his throat and looked the other way as the plane soared out of terrestrial dampness. The rain assailed the window in splashing waves.

"Glad I'm going back to God's country," said the promoter. "You couldn't *give* me Ireland if you put a glass roof over it."

The other man observed discreet silence.

"This is a hell of a country. It's all Gaelic opera as far as I'm concerned. Now tell me what *you* would do with ten thousand Christmas trees?"

The alarmed air voyager coughed again. It was the unhappy, nervous cough of a man who faced ten hours more in the company of an uncaged maniac over the Atlantic Ocean. He looked around nervously for the steward, a man named O'Hehir, with apostrophe. He was busy in the pantry serving corned beef and cabbage.

"I . . . I . . . well, I guess I'd maybe decorate them," he replied by way of humoring the dangerous man, who might even murder the pilots.

"Skip it, pal." The promoter shrugged.

With the dawn that came in green steel streaks the luxury American Airlines Stratocruiser was flying the Northern route out of the gloom of the midnight sun of Iceland, speeding like a silver bullet of a palace above a bad dream, an ugly stricken cacophony that was felt by the skin. Thousands of feet below staggered the raw scarred peaks of a divil's nightmare, insolent violent monoliths, even handsome in their lonely horror, great, scairy legs of mountains kicking out of the sea and whipping at their bed sheets of icy snow. It was striving malevolence and a sight to inspire the awe of the gods.

"Whew! Oh boy!" exclaimed the passenger next the promoter as he stared in wonder. "Some rocks!"

"Don't mention *rocks* to me," exploded the other Yankee, "and O'Boys, neither!"

"I . . . didn't say nothin'. I . . . I meant no harm," the astounded passenger apologized.

"I take those things personally," replied the promoter grumpily. "And don't forget it!"

He was mumbling complex disturbances into his plunging vest line.

"These Irish donkeys!" he gargled away. "They think they came over on the Ark. If they did, they pulled it over."

His chance companion was suffering great discomfiture. The panorama of a lifetime was forgotten. He was a studious-looking, innocuous little man, and it was probably the first time he had ever said "Oh, boy" in all of his life. He had picked a very bad time. It made him forget his grammar and everything else he had ever learned. He corner-eyed the stranger in actual terror. He jumped against the side of his seat when the promoter turned to him again, and his specs fell into his lap.

"Say, fellow," the frightening crayture beside him asked with a weird light in his eyes, "do swans actually have vast blue feet?"

The studious character fumbled with his specs on the bridge of his nose. His eyes now were too big for them to fit. Nervously, he got to his feet.

"Pardon me, sir," he said timidly. "I think I'll go to the bar." Somehow he got past the knees into the aisle.

"Listen, fellow," he heard a feverish voice say, "don't go ordering Paddy's, now; that polemical brew! It 'tis me duty to tell ye that Irish whisky has no manners. Faith, it'll be sure to talk back to ye. Paddy's will lay it on thick. 'Tis th' blairney, ye know; even in schnapps it gabs. Ire for Ireland, I say!"

The alarmed sowl started to bolt, but the promoter grasped him fiercely by the wrists and held him where he stood. He sniffed at the air.

"If you're running for Steward O'Hehir, that descendant of a long and ancient line of Irish kings and queens, as old as the Garden of Eden itself, He for Adam, Her for Eve—he's too busy with that corned beef and cabbage to help you."

A smacking odor, because corned beef and cabbage has no aroma, hit the promoter a powerful wallop in the nose.

"Wow!" he exclaimed, "you can't get away from it anywhere! Irish turkey! What strong wings *that* bird has. It even flies over Greenland. But, my friend," he said professorially to his trembling prisoner, "corned beef and cabbage actually *does* owe its origin to Turkey, although it was an Irishman, the first Irishman in the world, ould O'Noah himself, navigator of the Ark, who landed it in Turkey. That's why they call it Irish turkey. But you can win a bet that ould O'Noah never used any English mustard on that wild bird. Why, the Irish wouldn't even put English on a billiard ball."

"Bu . . . bu . . . but you were talking about O'Hehir and Adam and Eve," stammered the prisoner wildly, not knowing quite what he was saying or why he was saying it. "I didn't know Noah was O'Noah! I never dreamed he was an Irishman."

"Why certainly, man! It's easy to see you've never been to Blarney. *He* stands for Adam, the first man. *Her* stands for Eve, the first woman. Add He and Her and you get Heher. That O got in front of He and Her because O! was what Eve said when first she tasted the apple. Add O! to Heher and you get O'Heher! That is the actual origin of the O' in all Irishmen's names."

"Hey, leggo! I . . . I . . . I just don't get it. I . . . I mean I never knew Eve said anything."

"They do in Blarney, though. When she bit into that apple she certainly didn't say O'Hell. There was no such place at that time. The first O in the world, therefore, was that Irish apple of life. The apple was the first O in the world."

The victim was pulling away almost in a state of frenzy. He was pleading for his release from what he thought was a madman's clutches.

"Please, please," he begged, with all the control he could muster, "this is all Greek to me. Let's call Steward O'Hehir and let him get you something to quiet you down. You're suffering from some sort of shock."

"No, no! Don't you see, man, that at last I've discovered the true secret of the Blarney Stone!"

"You don't even spell O'Hehir *O'Heher,*" groaned the miserable tortured passenger.

"Oh, yes you do!" exclaimed the promoter. "That 'O!' Eve cried out when she tasted that apple got into O'Hehir by mistake. That *i* in O'Hehir is Eve's exclamation point upside down. The Garden of Eden was just a question of He and Her and nothing else, except an apple thrown in, that Irish O."

"Please, please, leggo my wrists!"

" 'Eat that damned fruit,' the old snake urged He and Her, Adam and Eve. 'That apple will open your eyes and make you gods. It is good for food. It is pleasant to look at. It is something to be desired and something to make both of you wise.' All the time, that old snake knew that apple had a worm in it, but he blarneyed He and Her, Adam and Eve, like a viper would."

The promoter was shaking the other passenger bodily.

" 'The serpent *beguiled* me,' Eve told the Lord, as she trembled in her fig leaf when she saw that the worm had made her naked. Man alive, don't you get it! That was the first blarney in the world, and it was a snake that did it."

Now, with a miserable howl and superhuman strength out of the brawn of sheer terror, the little mouselike man wrenched himself free and escaped to the bar.

The promoter did not pursue him. Greenland slid out of sight with the caprice of speed.

"I guess I'm one of the few men in the world," groaned the bitter wretched American in terrible reflection, "who *ever* saw a swan's *foot*. Everybody else sees their necks. It would have to happen to me. Or, did it? What a goose I am."

It is readily seen that O'Hewlett, the author of this volume, was ending his dismally futile adventures with the Palladium of Ireland—that stone of blarney, that Gaelic saga, if there can be such a thing, that attempt to lease the ould block of destiny for the mouths of his American compatriots to buss—in a terrible and shaken state. He hopes that some day that terrified crayture who sat beside him on the stratocruiser over Greenland will read these words and accept them as humble apology for his irrational conduct.

And that Puff will forgive him for ever stepping on his tail and drenching him with that Bond Street coat full of Irish rain.

And here, dear reader, is a last note for this book from County Cork, Ireland, which we know will be considered a sad note to this history of that gay pebble, the Blarney Stone, for an old friend since the writing of this volume has left this worrld. But the letter will break the news of the death of one of our heroes with whom we have labored, but at whom we have never whistled, for fear of a Mandarin temper too terrible to provoke:

> You will be very sorry to hear that dear Puff is gone. The minute after he had been seen by half the village, galloping down the street, his body was found a mile away. He was lying as if half asleep. No mark or bruise anywhere. The vet says that his heart just suddenly gave out.
>
> He was such a character and such a real friend. Blarney people have had letters from all around the country, from friends he knew here, and others of his own and of his own making whom he used to visit. If he were a human being, he could hardly be more mourned or missed. And alas, he left no heirs.

The stratoswan on which the promoter flew was gliding into the green blaze of Gander and Newfoundland's growing Christmas trees. He collapsed into a slumber, the sort which no words of O'Hewlett will ever describe. Nor the sadness he felt when later he learned that Sir George had died.

Chapter Twenty-Six

Love Master

Sadly, the O'Boys returned from their futile search for the Yankee to O'K.'s Snug Pub on the leafy little lane now sparkling with pearls on the leaves and as refreshed as a bud in a summer shower; but their own spirits were drooping.

That evening they sought to make amends by proxy, and in the rather obvious direction of the Kentucky man, Kane.

They found him still deep in tragic reverie.

Kind and tender Irish hearts, as quite no others in the world, respond to sowls in despair, O! and come a-rallying with their sympathy and their tears.

Kane now began to receive a double portion, that which would have been his anyway under all normal conditions, and a bounty from sincere contrition.

The burden of the barmaids, which had for so long made their eyes briny, now was shared by a stronger sex willing and able to lighten their load. No more did raucous voices ring out in song with such lyrics as "Paddy's Pastoral Rhapsody," a foine number when rendered to the tune of "The Night Before Larry Was Stretched":

> Here's a health to you, my darlin'
> Though I'm not worth a farthin'
> For when I'm drunk, I think I'm rich,
> I've a feather bed in every ditch.

334

The silence, in due consideration for Kane's grief, was clumsy, embarrassing, and awkward.

The O'Boys tiptoed in and out of the bar, and their consideration was magnificent to behold. Some of their noses were red from honking, although it was summertime and not the winter season when most of the Irish are inclined to sniffle a bit anyway. Kane's face was enough, however, to make anyone sniffle in any season. It was like the notes of sad music, like a wedding, somehow, yet no one even with a word violated his melancholy.

The O'Boys just stood respectfully staring at him with solemn, torn expressions reflecting the commiseration in their true Gaelic hearts. But this worked a considerable strain on the nerves, and O'K.'s customers kept him busier than ever behind the bar.

"Do ye'self good," they would say to each other in whispers, but they drank only silent condolence to the American sufferer in their midst, reasoning in their own way that this was the very least they could do to comfort him. To such extremes was this unselfish comforting carried that night after night they went to their beds heavy with stout and porter.

And the very divil some of them caught from their women who, arch and wifely and fussy, shattered their lofty spells with worldly abuse.

One night when a drunk but chastened O'D. staggered home, Herself greeted him sarcastically.

"Morra, Mister DeValera, holdin' anither one o' yer cabinet meetin's, I see! Time ye got home before 'twas makin' day!"

"We're tryin' to make amends," O'D. pleaded piously. "Faith, 'tis that poor bugger, th' American."

"Heigh ho! There ye go now, still a-meddlin' in worrld affairs. 'Twasn't but a whiler ago 'twas all for Ireland declarin' war on America single-handed th' lot o' ye were!"

"Aye," said O'D. meekly, trying to give his unsteady knees a futile measure of dignity, " 'twas th' turrible Saison o' th' Pooka."

"Pooka poof!"

"But somethin' foxed us up. Somethin' got into us, anyway."

"Plenty!" his wife shouted heartily. "And I know plenty o' *what!* Rightly I'd be a-callin' it th' Saison o' Paddy's if called upon to give it an indaycent name!"

"Woman, now, ye don't understand. Furrst 'twas *Top O' Th' Marnin'* . . ."

"Th' top o' yer heads! Oh, fie, fie! A lot o' Blairney Guinness politicians actin' like a flock o' clueless ould woman biddies that you resimble, takin' charge o' th' givernment, th' whole worrld, and th' cinema, too!"

"Just one wretched American now," O'D. explained thickly and lamely. "Just one, now. We've (hic) been tryin' in th' wurrst sort of way to help him."

"In th' wurrst sort of way, is dead right," exploded Mrs. O'D. "It's up to *him* to drown *his* own pairsonal sorrows! Sweet Son o' God! What airthly good can *your* belly full of Paddy's do his sorrowin' stommick!"

O'D. cringed under the stinging logic, and blurted an ineffectual and meaningless answer.

"Bejabbers! But he's here! We cannot lave him to die without a daycent send-off!"

"Aye! And what a send-off 'tis he *should* be gettin! If th' sad crayture was not so pathetic, 'twould be me own idea for th' wives o' Blairney to chase him back to Cork City with their brooms! Divil a dhrunk iver I see die in his due time!

"Since he came there's no reapin' o' corn, no cuttin' o' wood, no groomin' o' horses, no sellin' o' meat, no gatherin' o' vegetables, no milkin' o' cows, no gradin' o' wool, no drayin' a dray, no dippin' o' sheep, no herdin' o' cattle . . . and heifers low for th' bull to break a body's heart. 'Twill soon be meself who'll lead th' poor gruntin', slobberin' and sufferin' crayture to a heifer by his nose. And not a hand o' bywork's turned in Blair-

ney by a man with an O' before his very name! Not one O'This,
O'That, O'Tuther. . . ."

O'D. interrupted her fine point emphatically.

"O'Hell!" moaned the harassed O'D.

"Pairfect!" shouted his wife triumphantly. " 'Tis th' place
th' lot o' ye scallywags belong. Pairgatory ye've long since passed
by. Only blissid O'Somethin' in Blairney who hits a lick o' work
is O'K!"

"Och, whisht! And that he is!" laughed O'D. alcoholically.

"Is *what,* now, ye say?"

"O'K.'s a *cinema* worrd, woman," explained a condescending
O'D. "Meanin' i . . . identical, well, just what th' blissid worrd
says—good!"

"Expairt as ye are on such subjects, ye should know th' main-
ingless worrds, too. There's nothin' O'K. or good about any man
beginnin' with O'. O itself is a great gapin' empty vacancy o' air
with a hole through a hollow void and nothin' in it whativer
besides!"

"Woman alive!" protested O'D. "That is a far-stretched cavity
ye dig with that yawnin' mouth! But is it inhospitable ye're askin'
us to be? Drinkin' a drop to th' wretched bugger like they say
in th' newspapers 'hands across th' sea!' "

"Hands across th' pub!" snorted Mrs. O'D. disgustedly. " 'Tis
up to Dublin to reach across th' sea! Yer drinkin', me foine
ambassador, isn't helpin' th' darlint one whit."

"Then neither's his own! 'Tis good liquor wasted on him!
'Tis a drum he could drink, now, without turnin' a hair. 'Tleast
what *we* drink's not wasted a drop o' it."

"That I *do* see." Mrs. O'D. laughed in spite of herself. "Still,
here I work me hands to th' bone polishin' up th' house until a
fly can't light on it without breakin' its neck, and niver a hand ye
turn."

But a broken heart in Ireland has a certain immunity from any
form of harshness, and men, women and children alike are quick

to sense the sanctity of it, and even Irish dogs often whimper their understanding and lick the hands of the lovelorn. Mrs. O'D., as kind and sentimental as the next one, meant not an unkind word she had said, and her husband knew it, without even a look at her wiping away the tear which came when she thought of the poor lonesome American eating away at the very caul of his heart among strangers in an alien land. She forgot to scold her husband any more as pity welled in her deep bosom and softened her woman's thoughts.

O'D. was quick to take advantage of her mellowing mood.

"A foine man he is, too, a gintleman altogither, a Southern American like George Washington, a furrst-rate gineral!" he said loudly, glad to change the subject from drink. "Begob a *great* gineral!"

"But 'tis said th' American doesn't eat enough to keep his sowl hooked onto his ribs." Mrs. O'D. sighed.

"Ye've been rightly told."

There is a shameful railroad strike in Ireland now, a strike for higher wages in English shillings. Poor O'D. grasped the popular subject to change Herself's trend of attack.

"They should shtop th' strike," he said. "Passengers have to go backwards and forwards."

"Th' railroad men also have to eat," said Mrs. O'D., taken somewhat by surprise. "Victuals goes backwards and forwards, too."

But Herself pursued graver things and she was not to be deterred by this Irish gab of her man.

"True love and appetite niver travel in this worrld togither, though," she said. "No jarvey iver had them as passengers at the same time in his jauntin' car what wasn't a liar in th' whole cloth."

" 'Tis a passenger in a hairse he'll be comin' up soon if somethin' isn't done."

"And th' blood will be on th' American hussy's hands," decided Mrs. O'D. angrily.

"Where 'twould rightly belong!" O'D. agreed sleepily and pulled the covers up over his head, to dream of the convenient George Washington.

"Mary th' Vairgin pity him!"

It was very late, so the good woman made a sigh of a yawn, snuffed out the candle, and undressed in the glow of the turf fire.

"Now I wonder," she said half to herself, "why *did* he lug his grief to Blairney?"

O'D. was dozing off, but he mumbled a drowsy answer.

"Why all furriners come here, I guess—to kiss th' Blairney Stone."

Mrs. O'D. dropped her nightgown and her face froze. She emitted a blood-curdling cry as though she had seen the terrible features of a peeping Tom at her window. O'D. sprang out of bed as though he had been shot by one.

"Yirra!" he shouted in a wild stupor. "Up, Kerry! Th' British are comin'! Which way did he go?" and lunged toward the door in hot pursuit. Mrs. O'D. grabbed her husband by the shirttail, from Manchester mills.

"Wait! Wait! It's nobody. Sober up! Don't ye see, man, ye've hit th' nail square on th' head!"

O'D. looked around the room suspiciously, scratched his own little head to see what had hit it, and staggered stupidly toward a chair.

"Begob, woman . . ." he asked foolishly, "ye say now who hit who?"

"Sit down! Sit down!"

In high excitement, Mrs. O'D. relit the little bedside candle with a shaking hand, but light with a candle power of vastitude had flashed across her mind. She rushed to her wavering husband, seized his shoulders in a grasp approaching frenzy and pushed him into his chair. Poor O'D. howled.

"There now," Mrs. O'D. said soothingly, "and it 'tis a spot o' tay ye need, and desairvin' o' it ye are, too!"

"Th' Lord save us," moaned the mystified carder, " 'tis a suppeen o' whisky that I be needin' now."

"Tay!" the woman said firmly, lowering the teapot over the turf ashes and reaching for a cup on the mantel in one operation.

"All this time," she babbled, " 'tis like a blind man ye've been, walkin' around sairchin' for somethin' dark with th' lights snuffed out!"

O'D. scratched his head again.

"Ha, woman, and what a foine difference 'twould make what color 'twas I was lookin' for if I was blind!"

" 'Twould if 'twas in anither room," rejoined Mrs. O'D. mysteriously. "And as blind as a sightless mole ye've been without th' eyes o' a bat to see it. Not that ye know in yer sad condition what it 'tis, but this very night it 'tis a poor man's life ye've saved!"

O'D. gulped foolishly at his cup.

"Begob, not *that* blind?"

"Blind enough! Not knowin' Americans come to Blairney to kiss th' Stone."

"Yirra! Woman," O'D. sputtered, "are ye mad? They *all* do!"

"Aye," whispered the wife triumphantly, "but tell me, has *Himself* kissed it?"

O'D. recoiled like the parliamentary backfire of a Cromwell culverin in a long-port siege train of the Sassenachs.

"Kissed it? Why, woman, Himself's not left that table in O'K.'s pub long enough to kiss anything. I'd go bail he slept there last night. And as for kissin' a body, I don't think Himself's iver even kissed *her!*"

"Not even Maggy! It 'tis th' picture o' that American gurrl ye mean. Th' way he looks at her likeness I do not think she's iver even kissed *him!* And there is th' trouble o' it 'tall! Where pray tell me anyway does th' kissin' bug grow?"

Poor O'D. struggled with the confusion in his mind and throat in a splash of understanding.

"Woman," he said, "plaise heaven, ye mean th' Blairney Stone!"

Herself nodded her great affirmative Irish head and burst into the happy jow of that song so well known in Blarney, O!

> "Oh! say, would you find this same 'Blarney'?
> There's a Castle not far from Killarney,
> On the top of its wall, (But take care you don't fall)
> There's a stone that contains all this Blarney.
> Like a magnet its influence such is,
> That attraction it gives all it touches;
> If you kiss it, they say,
> That from that blessed day
> You may kiss whom you please with your Blarney."

Mrs. O'D. was as radiant and as glowing as a Delicious apple.

"For th' furrst time since th' Irish came from Phoenicia," she said, with the last note of her song ringing through the thatched roof of the Irish cottage, "O now has finally accumulated something inside its gapin' zero. Look what th' Blairney Stone did for dumb ould Puff! Just look how that crayture was affected."

"A whileen ago ye ridiculed th' pooka though."

"Th' Blairney Stone is no pooka. A man has to have th' blairney to get a kiss and get a wife. 'Twas th' blairney dumb ould Puff used. Th' wretched American afther kissin' th' ould block can go back out there to America and talk himself into anything! He can win her then. Our problem is to make Himself kiss th' Blairney Stone."

"Poor Maggy," sighed O'D. "If he goes away and gets that American gurrl . . . leavin' poor Maggy behind . . ."

"It 'tis too bad for poor Maggy," said that hearty wife. "If that talkless American stays on here in Blairney, 'twill be th' ruination o' th' Irish! Th' all-night drinkin' will niver stop."

"But if he is dumb as ye say, and cannot talk, what good will it do him kissin' th' Stone? Blairney is not for th' mum. Th' Blairney Stone can do anything except make th' Sphinx talk. That's askin' too much! Puff can bark and Puff can sniff. That's dog talkin' right on. Th' Sphinx has no nose except that th' elements has chewed away. So the Sphinx can't smell. No sense comparin' th' two."

"Smell o' snort, nose o' no nose, mouth o' no mouth, and deaf o' dumb," said Mrs. O'D. firmly, "that Kentucky man Kane is goin' to put his snoot against that rock if I have to push it. Th' wives o' Blairney will have to get rid o' him some way. We've got to get him out o' town. Meself'll lead that American with th' big pocketbook and no brains as I would th' gruntin' bull to th' heifer."

"Th' heifer's usually taken to th' bull," said O'D., "but th' blairney takes th' bull to th' heifer."

Chapter Twenty-Seven

The Pebble of Destiny

"Plaise heaven, *don't,*" begged O'D., but Herself was adamant.

"God's own truth," said Herself's husband, "yer voice is like th' rattlin' o' a pear in a drum."

It was a wonderful day. There was a reddish mist in the air and around some of the young trees, and under them were the snowdrops and calandines, and the blue scillas seemed almost to dance in the sun. The tulip bulbs had shot up eight inches high, so rich and green and sappy and full of their last life. The somber hues were dying into a lighter green, and the tennis court, forgotten by the spring, was brown with daisies dying, their petals tinged with the age of the season going by. Everywhere the grass was growing the age of color that ends all things, even the green grass of Ireland.

Mrs. O'D. went down to O'K.'s Snug Pub and took that mysterious Kentucky man Kane by the nose. O'D. was fearfully at her heels. Maggy was aghast and fit to faint, she was.

"Come with me," shouted Mrs. O'D., "and kiss th' Blairney Stone! Let's get right down to business." Like a bull she squeezed his nose.

Kane's gin-and-mix shattered in alcoholic vermouth, water and glass as he jumped to his feet. He sneezed on her fingers.

"Hey . . . hey!" he cried. "St . . . stop! I ca . . . came here to ki . . . kiss the Blarney Stone in the first place, but I've got crem . . . cremno . . . pho . . . phobia."

"Ye've got cr . . . cremno what?" demanded O'D.

"Crem . . . no . . . phobia. It is fear of precipices."

O'D. tapped his wife's shoulder.

"No use o' *him* iver kissin' th' ould block," he said. "Ye can't *stutter* blairney!"

Maggy and Kane walked toward the River Blarney. So we do not have to drag them and you, dear reader and author, again past that outflanking bawn of an enceinte, over that oubliette of a murthering hole, up that slender peel of a keep, up those 118 cruel steps of old Blarney Castle. The pain of that terrible climb, O! Miss Japgess, Tex, Puff, the Seven Dwarfs of Snow White have been up there and have come down, O!

The nightingale has flown up there. The bee and the wasp in Daniel O'Connell's mouth have buzzed and bussed up there drinking the honey from that errant blackberry vine. And a cannon ball of Cromwell did pommel it O! What happens to a cannon ball that kisses the Blarney Stone?

It is raining again in coughing Ireland.

Up on the hill, the Castle faces the usual Sunday prospect of jolly well nearly twenty people to tea.

Adrian, Valerie and Deborah are in the nursery making raffia mats and playing Swing on the gramophone.

"We don't need a million dollars," says Adrian. "We have more than that in the lake. Cormac McCarty showed me where it is, too. Mummy does not need that Russian nylon divining rod. When the time comes, I'll show her where the gold is."

"But what about the curse of the McCarties?"

"That won't work with us," Adrian replies tartly. *"Actually,* we are all somewhat McCarties ourselves. Our ancestresses, Ladies Lanesborough and Charlotte Fitzmaurice both married McCarties all sorts of generations ago."

It was so mysterious and exciting for a while. They got tired of their raffia mats and the Swing music after a brief time and became interested in the books on the shelves, *The Wind in the Willows,* some of Louisa Alcott, Ballantine, E. Nesbit, Beatrix Potter and Enid Blyton. They were searching for a special volume.

"Hurry and find it," urged Deborah.

They wanted to cry for a while over *Uncle Tom's Cabin.* It was so adorable to cry in Blarney Castle.

And it was such a nice and rainy day to enjoy a good cry over Topsy.

Maggy and Kane were walking arm-in-arm down to the banks of the River Blarney. They were oblivious to the rain, but Kane seemed nervous and shaken by his rough encounter with Mrs. O'D. His lips were trying away. Maggy placed a tender forefinger upon them.

"Don't talk," she said. "Ye don't have to."

Kane pulled Maggy close to him. In surprising suddenness he did this thing. He traced a forefinger of his own through the part in her hair all the way down to the top of her spine. Maggy's eyes, like her lips, were half parted in the waking from slumber, the slumber of passion that had been asleep since it was born. His mouth and his eyelashes, the eloquence of unsaid blarney fluttering in them, O! swept her flowing face without a word, swept it with a breeze of love, the same breeze that swept the photograph of another girrl fluttering from his hand to the sward of Ireland.

"I . . . I . . . I wish I co . . . could ki . . . kiss the Blarney Stone too," Kane said, as he watched the rain of Ireland wash away at the likeness on the sward, that long-looked-at photograph of the girl back home, the girl with the speckled brown eyes of a doe that had been frightened while drinking from a pool. The girl who had run away.

"I . . . I . . . I . . . I had my heart set on it," Kane said, "ki . . . ki . . . kissing the Blarney Stone."

Maggy laughed like the rain that made the river dance and ripple.

"Someday, ye will," she said with the gaiety of a bubble, and some wisdom, too, "someday when ye're just a bit short o' crutches, at an age when there won't be any harm in it. That's th' day I'll take ye up there and let ye kiss th' Blairney Stone blindfolded. Blindfolded so ye won't be scared o' th' heights. Then ye can blairney any colleen ye wish."

"Wha . . . wha . . . what age?"

"To be sure, no one knows what age that is," said Maggy wisely. "We'll wait and see in yer own individual case."

Kane hugged the blarney out of the girrl's own breathless lungs. And his mouth told an old old story against the lips of a girrl who had the reddest cheeks in Erin.

Never again would that Kentucky man Kane shed a tear when he heard this song:

Last night when we parted, his gentle good-by,
A thousand times said, and each time with a sigh,
And still the same sweet words he whispered to me,
My Aileen, Mavourneen, Acushlamachree.

The friend of my childhood, the hope of my youth,
Whose heart is all pure, and whose words are all truth,
Oh! still the same sweet words he whispers to me,
Are Aileen, Mavourneen, Acushlamachree.

Oh! when will the day come, the dear happy day,
That a maiden may hear all a lover can say,
And he speaks out the words he now whispers to me,
My Aileen, Mavourneen, Acushlamachree!

(1)